KEN RAGGIO

Long Winding Road
A Very Personal Story

By Ken Raggio

ISBN-13: 978-1475262773
ISBN-10: 1475262779

Copyright © 2012 by Ken Raggio

Edited by Pam Eddings

All scripture quotations in this book are from the Authorized King James Version of the Bible unless otherwise noted.

ALL RIGHTS RESERVED. No part of this publication may be reproduced or transmitted in any form or by any means, electronic or mechanical, including photocopying, recording, or by any information storage and retrieval system without prior permission of the author, with the exception of short quotes that are properly credited.

For Information, Contact:
Ken Raggio, 3312 Hwy 365, #219, Nederland, Texas 77627

VISIT my major WEBSITE at:	http://kenraggio.com
Read my BLOG at:	http://kenraggio.blogspot.com
FOLLOW ME on TWITTER:	http://twitter.com/kenraggiocom
FRIEND ME on FACEBOOK:	https://facebook.com/ken.raggio.9
LIKE my FACEBOOK FanPage:	Ken Raggio Bible Resources

Dedication

I dedicate this book to you.

This book is for you. It is for people who really, really want to be saved, but who may be struggling with the way things are in Christianity today.

I dedicate this book to seekers of Truth; especially to anyone who is exasperated or distressed by the tsunami of contradictory or mixed signals that are flooding Christianity.

If you really want to know the God of the Bible, I urge you to fasten your seatbelt and hold on tight. I want to take you on a wild ride down a long winding road. With God's help, I want to help you make sense of the maze. You will never see the Church or the world the same again.

I have already been advised that I am too transparent about myself in this book. That may or may not be true. You can decide for yourself. Parts of my story are certainly not flattering. I only know that it is the story of my life-long search for Truth, and I am compelled to tell it. I believe that many will identify very strongly with some of the struggles I have faced. Perhaps you will recognize some of your own struggles and find answers for your own questions. I hope you can handle it. I pray that you will.

It has been a long winding road. At times, it has been wonderfully joyous, at other times, unbearably difficult. Reality does not have a candy coating.

WARNING: This book is not for the faint-of-heart. It is not for part-time Christians. It is not for people who make excuses or lie to themselves about God, the Bible, Church or Christianity.

Well, perhaps it really is. But if you happen to fit into any of those categories, I warn you now. This book will rattle your cage. It will be brutal with flimsy theology. It may even raise a few hackles, because silly thinking about God or religion may not fare well here.

Say a prayer. Ask God to open your eyes and show you something that will genuinely help you. In Jesus' name.

Let's go.

Contents

Dedication	3
What's A Life For?	5
The Groves	7
The Call	17
Facing The Music	27
Apprenticeship	43
The Work Of An Evangelist	53
A Word, A Dream, A Miracle	67
Planting A Church	81
A Major Paradigm Shift	89
Which Way From Here?	97
Catch The Spirit Of Love	107
Holy Ghost Or Nothing	115
Crash And Burn	125
Truth Or Consequences	143
House-Cleaning Time	155
Eat No Bread, Drink No Water	167
This Time, We Are Going By The Book	181
Beware The Leavening Of Hypocrisy	201
Purge Out The Old Leaven	213
Decision Time	225
Crossing The Bridge	237
The Rest Of The Story	249
The Long Winding Road	261
No Going Back	287

Forward

What's a Life For?

A man is created in the image of God. He is supposed to look like God, but for whatever reasons, none of us really do. Our would-be-perfect lives are malformed by our experiences, our education, our upbringing, and countless other influences. Even the very, very best you can do never comes out perfect. We are only legitimized by His grace and His call, certainly not by our own credentials.

Nevertheless, when God lays His hand on you and says, "I want you!" He has His own plan for your life, and He expects you to respond with complete and absolute surrender.

God is our Creator; therefore, He is also our rightful Sovereign Master. He has absolute, albeit benevolent control over our lives and destinies. He is free to exercise either goodness or severity toward us. Early Church leaders happily declared that they were bond-servants - love-slaves - of Jesus Christ. As His servant, a Christian has no sovereign rights of his own, but is dutifully obliged to do the will of God. Only as we submit unreservedly to His will can we find true, enduring happiness.

I am not a hero or a super-achiever. I'm not rich or famous. I do not hold myself up as a model for anybody. I, like you, am only legitimized by the grace and the call of God. I am here to serve the purpose of God, like a wick in a candle.

He said that we are made overcomers by the blood of the Lamb and the word of our testimony. I want to be an overcomer. So here is my testimony. Maybe, just maybe, something in this story will help you. I pray that it will – in Jesus' name.

Ken Raggio
September 29, 2012

Long Winding Road

Chapter 1

The Groves

Johnny Appleseed, the legendary apple-tree planter, must surely have had a pecan-planting cousin who passed through the coastal plains of Southeast Texas near the turn of the twentieth century. Actually, there was no kinship, but the man's name was Wiley Choat, and in 1919 he planted 2,500 pecan trees every fifty feet on a 385-acre tract of land. To this day, many of those huge old pecan trees still stand throughout the community that sprang up among them. It was my home town. Old-timers called it "the Groves."

In stark contrast to the pastoral nature of the pecan trees stood scores of ugly steel towers inside the local chemical plants, hissing and groaning as the oil and gases of a jillion gushers flowed through their bowels. Automotive and aviation fuels and countless petrochemical products and by-products were being derived from the 'black gold' found so abundantly in the oil fields of that region. It was at Spindletop, only fifteen miles away in Beaumont, that the first major oil discovery in Texas – the Lucas Gusher – was made in 1901.

Home was in the heart of oil refinery territory on the Gulf Coast, near the Louisiana border. Thousands of blue-collar refinery workers dominated the work force in the "Golden Triangle" of Beaumont, Port Arthur and Orange, even more-so than in the world-renowned oil kingdom of Houston, only ninety miles to the West. Because of a strong Oil, Chemical and Atomic Workers Union, and their demands for high wages, good benefits, and guaranteed contracts, the standard of living among ordinary working men without a college education was far better than that of many white-collar workers outside the petrochemical industry.

Giant oil and chemical refineries such as Gulf Oil, Texaco, Mobil, DuPont, Shell, Unocal, Fina and many others filled the night skies with the luminous glow of thousands of flickering lights. The foul odors of scores of peculiar chemical concoctions permeated the air day and night. Via pipelines and tanker trucks, river barges and ocean-going ships lined up in various local ports, their products inspired Port Arthur's motto, "We Oil the World!"

Long Winding Road

And this was home to me.

Daddy was at work in one of the local refineries the day I was born. Grandpa Raggio called to tell him that mother just had twins. Grandpa was always full of mischief like that. Daddy left work in a rush to go to St. Mary's hospital where his anxiety was relieved when he found that I was not a twin. On September 26, 1951, the Raggios had a baby boy. About forty years later, Daddy retired from the same refinery.

Both of my grandfathers spent years in the refineries. My mother's dad, Granddad Thompson, was killed in a refinery explosion at Fina in 1973. Before I finally broke away from the area, I did my own time working briefly in four refineries (Jefferson Chemical, Neches Butane, Unocal and Fina); in the labor gang, janitorial pool, lab tech, as an insulator's helper, a pipe fitter's helper, carpenter's helper, and finally as a journeyman boilermaker. I even worked on the docks at the Ports of Beaumont and Orange as a catch-out longshoreman for a few months. That just may have been the hardest work on earth - throwing 110-pound sacks of flour, deep in the hull of a ship on 12-hour shifts!

Two blocks north of our home lived my mother's parents, Carthol Cozelle (C.C.) and Lizzie Thompson – Granddad and Granny. Two blocks south of our home lived my dad's parents, John and Margaret Raggio - Grandpa and Grandma.

School was directly behind our house. From the first to the ninth grades, all I had to do was walk through our backyard gate onto the playground of the Groves Elementary and Junior High Schools. Then, for the three years of high school, I caught the bus on the corner to attend the Port Neches-Groves High School. Every morning, the bus rolled down "Sara Jane Road," a spooky, foggy road that crossed a mysterious bridge near the Neches River, where the locals said the ghost of Sara Jane lingered.

Church

Most of my childhood memories include experiences in and around Church. Church was the center of everything.

In the 1950s, the Groves Assembly of God Church was a huge old wooden structure on Main Avenue. Its congregation of about a hundred and fifty folks included our family of five, both sets of my grandparents, and two or three of my aunts. Going to Church was a family affair, and we went to every service.

Our pastor, C.T. Owens, was a tall, wide-framed country-style preacher who hollered and marched up and down the aisles when he preached. He always preached hard, and against sin, and rarely concluded a meeting without an altar call where everybody swarmed down to the front and prayed, cried and worshipped God.

Music at the Groves Assembly was a big part of every service. A.J. Duplissy, the song leader, always opened the Sunday services with the invitation, "Let's all come to the choir!" A faithful crew of fifteen or twenty untrained singers voluntarily filled the choir benches for Sunday song services. The bindings on the old MELODIES OF PRAISE song books would practically fall open by themselves to "When We All Get To Heaven" (page 111) or "Victory in Jesus" (page 164), because we sang them nearly every service.

Brother Cecil Ritchey played a big upright bass fiddle. Mona Lou Reed played the piano, and my aunt Norma Raggio played the spinet Hammond organ. We heard solos and duets and trios regularly. "I Bowed On My Knees And Cried, Holy," and "You Can Have A Song In Your Heart," burned permanent memories into my mind. And along with the singers, there were shouters and worshippers. It was not uncommon for us to stay as late as ten or eleven o'clock on Sunday night as some got carried away in the Spirit, praying and worshipping God.

Only in recent years have I realized where one of my deepest beliefs about God and Heaven came from. It began with the death of my mother's Granny when I was ten years old. Granny Hayes was in her late seventies when she died of cancer. All the family traveled to Mabank, Texas, just southeast of Dallas, to attend Granny Hayes' funeral.

She had lived down a red-dirt road far out in the country, in a small, unpainted old farmhouse that had a simple porch all the way across the front of the house. It was covered in brown asphalt shingles, and had a lean-to on the back of the house that served as a kitchen.

Scores of family members crowded into that little old house for several days during the wake. The coffin was set up in one of the only two rooms in the house. Each room had an old metal bed frame with a feather mattress. The little, low-ceiling kitchen had an old Hoosier kitchen cabinet, a large metal pan for a sink, and a homemade kitchen table. Out back was a chicken yard and an outhouse. Right beside the back door was a huge galvanized tank that served as a water cistern. It caught the rain water from the roof of the house, and that water served the entire household. There was no running water. Everybody drank from a large metal dipper that was in a bucket that had been drawn out of the cistern. During Granny Hayes' funeral, the funeral parlor sent out large water-tanks for drinking water.

When it came time for the funeral, they carried Granny farther out into the country to an old cemetery. There was a tiny community Church beside the cemetery. The preacher from the Assembly of God Church conducted the service, and a little choir sang.

It was their song that opened my eyes to another world that day. I was just a ten-year old boy, but when they began to sing, "I am going to a city where the roses never fade," they really captured my imagination. The words said, "I am going to a city where the streets with gold are laid, where the tree of life is blooming, and the roses never fade."

I became a believer right then and there. As a small child, I caught a glimpse of Heaven that has endured for a lifetime.

Music

As time passed, the music of the Church became a deep love, like blood in my veins.

My parents gave me an old upright piano at Christmas time when I was about seven, and I immediately began to play Gospel songs by ear. By the time I was nine, I could play nearly every song in the songbook. I sang my first solo in Church at eight - "There Shall Be Showers of Blessings." Aunt Norma accompanied me on the piano.

I soon found my way into usefulness at Church. Every Sunday evening, before the main service, the Christ's Ambassadors would conduct a youth service back in the fellowship hall, and they called me out of Children's Church to play the piano for their service. I still remember the words to the anthem sung by all the young people of the Assemblies of God Churches around the country. The lyrics would surely be considered awkward and "over-the-top" today:

> We are Christ's Ambassadors, and our colors we must unfurl.
> We must wear a spotless robe, clean and righteous before the world.
> We must prove we're free from sin, and that Jesus dwells within;
> Proving duly that we're truly Christ's Ambassadors.

After the song service, they sent me back to Children's Church.

The old ladies had a morning prayer meeting once each week. I went to prayer meeting with Granny, and played the organ while they prayed. I softly played "Sweet Hour of Prayer" and other hymns.

When I was eight years old, Aunt Norma left our Church, and became the organist at the United Pentecostal Church in Port Arthur. So at Brother Owens' request, I became the Church organist. I sat at the Hammond M-3 organ and followed along as Mona Lou played the piano.

At first, I did not know all of the keys, so I fumbled around until I found each chord. After lunch on Sunday afternoons, I would go to Grandma and Grandpa's house, and I would show Aunt Norma the chords I had used that day. She then told me the name of the chords I was playing, and showed me the other chords that went along with them. After a few weeks, I could play most of the songs in the right key.

In those days, I wrote my first song; it was called "Eternal Life." I remember singing it for Brother and Sister Owens when they came to visit in our home. I sent a copy of it to the Library of Congress and had it copyrighted. It was a good song, and I still sing it occasionally. Another song I wrote when I was about ten years old was called "Peace Be Unto You," and I still sing that song.

Reading The Bible

It was in Sunday School that I first was motivated to read the Bible. A lady named Estelle asked permission to speak to the children, and she told us all about the American Bible Society. She said that if any of us would read the New Testament during the summer months, she would reward us with a new Bible. So for the first time in my life, at age 9, I read the entire New Testament, and received a new Bible. It was an inexpensive little black Bible printed on cheap paper, with red edges, but I carried it for years, until it wore out. The greatest reward of that experience, however, was not the new Bible I received, but the Word of God that was planted in my heart at that early age. What a priceless experience! I loved that Bible, and to this day I can still recall the smell of its pages as I read it in my bed at night.

When I was in the sixth grade, Daddy started selling Thompson Chain-Reference Bibles, and I got one of my own. I loved that Bible and often carried it to school among my other books. I wore it out completely over the years. That Bible probably played as big a role in my learning all about the ways of God as anything in my life. I was fascinated by the topical chain reference system that helped me follow a topic all the way through the Bible. I studied it constantly and learned enormous amounts of things about God in those days.

Miracles

During those days, I had another defining moment in Church. For years, I repeatedly became sick with tonsillitis. During my elementary school years, I often missed school because of tonsillitis, infection and high fever. Missing school wasn't so bad, but I didn't want to miss Church.

We were in the middle of a series of revival services with Evangelist Melvin McKnight from Houston, one of the best-known evangelists in the Assemblies of God at that time. For three or four weeks, services were held every night but Saturday. A lot of sinners were coming to the altars, and many were receiving the Baptism of the Holy Ghost. It was very exciting!

Unfortunately during that time, I came down with tonsillitis. I was so sick, I felt like dying. My fever reached 105 degrees, and I was nearly delirious. I was nauseated and dizzy, but I begged Mother not to make me stay home from Church. After much pleading, and promising that I would lie on the old homemade pew and be still, she consented.

All through service that night, I lay there. I was wretchedly miserable and sick. I couldn't sit up even when I tried. But I listened to the singing, and then the fiery preaching of the evangelist. That night he called for a prayer line. Everybody who had a need was invited to come through the line, and the Pastor and the Evangelist would pray for God to meet their need.

I determined that if I would go through the prayer line, God would heal me. So I got up and dizzily stood in line. I waited and waited. Finally, the preachers laid hands on me and prayed. I guess that since I was just a little kid, they figured a short little prayer would suffice, so that's what I got - a short little prayer. I was so disappointed, because I didn't feel a thing. As I turned to go back to my seat, I felt worse and worse. It didn't make sense. I was supposed to get healed, but I wasn't healed!

So after deliberating a minute or so, I decided that they didn't pray well enough, so I went back to the end of the line, and waited again. I don't remember the look on the preachers' faces when they saw me again, but I distinctly remember Brother McKnight's response when he laid his hand on my forehead and felt my high fever. He exclaimed, "My God, this boy is really sick!"

He then entered into a diligent prayer for the Lord to heal me. Instantly, my fever vanished, and I broke out in a cold sweat. As I walked back to my pew, I felt myself becoming well. The dizziness and nausea vanished. I immediately felt normal again. I went home that night feeling fine, and got up the next morning and went to school without any sign of sickness.

All these many years later I can testify that that miracle made a very profound impact on my life. It convinced me once and for all time of God's ability to perform miracles. I am still convinced today of God's miraculous healing power.

When I was about the age of eleven, the Church experienced some turmoil, and the pastor resigned. Due to some conflict in the congregation, we began seeking out another Church.

We visited several Churches, including the First United Pentecostal Church in Port Arthur, where Brother J.T. Pugh was Pastor. There was a tremendous revival going on at the time. The Church was completing a new building, and a few times my dad and I went to help the workers who were building it.

When they had their dedication services, we went. The place was packed with six or seven hundred people. The special singers were the O'Brien trio, from Starks, Louisiana. I had never heard anything like it in all my life. They sang "Lead Me To That Rock That Is Higher Than I." The congregation came to their feet as the trio sang, and sang, and sang. The sight of that worshipping crowd was awesome to behold.

My little brother and I sometimes sang together, and Brother Pugh invited us to sing at one of the dedication services. I played the big Hammond organ, and David stood beside me as we sang, "I Wouldn't Take Nothing For My Journey Now," and "It's Different Now" in front of that huge crowd. I was eleven, and David was six.

I didn't know a lot about what they believed, but I remember that they made a big deal about some people that were being baptized. The baptistery was built so that it came down the left side of the platform, and across the front a little way. The preacher didn't even have to leave the platform. He merely stepped over a few feet from the pulpit and baptized the candidate. Everybody was very enthusiastic with praise and shouting any time someone was baptized.

Still, we continued to visit other Churches in the vicinity. A small Assembly of God Church in Pear Ridge seemed to really need someone who could help out, and it appeared that we could be more helpful in a small Church than in a big one. At least, that is the reason I thought we decided on it. I learned later that the big Pentecostal Church was preaching different doctrine than we were accustomed to and different teachings about holiness, especially regarding outward appearance.

Right after we settled in the Pear Ridge Church, a distant cousin of mine was invited to come preach a revival there. Donnie Bell and his sister, Patricia (we called her Trish) traveled in trio with a widely-known evangelist at that time, Paul Emerson. Donnie played the electric guitar, and Paul and Trish each played accordions, while the three of them sang together. Donnie's strong preaching was very exciting to hear. I loved to hear him preach.

On a Friday night, the little Church was full. A youth group from Pastor Andy Radke's Church in Vidor came to join us. Donnie performed a very moving one-man musical skit based on the song, "A Child of The King" which was about a rich lady and a poor ditch-digger. Then he preached a powerful sermon.

When the altar call was given, I went to the organ as was my custom, to provide music during the prayer time. Within minutes, several young people had responded to the call, and were kneeling in the altar, praying. Some received the baptism of the Holy Ghost and began speaking in unknown tongues.

As I sat on the organ bench observing the tremendous response, I was suddenly overcome with desire to receive the Holy Ghost experience for myself. Three singers were standing beside me around the organ, singing worship songs, and I thought that I was duty-bound to continue playing. But the more I saw what was happening to the people who were praying, the more I knew that I wanted to be baptized in the Holy Ghost "tonight!"

With tears rolling down my face, I turned to the singers and made some flimsy apology. I stopped playing and jumped up from the organ bench. The silence was deafening for a few moments, but the sounds of people praying soon compensated. I hurried around to the altar bench, fell on my knees, lifted my hands, and began to worship the Lord. In about two minutes, I found myself speaking in tongues, laughing and crying simultaneously, as the Spirit of the Lord filled me for the first time in my life. It was an incredible experience. I must have talked in tongues for at least half an hour. When I finally stopped, I really didn't want to leave.

All the young people who came that night had planned to go out to the country after Church for a "moonlight hike." After all the prayer and praise calmed down, several carloads of young people struck out for Beaumont. We stopped by the Holsum Bread bakery and went inside and bought a few dozen loaves of fresh, hot bread that hadn't even been sliced yet. Then we went down Railroad Avenue to a grocery store and bought several sticks of butter, and everybody ate hot bread and butter.

We then headed for a deserted old farm road outside Vidor, and we all went for a "moonlight hike." In spite of all the activity, however, I couldn't get my mind off the fact that I had just been baptized in the Holy Ghost!

As we walked down that old road that night, I looked up at the star-filled skies and the shiny moon, and began to cry and worship the Lord all over again. "I got the Holy Ghost tonight!"

I couldn't get my mind on the rest of the goings on. I was no good for anything else. So I just thanked Him for filling me with the Holy Ghost.

I believe that night in 1962 was the most defining moment of my life. God began something in me then that would impact everything about me for all of time to come. Not only that, but I also believe that being filled with the Holy Ghost had everything to do with my being preserved and protected through many unspeakably difficult trials throughout my life.

Speaking of the Holy Ghost, Jesus said, "He that believeth on me, as the scripture hath said, out of his belly shall flow rivers of living water," (John 7:38).

That night, I got The River.

Chapter 2

The Call

Church Youth Camp

After I received the baptism of the Holy Ghost, I heard about summer Church Youth Camps. I desperately wanted to go, so I made reservations for my first camp. I had to get special permission from the District Office to attend, because I was not quite twelve years old - the minimum age for campers. By the time school was out at the end of May, I was eagerly anticipating camp.

On Saturday night, before camp began on Monday, I went to bed with Youth Camp on my mind. I could not go to sleep. Before I knew it, I looked at the clock, and it was about 2:00 AM. I felt the presence of the Lord in my room, so I got down on my knees beside my bed and began to pray about the coming week, that the Lord would bless the Camp, and let me be used for His glory while I was there.

As I prayed, I continued to feel God's presence. I felt that the Lord was speaking to me that night. I did not hear any audible words, but I felt in my heart that He was asking me to give Him my whole life for His purpose, and for His work. That night, I made a commitment to Him that I would give Him everything, for whatever He wanted me to do. I wondered if that meant I was going to be a preacher.

At Church the next morning, after service was dismissed, I stood in the aisle and told somebody that I thought the Lord had called me to preach last night. But they just looked at me with a blank stare and didn't respond to what I said. I wondered if I was wrong, or if I shouldn't tell anybody. But the feeling would not leave me. It just got stronger as time passed.

When I finally arrived at Youth Camp, I was asked to play the piano for all the night services. After the preaching each night, the altars filled with about 120 teenagers praying and seeking God. It was a wonderful experience for a young person. That entire week was awesome.

Bible Quizzing

About the time I turned thirteen, the young people in my Church joined the District Bible Quizzing competition. We studied the books of 1 and 2 Corinthians. For several months, I memorized almost the entirety of both books, and could quote most of it on demand. I have no doubt that learning all of those scriptures had a dramatic effect on my belief system for the rest of my life. Paul's epistles to the Corinthians contain some very, very important New Testament teachings on a wide variety of subjects, including preaching, baptism, the carnal mind versus the mind of the Spirit, judging, marriage, hair length, communion, the Gifts of the Spirit, Church discipline, and so much more. What a powerful initiation to the Gospel I received in those days!

My First Invitation To Speak

At the end of the Bible Quizzing season, Pastor Lindell Buck invited me to speak at a Christmas banquet for his Church youth group in Orange, Texas. That was in 1964. I was too young to drive a car, so Mother took me to the meeting. The banquet was held at a huge stone mansion, and the setting was very elegant. I delivered my first sermon to the young people and the adults who were present.

The first sermon that I have a written record of, I found notated in my Granny's Bible after she died. She always made a note in the margin when a preacher read his sermon text, writing his name and the date. "Kenneth - 4/24/66 - Sunday night." The text was Romans 8:11: "But if the Spirit of Him that raised up Jesus from the dead dwell in you, he that raised up Christ from the dead shall also quicken your mortal bodies." I was fourteen when I preached on that text. I preached that you needed to have the baptism of the Holy Ghost.

Preaching In My Home Church

My Pastor, N. Jay Broaddus, invited me to preach on a Wednesday night in my home Church. I worked feverishly preparing that sermon, and ended up with about twenty-five pages of hand-written notes. I wrote out everything I was going to say word-for-word.

When the Pastor called me to the pulpit, I stepped up, opened my Bible, and started to unfold my notes. As I nervously fumbled with the papers, they slipped out of my hands and fell on the floor, scattering in every direction! And the pages were not numbered! I panicked. I stooped down and gathered them up, laid them in a sloppy pile on the pulpit, and took a deep breath. I was mortified. It would take too long to sort the pages back into order, so I had to just speak from memory as best I could. The sermon only lasted about ten minutes. I was sorely embarrassed, but I really felt like I had something to say, so I just preached what was in my heart.

In all honesty, I cannot imagine why anybody wanted to hear a fifteen-year-old boy preach, but I was well received, and I was given many more opportunities.

Music Versus Preaching

Music was always a major part of my ministry. God gave me a special gift to sing and play the piano and organ. At 14, I was the organist for a huge South Texas District Youth Conference at Victory Assembly in Beaumont, attended by about 600 kids. I always had plenty of opportunities to use the musical gifts.

But music NEVER was as important to me as my desire to preach the Gospel. I NEVER believed that Gospel music was as important as preaching, and I never wanted to be known as just a Gospel musician. I believed that I was supposed to be a preacher.

Preachers Molded Me

Preaching molded me from my earliest days. Even as a small boy, I sat on the front row in Church and listened to the preacher. I said, "Amen!" and I went to the altar when the altar call was given.

In my childhood years, Christianity was FAR DIFFERENT than it is today. Preachers in virtually every Christian denomination still preached firmly against worldliness. It may have sounded primitive to our modern ears, but it was not wrong then, and it is not wrong now. Preachers in those days actually read their Bibles, and prayed and fasted. They preached against worldliness because God and His Word was against worldliness. Today, most preachers have never read the Bible as they should, so they don't feel the need to preach those things. They just pass around the latest, hottest feel-good sermons.

In earlier years, even the Methodists and Baptists preached against going to dances, pool halls, "picture shows" (movie theaters) and sporting events. Sin was black, and it made you feel guilty. That is what altars were for. People went to the altars, confessed their sins, repented and asked God to forgive them, and they promised they would not keep on doing those things. That was the way it should be.

Those preachers were not wrong. But over the years, they got outnumbered and overpowered by carnally-minded people in the pews.

Preaching Condemned Sin, And Called Sinners To Repent

In my childhood, every preacher I ever listened to preached against WORLDLINESS.

They preached against smoking, gambling, cursing, chewing tobacco, drinking, carousing, and plenty of other vices. They intended to straighten people up! When people came to Church, they expected to be CHANGED! If they weren't ready to be changed, they just stayed home. The preachers did not hesitate to say when things were sinful! And that was not wrong.

They preached against women looking like Jezebels with their makeup and jewelry and immodest clothes. They said that was sinful, too. They were not wrong. Again, they just got outnumbered and overpowered by carnally-minded people in the pews. The women did not want to look like prudes, and neither did their men, so the preachers just got replaced with others who did not object to makeup and jewelry and Jezebel ways. The women wanted to cut their hair and look sexy like the women on TV and in the movies, so they came to disdain the preachers who preached against those things. At best, they ignored the call to holiness and separation. At worst, they utterly rebelled against it.

Now, most preachers just wink at sin and let people get by with all those things. Our modern generation of preachers has learned that it is enormously profitable to comfort people in their sins. A preacher who will let people do whatever they want to do will soon have the largest Church in town, and the most money. These "come-as-you-are, do-as-you-please" Churches have siphoned off the crowds from the few Pastors who have tried to maintain their convictions, just like discounter Walmart has effectively shut down so many mom-and-pop businesses. The guy who preaches the Word of God with real convictions nowadays may just have to get a secular job and support himself after the cheap-grace Churches empty his congregation.

When television first came around, preachers everywhere went into a tizzy. I remember hearing preachers declaring war on men who stayed home from Sunday night services to watch "Gunsmoke" and "The Ed Sullivan Show." Nowadays, Churches don't even meet on Sunday nights. Instead, everybody goes to the movie theaters and watches every kind of corruption. Hollywood definitely won that round. But nobody cares. They are just glad they don't have to take the kids to Church on Sunday night.

Almost nobody thinks it is wrong to watch anything anymore. In the days before movie ratings, preachers tried their best to keep people from movies that, by today's standard, were totally innocent. But they weren't innocent. The oldest black-and-white movies constantly promoted lying, cheating, smoking, drinking, immorality, crime and all kinds of other vices. But because today's movie fare is infinitely more vile, the old movies look innocent by comparison. We have just become used to the dark. It no longer alarms us.

Television and Hollywood can now say or do anything and everything they want, and professing Christians just sit there and soak it up like a pump truck sucking up slime. And if a preacher raises his voice against television or Hollywood, he is blacklisted from nearly every pulpit in America. Christians used to refuse to watch any movie with an R or X rating, but those days are gone. Most preachers nowadays are as addicted to television and Hollywood and sports as any rank sinner was forty years ago, so you can never expect those preachers to condemn the many evils that are inherent in them. The ministry is FAILING mankind today, because the MINISTERS themselves are as WORLDLY and SINFUL as common sinners were in previous generations.

Preachers Hated The World, And The World Hated Preachers

The men who pastored me when I was young told me that I should not participate in organized sports because it would turn my heart away from God and Church. (Most denominations have in the past had official statements condemning organized sports!) They said it was one thing if you had to work around sinners, but if you had a choice, you should not hang with sinners in your free time. Christians were not supposed to be friends with the world, or spend their time hanging around ungodly people, listening to their cussing, and running around with them while they talked about drinking, and partying and carousing. They said that participating in football, or basketball, or the other sports turned your heart away from God, Church and righteous living. It took away from your spiritual man.

I believed them! I believed that if I ran with the ungodly crowd at school, I would lose my desire to be what God wanted me to be. And I was right about that. It is still true. You can't pray and read your Bible and do the things that God wants you to do when your heart is wrapped up in the things of the world.

Preachers preached, "touch not the unclean thing." Dancing was taboo. Dancing was rightfully labeled as something that unnecessarily stirred up the human passions. It made young people lust for each other, and tempted them to other sins. Young Christians did not go to the Proms or the school dances. But nowadays, Christians spend more time raving about "American Idol" and "Dancing With The Stars" than they do discussing the Bible or the things of God. Now, many of our little girls are enrolled in ballet dance lessons, and we put them on the Church stage to dance for us in their skimpy little costumes. And increasingly, "Christians" are the winning contestants in the latest dance contests, band contests and singing contests. Once the world has put their stamp of approval on them, the Church treats them like celebrities! They end up becoming the Praise and Worship leaders in the mega-Churches, or worse, they migrate out into the secular entertainment business where a nickel's worth of Christian lyrics mixed with a dollar's worth of worldliness will make them a big celebrity. What is wrong with this scenario?

Now, in most Churches, it is perfectly permissible to come to Church looking like Jezebel, with all the makeup, jewelry and immodesty that you want. Any and all hairstyles are welcomed, except any hairstyle that is clearly modest and conservative, or (God forbid!) makes you look like a Pentecostal. In that case, you will almost certainly be told that you need to be loosed from the bondage of legalism.

As a young boy, going to Church, reading my Bible, praying, living a holy life, and working to bring people into the Kingdom of God was LIFE!! Going to Church was the most important thing in life. If the Pastor called a revival meeting to run seven nights in a row, we were there ALL SEVEN NIGHTS!

If the people were responding well to the preaching, the Pastor was likely to extend the meeting for another seven nights. It was not uncommon to go to Church every single night for two or three weeks at a time! And we were happy to be there every night!

I thought the whole world needed Church! The whole world needed God! Everybody needed to be delivered from their sinful ways to serve the Lord!

And that made me want to preach! I wanted to be a part of the divine process of leading people OUT OF THEIR SINS into a HOLY LIFE in Church -- the FAMILY OF GOD!

A Faithful Preacher Will Convict Sinners Of Their Sins

I marvel in disbelief at how well modern preachers justify the very things that were ALWAYS WRONG for centuries before. Preachers do not call people to the altars any more. Most Churches do not have altars. We rarely, if ever, see a man or woman weeping sorely in repentance for their evil ways.

All you have to do now, (according to the new generation of preachers) is "accept the Lord Jesus Christ," by showing your hand and saying a 25-word prayer. Then you are free to go home and catch the afternoon football game on TV. No big deal. Go on and hurry home. Forget the sermon as fast as you can. You can sign your annual giving pledge next Sunday.

I have no doubt whatsoever that those old-time preachers were exactly right about worldliness. I have watched the entire evolution of Christianity very closely through the years, and I have seen NOTHING spiritually beneficial about letting "Christians" be more "worldly." I have watched two generations of young people drop out of Church because they got too close to the world. Anybody who thinks the modern Church is BETTER OFF NOW than it was forty years ago is blindly deluded. The modern Church is FALLING AWAY - exactly like the Bible prophets said it would.

Nowadays, the preachers are OK with worldliness. They don't preach against those things. In fact, many preachers nowadays are sports fanatics, and actually encourage Church events in tandem with major sporting events. One start-up congregation I heard of recently received one million dollars in start-up cash. And their evangelistic strategy is staging BIG-SCREEN FOOTBALL EVENTS on Sunday evenings to attract crowds. Then they teach Bible studies during half-time. God and sports idols are being worshipped together.

Preachers and Church members now spend their Sunday nights at the movie theaters. It is common to learn of Pastors who drink, and it is not surprising to find that many Pastors' offices in the larger Churches have wet bars!! Dancing is now done IN THE CHURCH, with ballet and dance classes considered WORSHIP! Many Churches sponsor events for young adults and/or married couples where dancing and drinking are part of the evening's entertainment. Some Churches charter buses to NASCAR races, or other major sporting events. And I'm talking about PENTECOSTAL Churches!

"Follow ...holiness, without which no man shall see the Lord." There is going to be a sad, tragic and rude awakening on Judgment Day when all these "Worldly Christians" face Almighty God at the judgment and discover that HE WAS NOT OK with those things.

Jesus said, "And then will I profess unto them, I never knew you: depart from me, ye that work iniquity," Matthew 7:23. If you don't depart from the world, you will eventually be forced to depart from God.

If my earliest Pastors had not preached the way they did, I would have almost certainly gone the way of the world. And I am absolutely convinced that MOVIES, SPORTS, and all the other WORLDLY HABITS have COST THE CHURCH thousands upon thousands of potential young preachers who NEVER HEARD THE CALL OF GOD, because the WORLD drowned it all out.

Worldliness in the Church is the equivalent of ABORTION among America's youth. Worldliness has aborted more young men and women of God, (and older people, too) than all the fetuses that have been aborted in abortion clinics.

Worldliness in the Church produces an IMPOTENT CHURCH in which young people no longer hear the call of God to separate themselves unto holy living. Our young people desperately need to hear the kind of preaching that some of us older people were raised on. It helped us to stay in Church for decades, and it would have the same effect on them, too.

The call of God is to PREACH ALL THE COUNSEL OF GOD (Acts 20:27).

I believe that is The Call I received when I was 11 years old, and that is the same call I am trying to follow at this very moment.

Long Winding Road

Chapter 3

Facing The Music

Musician

By the time I was fifteen, I had learned how to play the piano, organ, accordion, guitar, and bass. I bought my first Fender electric guitar and Fender amplifier when I was fourteen. I practiced at home with recordings of Gospel groups until I could emulate every guitar lick on the records. As a result, I was on the stage making music in every Church service. I alternated playing the piano, organ, accordion, and guitar.

I learned about music theory and got my vocal training in the Junior High School "A" Choir for three years. Because I was performing music and singing every time I went to Church, I had much more experience than all the other Choir members, so the teacher often expected more out of me. I received awards in Interscholastic League contests each year, and sang "The Lord's Prayer" for the Junior High Commencement. The High School Choir teacher came to the Junior High to conduct auditions among the 9th graders. She drafted me for the Senior Concert Choir, which I was in for three years. I sometimes directed that Choir.

At contests, I scored a First Place in Regional and Statewide Competitions, in solos and ensembles, and had the privilege of performing in three nightly concerts with the 200-voice Texas All-State Choir, accompanied by a 450-piece All-State Band and Orchestra before 7,000 people in the Austin Municipal Auditorium. That was an exhilarating experience. Afterward, I was offered a full music scholarship to Sam Houston State University, but I declined it, because I felt that I should pursue the ministry.

As a companion to my music studies, I also took several years of speech and drama classes from sixth to the twelfth grades. I participated in poetry and prose speaking events, was on the debate team, and worked on the High School tabloid newspaper, as a reporter, in layout, then as an Editor.

But singing and playing music was my passion. Everyone who sang Gospel music was my model. Mike Murdoch, who is now a widely-known television "prosperity" evangelist, held revivals in our little Church, playing and singing with his first wife, Linda. I had all their albums.

I remember my Pastor's wife bringing an album to Church with her one night because she wanted Mother to take it home and listen to it. It was the first release by an Assemblies of God evangelist from Ferriday, Louisiana. Everybody was talking about his tremendous revivals. His name was Jimmy Swaggart.

In those days, Swaggart still traveled from Church to Church by car, and sang by the hour, pumping a huge, black accordion as he sang. I saw him sing and preach for the first time when I attended the 1969 General Council of the Assemblies of God in the Tarrant County Convention Center in Fort Worth. His "Camp Meeting Hour" radio broadcasts were just beginning to be heard nationwide, and his dynamic stage presence was taking the Assemblies of God by a storm. At first, I thought his style was really behind the times, and I didn't really like it, but then it occurred to me that he was making an impact on the whole country, so it couldn't be all bad. So I got on the Swaggart bandwagon, too.

Gospel Quartets

From my elementary school days, I must have attended every Gospel concert that came to our area. Those were the days when the Statesmen Quartet with Hovie Lister, and the Blackwood Brothers with James Blackwood were traveling together, doing concerts with simple piano accompaniment. I'll never forget their appearance at Woodrow Wilson High School auditorium in Port Arthur. "Whitey" Gleason was the pianist for the Blackwood Brothers, and he was exceptionally talented. Those quartets could rouse an audience to their feet as they dramatically swooned their voices into the huge, rectangular RCA ribbon microphones, blaring powerfully above the cheers of the crowd through the monstrous "Voice of the Theatre" speakers. Music like this had never been heard before.

Gospel quartets sprang up everywhere: The Oak Ridge Boys, the Tennesseans, Jake Hess and the Imperials, The Sego Brothers and Naomi, The Dixie Echoes, The Florida Boys and many more. The Stamps Quartet and the Jordanaires backed up Elvis Presley. Even secular entertainers were getting in on Gospel acts. Louisiana Governor Jimmy Davis, Jimmie

Dean, Tennessee Ernie Ford, "Gentleman" Jim Reeves, and of course, Elvis produced Gospel albums that were enormously popular.

The Oak Ridge Boys came through town singing Gospel music several times, long before they ever performed country-western music. Little Willie Wynn was their featured high tenor singer, and few men in the business could stir the crowds like he did in those days. My bedroom walls were lined with autographed photos of many of the groups, including the Statesmen, the Blackwood Brothers, the LeFevres, the Stamps, the Happy Goodmans, the Galileans, and others.

Gospel music mesmerized me. In our home, Gospel music played loudly on the record player day and night. Nearly every song that was recorded in those days became a part of my repertoire. My younger brother David and I practiced singing at the piano in the living room with our front door wide open. Across the street, the neighbors would come out on their front porches to sit and listen to us sing.

When I was 12, my parents purchased a Hammond Organ for me. I spent countless hours alone in the living room playing the piano or the organ. Often, as soon as I came in from school in the evenings, I would go into the living room, close all the doors and curtains, and sit and play music for hours at a time. I still remember the glow of the orange pilot light on that organ as I made music in the dark. I would sing and play and worship God. Occasionally, I felt inspired to write a song. A lot of that time was intimate time between God and me alone, and intensely personal.

Children's Ministry

At thirteen years old, I received my first job as a "professional" Gospel musician, traveling with Kids Crusade evangelist, Don Hicks, for an entire summer, providing music ministry in his Kids Crusades and revivals. We toured Churches in Texas and Louisiana, the highlight being the Louisiana District A/G Kids Camp in Tioga. Along with singing and playing, I learned from him the methods of Child Evangelism, including Ventriloquism, "Magic" (sleight-of-hand), and story-telling.

The summer following my ninth grade in school, I traveled briefly with a Gospel group around the Houston area, playing guitar and bass. Then I accompanied another family singing group down to the Rio Grande Valley for a series of meetings, preaching, and playing the piano for them.

Licensed To Preach

I had begun preaching when I was thirteen, so I made application to the District Board of the South Texas Assemblies of God for my Ministerial Credentials for the first time in 1966, at the age of 14. They refused my application, saying that I was too young. I applied again in 1967 at the age of 15, and they refused again. I had already preached in scores of Churches. Finally, in 1968, at the age of sixteen, I received my "Exhorters Permit."

As I entered into the tenth grade, I formed another trio, and sang and played the piano with them. We were invited to sing in several Churches, and in most cases, I also preached. The Evangel Trio consisted of me, another guy and a girl from our local Church. We sang, and I preached in many of the nearby Churches at first.

Then we were invited to sing at a South Texas District Conference in Houston. Over 500 Churches were represented in that conference. Our state Youth President asked us to represent the District Youth Department in every Sectional Rally that year, promoting Summer Youth Camps. From there, our services took on the nature of youth crusades.

So at the ripe old age of fifteen, I ended up preaching and singing in the presence of hundreds of pastors in the South Texas District. The trio conducted services almost every weekend around the state for about a year and a half. We appeared on television programs on two local stations during that time, and became well-known among our peers.

One of my first big preaching opportunities came when I was 17. The trio sang, and I preached Sunday morning and Sunday night to over a thousand people at Lindale A/G in Houston, pastored by James McKeehan. It was quite an honor to be in that pulpit at 17, considering that the last revival they had there was a twelve-week revival with Jimmy Swaggart, and previous to that, the famed Jerry B. Walker, who was known for his sign-gift ministry.

Drama

As my Senior Year at Port Neches-Groves High School came to an end, I became heavily involved in extracurricular activities at school. I had enjoyed being in the Drama Department for two years previously, and had performed in the cast of a satire called "The Pot Boiler," and in William Shakespeare's "The Taming of the Shrew," both for Interscholastic League competition. Both years, our school won high honors in our region.

My drama teacher and my choir teacher drafted me to play the lead role in the Senior Play, a Broadway show called "Bye-Bye Birdie." I refused to do the role at first, because it had several dance routines, and I told them I would not dance. When they agreed to cut the dance segments, I consented. I had the same role that Dick Van Dyke played in the movie.

For the first time in my life, I began to spend more time on worldly activities than in Church activities. The energy that came from being in the spotlight and singing with a live fifty-piece orchestra was mind-altering. Not until the production was finished, and we had performed it for the last time to a full house, did I face the reality of how I had compromised myself spiritually for popularity with a secular crowd. But soon, I graduated, and that stage of life was over.

Youth Ministry

I immediately went back to my old priorities. I prayed earnestly for God to give me direction and a course to take upon graduating from High School. The South Texas District's C.A. (Christ Ambassadors) President approached me again, and asked me to be the Assistant Camp Director for five weeks of summer youth camps - four at Camp Pearl Wheat in Kerrville, and one at Camp Victory in Silsbee. I jumped at the opportunity.

For a seventeen year-old preacher, this was a valuable leadership role among ministers and youth from hundreds of Churches. As a result of my involvement in those camps, I received invitations to minister all over the district. I quickly booked the remainder of the summer with revivals and children's crusades.

That summer, I conducted five weeks of Children's Crusades, incorporating ventriloquism with two characters - Danny O'Day and Louie the Lip - to teach Bible lessons to the children. I made Gospel lessons out of sleight-of-hand "magic" tricks and told lots of stories using large flannelgraph illustrations. I also preached numerous revival services in A/G Churches around the district as I had done for almost four years.

Future Unknown

I met Dixie Weiler for the first time in the summer of 1969, at Camp Victory in Silsbee. She was sixteen.

Church camp. That says a lot. Church was the central part of both of our lives. We were both key players back in our home Churches, at least among the youth. Dixie sang in the Church Choir, and also sang with a girls' trio. She was a role model to several of the other girls in Church. Camp Victory was owned by Victory Assembly of God in Beaumont, pastored by B.H. Clendennen. That was Dixie's home Church, and he was her Pastor.

Dixie was a favorite camper. The year before, she had attended Camp Pearl Wheat and was honored as "Most Beautiful" girl. That honor rewarded her with free tuition to the camp of her choice this summer. She won that title, "Most Beautiful" again this summer at Camp Victory. Everybody loved Dixie. She loved God deeply, prayed earnestly, read her Bible, and loved to sing and worship God. She was a model young woman.

Dixie grew up in Church at Sabine Tabernacle in Beaumont, a large "Full-Gospel" Church pastored by Harry Hodge. Brother Hodge had been on a local television station for many years, and had a huge following. He also presided over a fellowship of about twenty-eight "Full-Gospel" Churches in East Texas and Louisiana.

Dixie's mother and grandmother were very faithful to that Church, and always helped with the annual "Convention" that attracted over a thousand people each year. They worked in the Church kitchen feeding the crowds that stayed in the dorms there for several days. When Harry Hodge died, Dixie's family eventually migrated to Pastor Clendennen's Church, Victory Assembly of God.

I think Dixie was the brightest light at Camp Victory. She was the center of attention in whatever she was doing. She had the brightest smile and contagious laughter. She always looked picture-perfect - impeccably groomed. Her clothes and shoes were always attractive; her hair was always perfectly styled, and never a hair out of place. She loved interacting with people and playing innocent pranks that would get a laugh. But after Youth Camp was over, I did not see Dixie again for two years. Little did I know that she would become my wife some day.

College

That fall, at my parents' urging, I attended Lamar College in Beaumont. My S.A.T. exams had shown that math was my strongest aptitude. I was definitely interested in the new field of computers, so I enrolled in 21 hours of computer programming-related subjects, learning to write programs in FORTRAN and COBOL, and training on all the current IBM Data Processing equipment, including a 1401 mainframe. The career track there was to become a Systems Analyst. It would have been a very lucrative career, had I stayed with it. I was elected the President of the Lamar Data Processing Society. As such, I was one of the first people in Texas to be introduced to the IBM System 3 Computer, the first of the third-generation computers. My future in computers looked interesting and bright. I received a personal guided tour of Exxon's Houston Data Processing Center and their IBM 360 mainframe.

During those college days, while hanging out at the Chi Alpha center, (the Assemblies of God student organization) at Lamar Assembly of God Church, Pastor Cleddie Keith invited me to come to work at the Church as his Assistant, and as teacher of the Adult Bible Class, Church Organist and Choir Director. It was a Church of about 125 to 150 members, and that was my first paid staff position ever.

By the end of that semester, however, I was unhappy with my decision to pursue a career in computers. I felt certain that my call to the ministry should take precedence over my interest in computer programming, so I fasted and prayed about it and asked God to show me what to do.

During a Wednesday night service, while I was sitting at the organ, someone gave a message in tongues, and the Pastor interpreted the message. These forty years later, I do not remember the exact message, but I know that I believed that message was my confirmation that I should fully pursue the ministry. In that service, I came to the conclusion that I should leave Lamar and enroll in Bible College.

I left Church that night and drove immediately to Port Arthur where Daddy and Mother were still in service at their Church. I walked into the auditorium as their service was ending, and sat down on the pew with them. I told them that I had received an answer from the Lord, and that I had decided to leave Lamar and go to Bible College in Springfield, Missouri. It was Christmas time, 1969, and enrollment at the Bible College began the very next week. My folks asked, "When do you plan to go?" I said, "Immediately."

The next day, I informed the Dean of the Computer Department at Lamar that I intended to leave and attend Bible College. He was very upset. He and I had worked very closely together, and I was his star student. He believed I had big potential in computers. He tried to persuade me to stay. He said, "If you will stay for another year, I will PERSONALLY pay for it!" But I could not be persuaded.

I called my old Pastor from Groves who was then pastoring in Farmers Branch in the Dallas area. I told him that I would be passing through Dallas on the way to Springfield and would like to stop by and visit him. He invited me to preach in his Church that Sunday morning and Sunday night, so that is what I did. The following day, I arrived in Springfield, and enrolled for classes at Central Bible College.

Revivaltime

I was immediately inducted into the radio Choir for REVIVALTIME, the international radio broadcast for the Assemblies of God. On the REVIVALTIME set, I met and listened to C.M. Ward, one of the most widely-known preachers of the day. He preached every broadcast on Sunday nights in the 400-seat radio auditorium at the International Headquarters of the Assemblies of God, 1445 Boonville Ave, Springfield, Missouri. Every Sunday night, our Choir sang live on 650 stations of the ABC RADIO network, and later by tape to hundreds of other stations. I became one of the soloists in the Choir. Under the direction of Cyril McClellan, we toured that year through Missouri, Kansas, Colorado, and Nebraska during the weeks before and after Easter.

In February, Kurt Kaiser came from Word Records to produce the annual Revivaltime Choir album in the A/G Headquarters' studio. Cyril McClellan charted a solo part into one of the songs and called on me to sing it. We did three or four takes, and I was unhappy with the way I sounded, so I asked him to scratch my solo. The record was released nationally - without the solo. The female soloist for Revivaltime, Gloria Elliot, went on to become a well-known singer around the world. She recorded numerous albums and continues to travel, performing in concerts and TV appearances. I can only wonder what might have happened differently in my life if I hadn't declined that solo opportunity. I have learned, however, that there are no mistakes with God in control.

Bible College

Meanwhile, on the campus of Central Bible College, I associated with several different crusade teams, traveling on weekends to points in Missouri, Iowa, Illinois, Kentucky, and Tennessee - playing, singing and preaching. While there, at the age of eighteen, I received my General Ministerial License from the Missouri District of the Assemblies of God. I preached out nearly every weekend while at Bible College. Two men in my home Church in Springfield were interested in forming a male trio. Those were the days when "The Couriers" were especially popular, and we adapted their style of music. We formed a trio and evangelized for a while.

One day, as I walked down the hallway of my fourth-floor dormitory, I heard a song coming out of one of the dorm rooms.

> I've got confidence God is gonna see me through.
> No matter what the case may be,
> I know He's gonna fix it for me.

I had never heard that song or that group before. I knocked on the door and asked who those singers were. It was Andrae' Crouch and the Disciples. January 1970. I remember that day as well as the day John F. Kennedy was shot, or the day that Elvis died. Andrae' Crouch's music not only electrified Gospel music, it radically revolutionized it overnight. "Through It All," "The Blood Will Never Lose Its Power," and so many others became legendary classics. From that day, I learned to play and sing just about everything Andrae' ever recorded.

Toward the end of the first semester, I began to play the piano occasionally for a girl in the Revivaltime Choir who was an outstanding singer. She had already recorded her first album, and had several singing engagements in surrounding Churches. We did several weekend meetings together. She sang, and I preached. At first it was strictly a platonic relationship, but after a while, we began to date.

During the summer months, I returned home to work in a local refinery to earn some money to take back to college. I proposed marriage to my girlfriend toward the end of the summer, and we became engaged. When I returned to Springfield, she chose not to return to college in the fall, so I decided to go to Kansas City where she lived. The A/G pastor there took me into his home, and I became something of an assistant to him.

Teen Challenge

One of my first projects there was to work with him on a city-wide Youth Rally featuring Nicky Cruz. David Wilkerson's book, "The Cross and the Switchblade" was a national best-seller at the time, and Nicky was one of the worst street-gang members who was converted under Wilkerson's ministry. Nicky's story was featured in "The Cross and the Switchblade."

I had recently been an altar worker in Wilkerson's crusade in Beaumont, and had done some street evangelism among the hippies at the Teen Challenge Coffeehouse on Allen's Landing in downtown Houston. I knew of nothing in the United States at that time that compared with the dynamics of what God seemed to be doing through David Wilkerson and the Teen Challenge ministries.

We rented the Broadway Theater in downtown Kansas City for Friday night, and packed about 800 teen-agers in. Nicky's testimony was provocative, and hundreds of kids responded to the altar call that night.

Trio

I soon formed another trio with my fiancée and a guy in the local Church. It immediately began to attract a lot of attention, because all three of us were seasoned musicians. Both of them had already recorded their own Gospel albums, and all of us had extensive backgrounds in music ministry.

Long Winding Road

We added a fourth member who served as our organist. I played the piano and sang.

The Kansas City Youth for Christ auditorium became our hangout. About 2500 teen-agers from a 100-mile radius packed the huge auditorium every weekend. They literally came in bus loads. We became the house talent in the Saturday Night Youth Rallies and performed every Saturday night. There was also a recording studio in the headquarters where we rehearsed every song for hours and hours. From there, we were invited to sing in Churches of nearly every denomination.

We sang on a Sunday morning to over a thousand at Baptist Temple. Then, we performed for a big Sunday afternoon concert at the gilded Methodist Church downtown. The huge Nazarene Church in Kansas City, Kansas insisted that we sing nothing but Bill Gaither's songs, and not surprisingly, we had several Gaither songs in our repertoire. We also performed songs by Lanny Wolfe, Dottie Rambo, Andre' Crouch, and used some arrangements by the McDuff Brothers (John, Coleman and Roger), who were outstanding ministers and singers in the A/G. We traveled around the state, and the neighboring states.

Going Pro

A brother of one of the trio members owned an insurance company, and he became our financial backer. He loved our sound, so he purchased a complete video camera and recording system (in 1970 they were reel-to-reel and black-and-white) and began video-taping our events so we could review them and "polish" our act. Eventually, he became our manager. The Dean of Music at Central Bible College helped arrange for us a recording contract with a national rock-and-roll label which was opening a Gospel division. Being their first Gospel group, the musicians they hired to back us up were strictly rhythm and blues - they sounded more like Janis Joplin's band than a Gospel group, but we were enjoying the possibilities. It was quite an experience to have our songs take on a new dimension, with a full band behind us. Only two groups in the country traveled with a full band - Jake Hess and the Imperials, and Andrae' Crouch and the Disciples. Everybody else simply used a piano. We cut three songs and were working on the fourth.

Our trio became well-known in that region very quickly. We did warm-ups in concerts with several of the best-known Gospel groups in those days: the Blackwood Brothers, the Statesmen, the Imperials, the Oak Ridge Boys, the Spear Family, the Downings, the Florida Boys, the Galileans, the Happy Goodman Family, Rosie Roselle and the Searchers, and a few others.

W.B. Nowlin was the legendary "Battle of Songs" (Gospel concert) promoter, and probably the biggest talent agent for Gospel artists in those days. He helped Elvis Presley get his start. Nowlin came to audition us during a Friday night concert with some of his other artists, and we were on the verge of signing a contract with him as our agent.

We were well into the production of our first album when my fiancée and I began to have serious personal conflicts. I never expected it to end in a break-up, but one day I went to pick her up, and she sent word by her mother that she did not want to see me again. She refused to even speak to me. In one sudden, unexpected, shocking moment, the wedding was off, the trio was over, and EVERYTHING came to an instant halt. I was absolutely stunned!

Viet Nam?

That VERY SAME DAY, I went home and found a letter from the Selective Service - the Draft Board - in my mailbox. It told me to report immediately for a physical exam for the Army. After leaving Bible College, I lost my draft deferment. The Viet Nam War was not yet over, and suddenly, it looked like I was going to be sent to Viet Nam. I was literally in shock as I found myself driving to Houston, Texas to face the Draft Board.

On the way to Houston, I stopped in Fort Worth because I knew that my friend Rosie Roselle was in concert with the Searchers at the Will Rogers Auditorium. For many years, Rosie was the tenor singer for the Statesmen Quartet, but he had his own group at that time. I went backstage and told him about my shocking turn of events. I was very upset about everything, and asked him to pray for me. We had a good prayer together.

When I got home, miraculously, my family doctor wrote a letter to the draft board describing some back trouble I had during High School. Subsequently, their physical exam showed that I had an abnormality in my lower back that disqualified me from the Army. I was never so thankful to have a health problem. Otherwise, my story may have ended in Viet Nam.

Big Decisions To Make

Rosie Roselle asked me to consider coming with him and the Searchers as their pianist, but I didn't feel like that was the right thing for me to do at the time. Just a few days later, Rusty Goodman learned that I was available and called and asked me to audition for the Happy Goodman family. They were contemplating some changes and wanted to know if I was available to travel with them. I met them on-stage at one of their concerts and talked to him about the details, but I did not think, at the time, that I was ready to make a commitment to live on the road. I still had preaching on my heart.

Gospel music bid high for my soul in those days. I played the piano on various occasions for some of the best-known Gospel artists in the country: Howard and Vestal Goodman, Lulu Roman (from Hee-Haw TV show), Walt Mills, Big John Hall (formerly the bass singer with the Blackwood Brothers), and several others. But I did not want to forfeit my preaching ministry to be a professional Gospel musician.

My heart compelled me to follow the call to preach the Gospel. But the Gospel music business itself also left a little bit of a bitter taste in my mouth. The more I rubbed shoulders with professional Gospel musicians, the more I learned about things that I did not want to know. After a large concert one night, I was standing around outside with members of a very well-known group. Inside their tour bus, I discovered that there were girls traveling with them who were not their wives. There was some pretty obvious hanky-panky going on, and my mind was blown when I realized it.

On another occasion, in Little Rock, Arkansas, I happened to see the members of another well-known Gospel quartet coming out of a local bar. They were drinking and smoking after the concert that night. Again, I was shocked and disappointed to learn that they were not the real deal.

After a while, it occurred to me that a large percentage of the Gospel music professionals RARELY attended Church! A lot of them lived on the road almost year-round. Just about the only time they attended Church was when they were performing in a Church. That meant that they almost never heard any real Gospel preaching. That was very disturbing to me, because I believe that everybody has to go to Church to hear the preaching if they intend to live a godly life. The Bible says, "Faith comes by hearing the word of God..." and "Forsake not the assembling of yourselves together..."

Nevertheless, the lure of being a professional Gospel musician was a strong one. Certainly, not all the musicians were phony. Many were very sincere people. At last, it was a really BIG choice that I had to make to stay the course to be a preacher. Nobody knows how big (except God). I came very close to being a career musician.

The Voice Of Victory

I was 19 when I returned to Beaumont in May of 1971. With the threat of Viet Nam now passed, I looked for a Church to call home. I knew of Pastor Clendennen, and had seen him preach on local television over the years, so I decided to visit Victory Assembly of God - a congregation of about 500-600 at that time.

I visited on a Sunday night, and sat in the congregation. At the end of the service, an old friend, Chester Bethel, introduced me to Pastor Clendennen, and told him about my singing, music and preaching ministries. (I had traveled briefly with his family singing group years earlier.)

Pastor Clendennen was expanding his television ministry at that time to 150 stations across America. He told me that he needed to hire someone at the Church to travel with him in television crusades and to help in the local ministry. I accepted the offer on the spot, and went to work for him the next day. I became his Crusade Pianist and Singer, flying from coast to coast to auditoriums, civic centers and Churches in 1-3 night crusades in places like Spokane, Albuquerque, St Louis, Philadelphia, Rochester, Charlotte, New Orleans and many others.

At home, I became the teacher of the College and Career Class, the Choir Director, the Church Pianist, and occasionally filled the pulpit for the Pastor. Shortly, I inherited the job of Editor and Publisher of his monthly 16-page "Streams of Faith" magazine, and his weekly newsletters, which were sent to 12,000 households at first. His list grew quickly to 35,000 monthly, and we changed the name of the magazine and the television and radio programs to "The International Voice of Victory." Each month I edited and published a major sermon of his. I also edited his recorded messages for radio. He was on about thirty radio stations.

Many of the earlier events of that year had seemed very tragic and upsetting to me at the time, and nothing seemed to make sense. But forty years later I can see that God's hand was carefully guiding me in the direction that I needed to go. Many of the roles I played in those days prepared me for the ministry that I now have through my writing and publishing.

I view my time with Pastor Clendennen as having been divinely ordained. I felt that I was a kindred spirit to his message and ministry, and his vision for world evangelism far exceeded anything I had ever known any other Pentecostal preacher to have. In the few years I worked and traveled with him, we saw many, many people receive the Baptism of the Holy Ghost, and many miracles of healing in our Crusades and Camp Meetings around the country.

I was not the same person after that. I learned in those days that one man can make a difference. One man can preach, can write, can broadcast, can crusade, and can reach the masses if he will. In the forty years since then, I watched him from afar as he circled the globe in his old age, and planted Bible schools in about 150 nations before he died.

But in those early days, in that setting in Beaumont, a model for ministry was indelibly burned into my soul. The die was cast. I would never be like most preachers. I wanted to preach the Gospel to the whole world. And I still do.

Long Winding Road

Chapter 4

Apprenticeship

I have no doubt that God led me down the path that I took after leaving Bible College. At first, it appeared that I would become a professional Gospel musician and singer, but that was not what God had planned for me. The call to preach pressed on me night and day, and although leaving Kansas City and professional Gospel music at the age of 19 seemed extremely traumatic for me at that time, I now know (over forty years later) that I was never meant to travel that road.

Nothing Just Happens

Whenever you find yourself being ripped away from a course of action that you really thought you were supposed to pursue, you should remind yourself that "nothing just happens" in the will of God. Ask Jacob, or Joseph, or David, or Jonah, or any of the major Bible characters. Their lives were often abruptly re-routed because God had different plans than what they anticipated.

If you are honest and sincere in your walk with God, you will eventually experience something of that kind. You will be moving at break-neck speed in one direction, and suddenly, God will change your direction. Sometimes, it is because you were carnal and misdirected. Sometimes, it is because someone else threw an obstacle in your way. Sometimes, Satan lies in wait for your soul, and tricks you into a diversion. But ultimately, it is Almighty God who will move you in the right direction. And you will not always understand why. Satan may have meant it for evil, but God meant it for good. Sometimes, God will move you in a direction that you think is entirely wrong. But in the end, you will see that it was exactly right. It was providential.

I believe that my landing in Beaumont at Victory Temple in May of 1971 was providential.

The Apprenticeship Began

Pastor Clendennen's preaching was awe-inspiring to me in those days. I had never heard his kind of preaching. He was in great demand all over the country, preaching Camp Meetings and Conferences regularly. It was nothing short of revelatory to me. He stayed close to a number of themes, and preached them again and again and again. Prayer and Fasting: Pastor Clendennen preached and practiced prayer and fasting. We had prayer meetings every morning at the Church at 5:30; prayer services every Tuesday and Thursday morning at 10:00; fasting until 3 PM every Tuesday and Thursday; and an all-Church 30-day prayer and fasting vigil for the month of October every year. He preached constantly about being filled with the Holy Ghost, crucifying the flesh and walking in the Spirit.

It's All About The Preaching

Brother Clendennen preached hard against phony religion. He rebuked the prodigal Church for departing from its Biblical roots and chasing after fads and fashions. As an ex-marine who had fought on the front lines in the South Pacific at Guadalcanal, in World War II, he had a militant spirit, and he insisted the Church should be a militant Church. He decried the Charismatic Movement, the Ecumenical Movement, the Roman Catholic Church, and all the new worldly trends that were creeping into the Church. He stood for getting back to the basics of Biblical Christianity.

His preaching had the most profound effect on my ministry. I could preach much of his material almost verbatim, because it stuck in my soul. I not only believed what he preached, but I also felt the strongest urgency to say the same things.

For many years, Brother Clendennen had a weekly broadcast on a local television station. In those days, we did not yet have our own television production equipment, so every Monday night a large group of people would drive over to Channel 4 KJAC studios in Port Arthur to make a tape for the future broadcasts. Sometimes we would record two or three programs in one night. We turned the entire studio into a Church house. We set up a platform with chairs for the choir. All the musicians brought their instruments, and they all had to be miked. We set up chairs for the audience. Brother Clendennen preached with a hundred-foot microphone cord. He preached all over the place. We had total Church with singing and shouting and worshipping, while three cameras looked on. We typically had 100-200 people show up at the TV studio on Monday nights for taping.

Expanding Into A National Ministry

In late summer of 1971, we produced three television specials called "One Nation Under God" crusades. That is when we launched a national television ministry. Brother Clendennen hired the Beaver Agency of Akron, Ohio to help us get on stations around the country. They were the people who promoted Rex Humbard and the Cathedral of Tomorrow in Akron. After that TV Special aired in probably a hundred markets, the response came daily in mailbags full of letters.

We immediately started signing on TV stations for a regular weekly show. Those were the days before satellite television. There were no satellite networks. We purchased professional-quality Video Tape Recorders, and copied hundreds of two-inch reel-to-reel video tapes to be "bicycled" around the country - we always had one tape going and one tape returning because they were so expensive. Within a few months, we were broadcasting weekly on 150 TV stations all over America.

It was at the summer Camp Victory Camp Meeting in 1971 that Brother Clendennen set out to raise the money for our first TV cameras. They were $14,000 each, and he raised the money to buy three of them. Within a year or so, we had a complete production facility inside the auditorium, with the control room upstairs in the balcony. Not long after that, we bought an old Greyhound SceniCruiser bus, and put an entire production control room in it. From then on, we could take the entire television crew on crusades around the country.

Publishing The Gospel

During that time, I was editing and producing the magazine. For many years, it had been called "Streams of Faith." As the magazine grew from a circulation of 12,000 monthly to over 35,000, I added a byline under the title: "The International Voice of Victory." The name of the Church was Victory Assembly of God. Brother Clendennen often referred to the Church as "The Temple." So I gradually started putting "Victory Temple" on the return address. Within a few months time, everybody started calling it Victory Temple. After a while, they officially changed the name of the Church to Victory Temple. The TV program became, "The International Voice of Victory."

At that point, the sheer size of the magazine became more than I could handle in-house. We had two large offset printing presses that ran day and night. I had a complete darkroom where I produced all our negatives and metal printing plates. We had a ten-bin collator and stitcher that automatically assembled, folded and stitched the magazine. We had our own addressing equipment, plate-making machines, and a five-place Pitney Bowes mail envelope inserter. We also had a massive audio-tape duplicating set-up which produced thousands of tapes every month for our viewers.

Introducing Computers To The Ministry

Because I had contacts with some local IBM executives from my college days, I was privy to the inauguration of a new third-generation mainframe computer system being marketed in the Beaumont market in late 1971. I had observed the computer-generated letters being produced by Rex Humbard and Oral Roberts, and persuaded Brother Clendennen that we should adopt that process, too. I actually wrote a custom program to accomplish the needed tasks, and we arranged to rent the new System 3 mainframe in Beaumont periodically. I hired data-entry clerks to quickly keypunch our entire mailing list onto 88-column punch cards, loaded that database onto the mainframe computer, and began sending personalized letters to all our followers. That revolutionized our fundraising efforts, greatly simplified the entire direct-mail processes, and dramatically increased the amount of contributions.

A large staff of workers answered mail, fulfilled book, tape and record orders, prepared the magazine, weekly newsletters and other direct mail pieces for the post office. We sent over 100,000 pieces of mail every month to the post office.

At first, we did all our typesetting in-house on IBM Executive typewriters, because desktop computers had not yet been invented. It was enormously tedious. We finally started sending it out to a typesetter who delivered it all on photographic film. Then we transitioned the production of the magazine from using mechanical paste-ups, darkroom and negative-stripping to computerized typesetting. Once the circulation of the magazine reached 35,000, we sent it all out to a commercial publisher for hands-free production. It took on a new, much-improved look at that time.

How I Met My Future Wife At Victory Temple

On the first Tuesday morning after I arrived on staff in May of '71, I attended the 10 AM prayer service. The Tuesday and Thursday morning services were usually attended by a small group of Church members.

That morning, Dixie Weiler's mother was there. She went home that day and told Dixie that there was a new young man at Church that morning. She told her that he played and sang and carried a Bible. She thought I must be a preacher. The next Sunday, Dixie's dad saw me playing the piano on stage, and he later told me that he immediately began to think that I might be somebody for Dixie.

Dixie was interested. Although she was newly engaged at the time, she said that she believed she was supposed to marry a preacher; therefore she broke up with her fiancé and started going out with me.

As I began to show up in all the regular services, I saw Dixie and her friend, Billie hanging around. Dixie had won Billie to the Lord by witnessing to her at High School. She had mentored Billie spiritually, and had taken a personal interest in helping her assimilate into Church. They had become dear friends.

The young people of the Church regularly went out to eat on Sunday nights at Patrizzi's, a nearby Italian restaurant. I saw Dixie there. Another night, we all went to Mr. Gatti's, a new pizza parlor, and Dixie spent her time walking in and out among the tables, laughing and cutting up with everybody. She glowed like a shining light. It seemed to me as if she was the only person in the restaurant that night. That was the night I first took a serious interest in her.

Soon after I hired on at Victory, Pastor Clendennen had scheduled a crusade in Evansville, Indiana, at Calvary Temple, a large Assembly of God Church where Hansel Vibbert was the pastor. He and I took commercial flights to Evansville. He instructed the band to come on the Church's plane, an old Lockheed Lodestar, a 14-passenger twin engine. We had a great Church band. Donald Carver was the drummer, Donnie Dean played lead guitar, Russell Thibodeaux played rhythm guitar, Keith Spoonemore played clarinet, Keith Morgan and Mike Thibodeaux played saxophones, Jone Ray Carruth played bass guitar, and Scott Kamp played steel guitar. I played the piano. My brother, David, was a TV cameraman for the Church, and he usually traveled with us.

I urged Dixie and Billie to come along with the band, and they did. Their plane to Indiana went through some pretty bad weather, and they got tossed around quite a bit. But on that trip, Dixie had a talk with my brother, David, about me. David tried to tell Dixie to steer clear of me. He advised her that I wasn't ready for marriage. He knew me pretty well. But that advice didn't hold much weight, as time would tell.

Dixie experienced a stressful situation with a guy that she had once dated briefly. Early in their relationship, he assaulted her, and she immediately broke up with him. But a year later, he was still stalking her around town, causing her much anguish. Shortly after I met Dixie, he followed her to a shopping center across the street from the Church. While she was inside, he pulled the sparkplug wires on her car so that it wouldn't start. Then he waited on her to come out so he could harass her. Dixie ran across the street to the Church to call her Dad for help. I was in the office, and she told me what was going on. I went back to her car to confront the guy, and he became belligerent. Soon, her Dad arrived, after calling the police. Once the police arrived, they sent the guy on his way. The crisis was diffused, and we all went our separate ways.

Courtship Begins

Later that week, Dixie came by the Church office to visit. We talked briefly, and she told me that the Church was hosting a graduation banquet for all the high school seniors, and asked if I would like to go to that banquet with her. I told her I would like that. That is how our first date developed. The banquet was held on a Friday night at a popular local restaurant, and I enjoyed being with her. I took Dixie home afterward, but didn't give her any indication that I had any interest in her.

My feelings had been hurt pretty badly when my previous relationship had ended suddenly. I was pretty wary of girls at that particular point. I was not interested at all in getting involved with another girl just yet, and I told that to Dixie very plainly. That didn't stop her from talking to me, however.

Sunday came along, and C.M. Ward, the radio minister of REVIVALTIME, had arrived from Springfield as the guest minister for Brother Clendennen's annual week-long Camp Meeting that would begin Monday night at Camp Victory campgrounds. Since I knew Brother Ward personally, I was eager to go. He was the teacher of the Hermeneutics class at Central Bible College while I was attending school there, and being in the Revivaltime Choir, I often sat behind him as he preached on the world-wide radio broadcast.

I mentioned to Dixie that Brother Ward was scheduled to preach on Monday night at the Camp Meeting and told her that I would take her to the service if she was interested in going. That initial invitation turned into a nightly date for a week. Each evening I picked her up in Beaumont, went to Camp, then took her home. After services, she would join me on stage and sing along with me on various songs during the altar services. That was the germination of our future ministry together. She loved to sing and worship and pray.

Still, I deliberately refrained from showing any romantic interests. I was very determined that I wasn't going to rush into another romantic trap. I was downright adamant that I didn't want to get involved with another girl so soon. She seemed to understand that and didn't press the issue. She was a delightful girl, and I enjoyed every minute with her. I was impressed with her impeccable grooming and her high personal standards. She dressed especially well, and had good taste in everything. She loved to laugh. She always brightened the room wherever she went.

Not long after the Camp Meeting, I was invited over to Dixie's house for supper with her family. Fourteen months later, we were married.

During our courtship, one of our favorite pastimes was to go to the Church at night and sit at the grand piano and play and sing together. Dixie loved my music. I played the piano, and we often sang for hours at a time.

We began singing together in Church. She had always been an alto voice in the Church choir, and frequently sang alto in a girls' trio. Harmonizing was her specialty. She explained to me that as a little girl, she remembered standing beside her mother and listening to her sing the alto part during the Church song services. I became accustomed to her alto voice following me on every song. To this day, in the middle of a congregational song, I can imagine that I hear her harmonizing beside me.

For thirty-two years, we sang together in every service. People were always amazed at what a powerful voice came from such a petite girl. Not only that, but she always looked younger than her age, and I always looked older than my age. I can't tell you how many Churches we went to where people thought she was my daughter.

Laverne Tripp wrote a song in the late '60s called, "It's Worth It All." Dixie and I liked that song and began singing it together before we even married. The words were:

> I don't want a mansion on a hillside.
> I don't care for wealth or worldly fame.
> I don't worry when those around me prosper,
> for I have Jesus and that's worth everything.
>
> It's worth it all to feel this fire that's burning deep within.
> It's worth it all to know I'm saved and I am free from sin.
> Just to feel His touch and know that He is coming back again,
> It's worth it all. It's worth it all.

We sang that song together from Mexico to Canada, from the East Coast to the Rocky Mountains in hundreds of Churches and auditoriums. We even sang it on national television on Jim Bakker's PTL CLUB. We recorded it in 1973 with the Goss Brothers in Atlanta, Georgia at the LeFevre Studio and sold thousands of copies on 33 RPM records, 8-track tapes and audio cassettes.

That song not only became our anthem for our entire married life, it was also an omen.

We never had a mansion on a hillside.
We never had wealth or worldly fame.
We didn't worry when those around us prospered.
But we had Jesus.
And that was worth everything.

In later life, she sang more and more solos. Her ministry in music was powerfully anointed, and blessed many, many people. I have wished so many times that I had featured her solos far more often from the beginning.

Dixie passed away in 2003 at the age of 50, but now she has Jesus for all eternity. She really did get EVERYTHING - just like we sang! And it really was WORTH IT ALL.

When Dixie and I first began to discuss the subject of marriage and the ministry, I had contacts all over the country from my travels, and felt that we could make a life together in the ministry. So in the spring of 1972, I took Dixie to the finest restaurant in Beaumont and proposed marriage to her. She immediately responded with a delirious and tearful 'yes', and my fate was sealed. I had won the heart of one of the most beautiful, most precious, most devoted Christian girls anywhere to be found.

We set the date for August 25th and began making plans. Dixie's mother often catered weddings, and was a spectacular seamstress as well. Delma created and sewed Dixie's gorgeous wedding dress, baked a beautiful wedding cake and groom's cake, and catered the wedding reception at the new Red Carpet Inn. (Over the years, Delma sewed scores of absolutely beautiful dresses for Dixie to wear to Church. Thanks to her mom, Dixie was always dressed exceptionally nice.)

On Monday before the Saturday wedding, Brother Clendennen and I flew to Spokane, Washington for a two-night crusade in the Masonic Temple auditorium. We stayed in the Holiday Inn. On Tuesday afternoon, I told him I needed to go downtown to find a pair of shoes for my wedding. A couple hours later, I returned with a "high-fashion" pair of shoes - part patent-leather, and part suede, with huge elevator heels. I woke Brother Clendennen up from his nap to show him those shoes, and he nearly died laughing. He hee-hawed and rolled in the bed at those outrageous shoes. I wore them to the wedding anyway. Thirty-five years later, I saw him again just before he died, and he asked me if I had bought any new shoes lately. I was amazed that he still remembered those goofy shoes.

Our wedding was at Victory Temple, with Pastor Clendennen officiating. It was a beautiful event with a few hundred of our family members and friends in attendance. Dixie looked like a very angel from heaven. I always told her that she was like an angel to me. And God knows I meant it. I played the grand piano and sang a song to her -- the theme from "Love Story."

> Where do I begin to tell the story of how great a love can be,
> The sweet love story that is older than the sea,
> The simple truth about the love she brings to me?
> Where do I start?
>
> With her first "Hello!"
> she gave new meaning to this empty world of mine,
> There'd never be another love, another time,
> She came into my life and made the living fine,
> She fills my heart, She fills my heart with very special things,
> With angels' songs, with wild imaginings,
> She fills my soul with so much love,
> That anywhere I go, I'm never lonely,
> With her along, who could be lonely?
> I reach for her hand, it's always there...
>
> How long does it last?
> Can love be measured by the hours in a day?
> I have no answers now, but this much I can say,
> I know I'll need her 'till the stars all burn away
> And she'll be there... She'll be there.

We both teared up as we repeated our vows to each other. Dixie was 19, and I was 20. It was a once in a lifetime love affair. Our marriage was made in Heaven.

Four months later, we purchased a new car and a new travel trailer, and left Beaumont, to begin traveling full-time across the United States, preaching and singing in Churches, Crusades and Camp Meetings. I had finished my Apprenticeship.

Chapter 5

The Work Of An Evangelist

Answering A Specific Call

Back in my Bible College days, while I was living in a fourth-floor dormitory, there was a large, open prayer room where all the male student residents could find a place to pray. Altar benches were built all around the walls of that room, and a row of altars went down the center of the room, from one end to the other. I spent three days in that room in a prayer and fasting vigil, asking God to show me clearly what I was supposed to do with my life. At the end of the third day, God gave me several verses of scripture that I believed were His explicit answers to me. Among those verses was 2 Timothy 4:5: "But watch thou in all things, endure afflictions, *DO THE WORK OF AN EVANGELIST*, make full proof of thy ministry."

Dixie knew that I had no intention of staying in Beaumont after we were married. She knew that I felt the call to do the work of an evangelist, and she was ready to go with me wherever that call would lead. We knew that we would be leaving shortly after we were married.

As a wedding gift, Dixie's parents gave us their nice late-model car. I sold my car, and with the money, Dixie and I took a 10-day honeymoon trip to Colorado Springs, Colorado. It was early September 1972 when we returned home, and there was plenty of work to do back at the Church.

We rented a small, furnished apartment from a genteel old lady, Pearly Rogers, who had taught the Ladies Bible Class for forty years at the big Baptist Church downtown. She was delighted to have a young couple in the ministry living upstairs in her beautiful old two-story Southern home. We had only one bedroom, a bath, and a small kitchen. Having guests over was pretty funny, because our only chairs were four wooden rockers situated around the bed. As everyone began to talk, and rock in rhythm (or out of rhythm), it never failed to get a laugh. Music played on our stereo by day and night, especially the newest recordings by Andrae' Crouch and the Disciples, the Imperials, and others. Working with the choir meant I was constantly looking for new songs.

Long Winding Road

Gearing Up

For the next three months, we prepared ourselves to leave Beaumont and begin traveling in evangelistic ministry. I printed a multi-colored brochure announcing our entrance into full-time ministry, and mailed it with a postage-paid return-response postcard to several hundred Assembly of God preachers whom I knew. The response from that announcement produced our first preaching engagements.

We purchased a brand new full-size Ford, with a 400hp engine - big enough to tow a travel trailer - and installed a full towing package on it. We bought a nice 28-foot travel trailer, the top-of-the-line model built by Fleetwood, and moved all our belongings into it.

In those days, many Churches did not have adequate sound systems, if any at all. I went to a music store and bought a Shure Vocalmaster P.A. System, which was the state-of-the-art P.A. in those days. I already owned a small sound system, and I used those speakers for monitors. I purchased two gigantic Altec-Lansing Voice of the Theater speakers, the kind all the Gospel quartets were using. That system was powerful enough to preach and sing to an audience of thousands. Those speakers were so large that we could hardly get in the trailer when they were on board. I honestly think that some of the back trouble I have to this day traces back to loading and unloading those massive speakers.

Right after Christmas, Dixie and I headed out to start holding revivals. Every night, she and I sang several songs before I preached. I played the piano, and she played the tambourine.

The First Test

Our first week was in the heart of Dallas-Fort Worth. It was my first encounter with a new Charismatic-leaning ministry.

After two nights there, the Pastor took me into his office and told me that I needed to do some miracles. I sat across from his desk and listened incredulously as he proceeded to "teach" me how to stretch legs. He showed me how to set people in a chair so that you could see that one leg was shorter than the other. Then he showed me how to pray for the short leg to grow out. Then he showed me how to stand them against the wall to demonstrate to the audience how they no longer had one leg shorter than the other. It was a surreal experience. I couldn't believe this guy was for real.

I told that preacher that I believe in miracles as much as anybody on earth, but I wasn't about to resort to a bunch of nonsense like that to prove that God could do miracles. Boy, I was upset, and it showed.

You can imagine how wonderful the rest of that week was. I spent my days inside that empty auditorium, fasting and praying for God to give me the right things to preach each night. I gave everything I had to finish out that week, but we were glad to get out of town. That was my first encounter with the Charismatic-type Church, and I was completely turned-off by it.

The Influence Of Other Ministries

In my growing up years, I had been strongly affected by most of the best-known Pentecostal-style ministries of that day. As a child, my regular Sunday morning routine included sitting in front of the television watching Oral Roberts and A.A. Allen in their massive tent revivals. Daddy used to come in from his midnight refinery shift after stopping by the local donut shop. I would sit on the floor as a 10-year-old boy, eating hot glazed doughnuts and watching Oral Roberts preach and conduct his healing lines. Both of them were electrifying preachers in those days.

I loved hearing Allen's great mass choir, directed by Gene Allen. His organists, David Davis and later, Nancy Harmon, greatly influenced my own organ-playing style. Allen called it "Miracle Music," and it was. Allen was one of the first to incorporate the big Hammond organ, drums and tambourines as a notable feature of his music. It was shouting and dancing music. Thousands of people received every kind of miracle during those meetings.

Roberts and Allen both performed the most amazing miracles. I would call my parents and say, "Come look at this!" Over the years, a lot of people accused Allen of staging bogus miracles to maintain his popularity, and I cannot defend him in that regard, because I do not know all the facts. One thing I can ascertain, however, is that there were many, many bona-fide miracles performed by the hand of God, in the name of Jesus. Leroy

Jenkins, who later became a tent preacher, was instantly healed after his arm had been amputated by falling window glass. Doctors had sown it back on at his demand, without reattaching blood vessels or nerves, telling him that he would soon get gangrene and die. In agony, he went to Allen's tent crusade in Atlanta, Georgia, with a dead arm attached. He was instantly healed - his arm came back to life - in front of 8,000 people.

Nevertheless, both Allen and Roberts were controversial. I suppose that every preacher who ever sticks his neck out is controversial. I stopped endorsing preachers long ago, because I learned that a man who seems to be a great man of God today may turn out to be the biggest devil tomorrow.

Paul said, "Judge nothing before the time, until the Lord come, who both will bring to light the hidden things of darkness, and will make manifest the counsels of the hearts: and then shall every man have praise of God," 1 Corinthians 4:5.

We are indeed called upon by Jesus Himself to "Judge not according to the appearance, but judge righteous judgment," John 7:24. By the commandments of God, I must not judge men. But I MUST judge everything by true doctrine and divine principle.

I have no authority by God to judge you or any other man. But I have every authority to judge your doctrine and your principles. I cannot say where YOU stand with God, but I can certainly say where your doctrines and your principles (or absence thereof) stand, because I can compare them directly with the scriptures.

With all of that said, I will tell you that because of what I saw in Roberts and Allen's ministries, I became thoroughly convinced that God was in the miracle-working, divine healing business in these modern times. Some of the things that the early tent preachers preached were absolutely right, and other things they preached were dead wrong.

I bought Allen's biography (written after his death from alcoholism), entitled "Born to Lose, Bound to Win." Dixie and I read that entire book out loud on one of our road trips. The author obviously attempted to whitewash Allen's life and ministry of many negatives and contradictions, but certain truths were undeniable. God does heal people when men preach His Word and act by faith.

I read so many of Oral Roberts' books, including his biography, "The Call," and the enormously popular, "Seed Faith." I also followed T.L. Osborn, a world-renowned missionary, who was also from Tulsa, Oklahoma. I received his monthly magazine, and read many of his publications. Osborn and his wife Daisy were significantly influenced by the healing ministry of William Branham. They were one of the first Pentecostal-type ministries to invade the African continent, beginning in Uganda, conducting giant crusades where literally hundreds of thousands of people were in attendance. Enormous multitudes of people had received the Holy Spirit under their ministry, as well as every kind of miracle and healing you could imagine, including many, many people raised from the dead.

Dixie and I visited Osborn's offices, met his wife, and toured his world-class museum which contained thousands of artifacts collected from his global missionary travels. Dixie and I also ministered for a week in a Church pastored by Osborn's sister, Mrs. O.C. Gillock, in Odessa, Texas.

In the 1950s and 60s, two large "Clear-Channel" 250,000-watt AM radio stations in Mexico broadcast Gospel preachers all night long who could be heard all over America. As a boy, I often put on my earphones and listened to the all-night radio preachers on my transistor radio. They called them "border-blasters," because the FCC did not allow American radio stations to operate under that much power. XERF in Ciudad, Acuña, and XEG in Monterey provided enormous audiences for those preachers.

One of the radio preachers was Lester Roloff, a straight-shooting Baptist preacher who quoted lots of scriptures and preached godly living. He operated a Children's Orphanage in Corpus Christi, and flew his own plane to preach all over the country. His messages were electrifying and convicting.

I often heard Bishop S.C. Johnson, an Acts 2:38 Oneness preacher who pastored the 2,000-member "Church of the Lord Jesus Christ of the Apostolic Faith," in Philadelphia. After he died in 1961, his programs continued to alternate with those of his successor, Bishop S. McDowell Shelton. Some of those programs can still be heard on a few stations to this day. Both men were staunch Jesus' name, holiness preachers who had great command of the scriptures. The large Church choir sang a theme song on every program:

> One, one, one – One way to God,
> One, one, one – One way to God,
> One, one, one – One way to God,
>   Baptized in Jesus' Name.

Another all-night radio preacher was the great charlatan, "Rev. Ike." Dr. Frederick Eikerenkoetter. He was one of the very first "get-rich-quick-in-Jesus'-name" prosperity preachers. He purchased the gold-leafed, 3,000-seat Lowes Theater in Manhattan, New York, and preached, "You can't lose with the stuff I use!" He promised prosperity and blessings on those who sent him generous love offerings. I have watched an entire generation of prosperity preachers recycle the kinds of things I heard Rev. Ike preach back in the beginning. In his place, we now have men like John Avanzini, Leroy Thompson, Peter Popoff, Robert Tilton, Mike Murdock, and far too many others.

Those old radio broadcasts inspired many, many world-wide radio ministries. In the 1960s, radio preachers began to proliferate. Kenneth Hagin and Charles Capps filled the airwaves with their "Word of Faith" teachings, which had originated largely in the writings of E.W. Kenyon. John Osteen was profoundly influenced by them. I heard Kenneth Hagin teach at John Osteen's "Oasis of Love" Church in Houston during the 1970s.

To people who were not well-studied in the Bible, their teachings were persuasive. Only as years went by, did the real heresy of their teachings begin to be manifest. I listened to them skeptically as a young preacher. I watched as they gradually spawned a huge industry of positive confession, divine health, "name-it-and-claim-it, blab-it-and-grab-it" preachers, including Kenneth Copeland, Creflo Dollar, Jerry Savelle, Frederick Price, Marilyn Hickey, Joyce Meyer, Joel Osteen and many others.

The old-guard revival crusade preachers of the 1940s and 1950s (besides Roberts and Allen) had included William Branham, Jack Coe, Aimee Semple McPherson, Kathryn Kuhlman, and many other lesser-knowns. After A.A. Allen died, two of his associates, Don Stewart and R.W.

Schambach went on to have worldwide crusade and TV ministries of their own.

William Branham and Jack Coe had specialized in calling out people and discerning their needs. Those practices, which are included in the "Gifts of the Spirit" of 1 Corinthians 12, quickly fell into misuse and abuse. While such practices, when genuinely inspired by the Holy Ghost, are entirely scriptural, those gifts were often exploited for sensational purposes, and quickly failed the litmus test.

All too often, the minister who operates in the Gifts of the Spirit begins to feel some necessity to operate the gifts "on demand." The Holy Ghost does not work in that manner. Any "discernment" or "prophecy" that is not genuinely inspired by the Holy Ghost is destined to produce an undesirable result. We simply MUST NOT attempt to artificially manifest the Gifts of the Spirit. I will defend to the death a genuine manifestation of the Holy Ghost, but will completely denounce a fraudulent version. I have seen both throughout my lifetime, and will stand resolutely behind what I say here.

Let The Miracles Begin

As a young man, I was never personally exposed to the operation of the gifts of the Spirit. I never witnessed first-hand a minister calling out anyone to discern a need or to perform a miracle on-the-spot like that.

My first experience came to me entirely unexpected. I stepped into the pulpit one night in a Church on the Outer Banks of North Carolina. As I opened my Bible to announce my text to preach, I suddenly felt an overwhelming impulse that there was someone in the audience who was suffering from a kidney disease. I tried to ignore what I felt, but it literally arrested me. I stood there for a moment, wondering what I should do with what I felt. Finally, I said, "I cannot explain to you what I feel right now, but I am impressed that there is someone here tonight who is suffering with a kidney disease. I can only assume that God wants to do a miracle for you. If you are here suffering with a kidney disease, I would like for you to stand and let us pray for you right now." Immediately, a lady stood up in the middle of the audience. "That's me!" she said. I wasted no more words. I asked the congregation to stretch their hands toward the lady and pray with me for her. Then she sat down, and I proceeded to preach.

The next night, that same lady asked to give her testimony. She said, "I have suffered with kidney disease for twelve years. One of my kidneys had completely failed. I was having increasing trouble, and my kidney function was getting worse and worse. But since last night, my kidneys have functioned wonderfully." After that night, she went to the doctor for an examination, and he found that her dead kidney had started working again.

I believe in the Gifts of the Spirit, but I believe they must be inspired by the Holy Ghost. That is all I will say about that for now.

Street Meetings, Church Suppers, And Missions

Our second revival was in Laredo, just across the border from the Mexican town of Nuevo Laredo. The pastor there arranged for us to conduct daytime crusades on the town square. There was a huge brick bandstand in the middle of the city square, and we set up all our sound equipment and musical instruments for afternoon services. Dixie and I sang, and I preached through a Spanish interpreter. Several hundred people gathered around as the service progressed. In the end I gave an invitation for conversions, and dozens of people responded. We also held nightly services at the Church for two weeks, with excellent results. The pastor was delighted with that meeting.

In those days, nearly every revival ran six or seven nights a week. Every night we sang several songs, I preached for an hour, and gave an altar call. There were periods when Dixie and I preached and sang without a single night off for over three months. In many of those revivals, especially in larger Churches, I also ministered in daytime services on weekdays.

We held a seven-night meeting in Victoria, Texas, at a beautiful Church. At that time, Brother Clendennen was planning a trip to Saigon, Viet Nam, and had invited me to go with him. I needed to raise the money for my own plane fare. I hoped to raise the money during that revival to help make the crusade trip to Viet Nam. Victory Temple operated a Christian Servicemen's Center in Saigon, and one of the preachers from the Beaumont Church was its Pastor. Brother Clendennen made several trips to Viet Nam to preach crusades. Hundreds of people received the Baptism of the Holy Ghost in those days - the first time anyone in Viet Nam had ever received the Holy Ghost.

Long Winding Road

On a Monday morning, I drove from Victoria to Beaumont to get all FIVE of my vaccination shots for the trip overseas. Then I drove back to Victoria that evening. Those shots made me violently sick. By the time I got in the pulpit that night, I had fever raging at about 105. I remember preaching as hard as I could that night, but I quickly found myself standing in front of the pulpit with my back leaning against it.

I discussed my plans for the missionary trip with the pastor, in hopes that he would help me raise the money for the Viet Nam crusade. He was a millionaire building contractor, besides being the pastor. The Church was very wealthy and well-able to help me make the trip. But he showed no interest whatsoever in helping. Ironically, they put on a big fund-raising event while we were there. It was Groundhog Day, so they had a "Groundhog" supper - sausage and eggs -- to raise money for the Church. But I learned a sad, disappointing lesson then. Some Churches just horde money, and have no real missionary vision. I don't know how God will judge that in the end, but I don't think it will go unnoticed.

Ken and Dixie Raggio - "Singing, Pentecostal!"

Dixie and I decided to produce a record album of our singing that spring. I booked a studio, and hired a professional photographer to meet us at Victory to take photos for the album jacket. We spent all evening taking pictures, but they did not turn out as good as we had hoped. Dixie hated those photos, and didn't want anybody to see them. But I argued that we were facing a deadline, and didn't have time for another photo shoot. I should have listened to her, however, because she knew better. Those less-than-flattering pictures were forever stuck on that album. On the back of the album, we used a black-and-white photo that we had made at a portrait studio in Laredo. It was only slightly better than the cover photos.

We parked our trailer in Beaumont and flew to Atlanta, Georgia to record at LeFevre Sound Studios. The Goss Brothers were some of the most sought-after Gospel studio musicians in those days, and they backed us up on that album. Larry played the organ, James played the guitar, Ronnie played the bass, and Joe Piscopo played the drums. Larry Goss is still a sought-after musician and producer, having produced countless albums for the Brooklyn Tabernacle Choir, and scores of other renowned musicians. Years later, I became the pastor of a Church near there, and James Goss was my Choir Director and Organist.

Dixie and I were very excited about producing our own album. We called it, "Singing, Pentecostal!" Naturally, "It's Worth It All," was one of the featured songs. We also used a song I had written on that album. We ordered 1,000 long-play vinyl albums and 500 8-track tapes. I later remastered it for audio cassettes, and eventually sold more audio cassettes than records or 8-tracks. I rented a large mailing list of people who had previously ordered Gospel records by direct mail from Word Records. I produced a direct-mail advertising campaign for our album, and sold almost enough records to cover the entire production costs of that album.

Camp Meetings And Revivals

Evangelist Melvin McKnight had been a friend for many years. He was preaching the night I was healed of a high fever and tonsillitis when I was a child. He also preached frequent revivals for Brother Clendennen at Victory Temple. He knew me and my music and ministry well, so when he learned that Dixie and I had entered the ministry as full-time evangelists, he wanted to help us.

He invited us to accompany him to three State-wide Camp Meetings where he was scheduled to preach. One was in Franklin, North Carolina, at the Assemblies of God Western Camp, situated on the Cullasaja River. The second camp was in Windsor, North Carolina, at the District's Eastern Camp. The third Camp Meeting was in Mars Hill, Maine. He wanted Dixie and I to provide the music each night in all of those Camp Meetings, and I would be given the opportunity to preach in the day services. During those camps, we scheduled about forty revivals in North Carolina alone.

The Aroostook County Camp Meeting in Mars Hill, Maine was a state-wide joint camp between the A/G Churches, the Pentecostal Holiness, the Foursquare Gospel, the Church of God, and some independent Full-Gospel Churches, and was superintended by Bill Wilson. The attendance was almost 1,000. Scores of pastors and Churches were involved. Brother Wilson invited me to preach several services in that camp, as well.

I was counting on our record album sales to offset the expense of pulling our trailer all the way to Maine. I scheduled the first shipment of our new albums to be delivered to the airport in Presque Isle, Maine, so they would be available for that Camp Meeting. As fate would have it, the albums did not come on time. After several urgent calls to Maurice LeFevre, the albums showed up on Sunday evening, just before the very last service of the Camp Meeting. We desperately needed those albums to make that trip profitable, so I made an emergency trip to Presque Isle right after the Sunday morning service.

Arriving back at the campgrounds just before the night service, I quickly set up a display of our records in the back of the Tabernacle. Before I finished, Brother Wilson came to notify me that he did not allow anyone to sell merchandise on Sunday. I was devastated.

Brother McKnight took matters in his own hands. He walked to the microphone just before I preached that night and told that large audience that Ken and Dixie's new album had just arrived by plane that evening. He said that he respected Brother Wilson's request not to sell anything in Church on a Sunday. So he said that he wasn't going to ask anybody to BUY anything. But he said, "If you will DONATE the price of the record to these kids, they will GIVE you a record after service!" Everybody laughed, and that sales pitch closed the sale. We liquidated several cases of albums that night, and nobody made a fuss.

After the camp, Dixie and I preached several revivals in Maine. All the Churches wanted to have a revival before the potato harvest in the fall. In Maine, they literally shut down businesses and Churches during the potato harvest because everybody participated in the potato harvests. They only had a narrow window of opportunity, or the potatoes would be lost. We had to beat that deadline.

In Presque Isle, we preached at the Foursquare Church originally founded by the famous Aimee Semple McPherson. The congregation of about 200 was without a pastor at the time, and throughout that revival they tried to prevail on us to accept the pastorate of that Church. It was very tempting, but Presque Isle was a very foreign climate to us Texans, and we couldn't imagine living in six feet of snow every winter. It was already 40 degrees in July!

In East Millinocket, we preached and sang for two weeks in a good Church pastored by Vinal Thomas. In Oakland, a lady pastor, Edith Morton, had a large congregation, and a strong youth group. We set up an outdoor service on the parking lot of the main grocery store in town, and Dixie and I sang, I preached, and several people responded to the invitation that day.

We wrapped it up in Maine and headed back to Texas for several meetings there in the fall.

More Crusades

We took a trip with Brother Clendennen on his Silver Eagle Bus to Albuquerque, New Mexico. He and I had been there in a crusade the year before, and we expected this one to be much larger. I helped drive the bus out to Albuquerque for a three-night crusade in the Albuquerque Civic Center. The guys in the Church band were on board with us.

The first morning we were in town, Dixie and I and the band decided to take the cable car to the top of Sandia Peak Mountain and have lunch in the lodge. While we were up there, it began to snow, so for safety reasons, they closed the cable car to the bottom. We sat for hours waiting on the operators to open up the cable car again so we could get down for night service. It was so late when we finally got off the mountain that we barely made it to the crusade that night. We came running into the Civic Center just a few minutes before the service, dragging guitars, amplifiers, drums and sound equipment. Brother Clendennen was just about livid. About a thousand people were sitting there waiting for service to start.

I led the song service, playing an old-fashioned calfskin tambourine, as the band furnished the music. It was a rousing, Pentecostal-style service, and Brother Clendennen's preaching had the crowd on their feet again and again. Dixie and I also sang that night. We booked several revivals in New Mexico while there, and made a return trip a few months later. While in Albuquerque, I preached daily on a Christian radio station and at night in the local A/G Church. One of the Churches was a Spanish-speaking congregation, and I preached nightly through an interpreter. Another revival was held on an Indian reservation with all Indians in attendance. In one city, the pastor dismissed a Friday night service because the youth had a skating party booked. I was astonished that the Church canceled a revival service for a skating party. Another pastor had a good Church in Socorro, where we had great attendance and many conversions.

Waking The Dead

I love to recall one occasion when Brother Clendennen held a crusade in a Church in Golden Meadows, Louisiana - down in the southern Cajun bayou country. Our Church band caravanned in several cars from Beaumont to Golden Meadows. Brother Clendennen went far ahead of us, and none of us knew exactly where the Church was located. Each car was loaded with guitars, amps, horns, and instruments, and we were running late, driving as hard and fast as we could.

We came into the edge of Golden Meadows just about service time. We saw a Church on the left that had a large crowd of cars around it so we all turned in, jumped out of our cars and started grabbing guitars and horns and drums and other instruments. The guys ran up the steps and burst in the back door of the Church expecting service to already be in progress. It was in progress all right. It was a Catholic funeral wake. We were in the wrong place! Red-faced and embarrassed, we all turned and ran out as fast as we could down the road to the right Church where we were truly late. Those funeral mourners never knew why that band of musicians had arrived and departed so suddenly.

At one particularly difficult Church in the vicinity of Tyler, Texas, I struggled to get any kind of response from the congregation. It was one of the deadest Churches I had ever been in. One day, I sat down at the piano and wrote a song called, "I'm Just Praising The Lord." It was a truly Pentecostal-style song about shouting, clapping, foot-stomping and dancing in the aisles in worship. We tried that song out on that congregation that night, and it literally brought the people out of the pews. I was amazed, thankful and relieved. Nobody but an itinerant preacher can appreciate the vast differences in people's manner in praise and worship.

Traveling For Jesus

Dixie and I pulled our travel trailer for almost three years from Mexico to Canada, from the Rocky Mountains to the East Coast, and hundreds of points between. Occasionally, we would meet Brother Clendennen for a crusade somewhere, and provide the music and singing. We booked additional revivals in those meetings. By the time I was 24 years old, I had ministered in hundreds of Churches, auditoriums, camps and conferences in 38 states. We saw thousands of people come to the altars to give their lives to God, to receive the Baptism of the Holy Ghost, and to receive every kind of miracle and healing.

But we were still kids, and that was only the beginning.

Long Winding Road

Chapter 6

A Word, a Dream, a Miracle

Our First Child

In October, 1973, Dixie and I were in Beeville, Texas holding a revival at a Church there. There was a young photographer in the Church who offered to do some publicity photos for us, so we spent an afternoon in the countryside taking some pictures. Dixie commented that it seemed like the dress she wore that day felt too tight on her. That week, she surprised me with the discovery that she was pregnant with our first child.

I was startled at first. I had not seriously contemplated having children, so the very idea was at first frightening. (I had just turned 22 years old.) But after a few hours of intense contemplation, I concluded that it would be wonderful to have our own child. I began to calculate how I could remodel the inside of our travel trailer to make room for a baby bed and accessories.

Having a baby was going to change a lot of things, so I began preparing. I went to work remodeling the kitchen area of our trailer to make room for a baby bed, tearing out the existing dining room area, and part of the kitchen cabinet. I custom-built a fold-away dining room table, and laminated it entirely with Formica. It was a quality piece of furniture. Then, we went to Foleys and purchased a nice sofa with a single hide-a-bed in it. I also re-carpeted the whole trailer with high-quality carpet, and added two handsome custom-built bookcases with fold-down desktops.

The Logistics Of Ministry

Audio cassettes were enormously popular in those days, but most Churches still did not record their services. Many people asked for recordings of our preaching and singing. Since we used our own sound system in almost every Church, I purchased a high-quality cassette recorder and installed it in-line so I could record the singing and preaching in every service. I also purchased a high-speed duplicator so we could make copies of the services available immediately after the service was over. We also had our songs on vinyl records, 8-track and Cassette tapes.

While traveling in television crusades with Pastor Clendennen, I had learned that there was a great demand for Giant Print Bibles, Study Bibles and Concordances, so I bought cases of all three, and had a display in the foyer at each Church we went to. In 1974, Jimmy Swaggart's music was enormously popular, so I started buying cases of his records to sell on the road. Every time I passed through Baton Rouge, I stopped by Swaggart's office and purchased several more cases of his albums and tapes. I sold hundreds of Swaggart's records and tapes, and hundreds of Bibles and Concordances, in addition to thousands of our own records and cassette tapes.

Dixie tended to the book and tape display after each service was dismissed. As a rule of thumb, our income from book and record sales was about equal to the offering for the week. Whatever amount we made in the weekly offering, we usually made a similar amount in sales. We did pretty well financially in the early 1970s.

Facing Spiritual Challenges In The Ministry

We held a revival in the western part of North Carolina, at a Church that was different from anything I had been accustomed to. Their services were very dry and formal. Oddly enough, however, they wanted to take us to a local inter-denominational fellowship dinner hosted by the local chapter of the Full Gospel Business Men's Fellowship International. I never felt more awkward than I did that night as I sat and listened to people give numerous testimonies and exhortations that I knew were biblically unsound. I tried my best to oblige our hosts without saying anything critical.

We really wanted that meeting to end. However, the Pastor's daughter and son-in-law visited one of our services, and amazingly, they wanted us to come and minister in the Church where they pastored in another part of the state. That young pastor was also the Presbyter over all the Churches in that Section. They had a small child, and a very modern-thinking, growing congregation. Unfortunately, it was too "modern" for me.

It was the first Assemblies of God Church I had ever attended where the women wore slacks to Church. Several of the young Pastor's liberal views were really out-of-bounds for me. We were scheduled to be there for two weeks. On the second day we took a day-trip to a nearby amusement park, and the Pastor's wife wore slacks. I was shocked! I had never seen a Pastor's wife in slacks. I had always believed that a woman should not wear that which pertaineth to a man. That came from Deuteronomy 22:5.

> "The woman shall not wear that which pertaineth unto a man, neither shall a man put on a woman's garment: for all that do so are abomination unto the LORD thy God."

Up until the late 1960s, every Pentecostal preacher of every denomination preached against women wearing slacks. Until the turn of the twentieth-century, it was virtually unheard of for a woman to wear slacks at all. In all of Western civilization, slacks were unquestionably a man's apparel, and dresses were a woman's apparel. Men did not wear dresses, and women did not wear slacks.

It was not until the first and second World Wars, when women were forced to work in the factories, that they were also required to wear pants, since they were doing men's jobs. Most women had never worn slacks before that time. Immediately, however, Hollywood popularized women in slacks, and it quickly began to eliminate any sense of Biblical instructions on that matter. They boldly broke that taboo. Not surprisingly, that era also spawned a huge surge in homosexuality and bisexuality.

In the simplest assessment, it was the United States government and Hollywood that successfully promoted women wearing men's apparel. That clothing revolution came with a high price tag. It evolved into gender neutral, same-sex apparel, or UNISEX clothing - the result that we now see throughout Western civilization. Although it may be commonplace in society, it is not commonplace in the mind of Almighty God. We have broken His rules for so long that we no longer believe that He cares, but make no mistake about it, He does care.

> "Because sentence against an evil work is not executed speedily, therefore the heart of the sons of men is fully set in them to do evil. Though a sinner do evil an hundred times, and his days be prolonged, yet surely I know that it shall be well with them that fear God, which fear before him: But it shall not be well with the wicked, neither shall he prolong his days, which are as a shadow; because he feareth not before God.
> Ecclesiastes 8:11-13

At any rate, I could not feel comfortable trying to preach the Gospel in a Church that so boldly broke the scriptures on that matter. Anyone could plainly see that they were taking a bold stand against a centuries-old Biblical teaching about women's apparel, and I could not ignore that. Dixie had always worn dresses. She did not even own a pair of slacks, and she was just as uncomfortable with the situation as I was.

It is the responsibility of men of God to hold to GOD'S standard, no matter what the WORLD'S standard is. I figured that if they did not have any respect for thousands of years of Biblical teachings and universally-accepted Church standards, then they were not going to take my Gospel preaching seriously either. They were in clear defiance of the beliefs of many generations of saints before them, and showed that they were very determined to ignore the Bible and history to do as they pleased, so I felt that I had no reason to stay and contend with such a mindset.

In those early years of my ministry, I was profoundly influenced by the writings of Leonard Ravenhill. I had several of his books, including "Meat for Men," "Why Revival Tarries," "Sodom Had No Bible," and "Revival Praying." Ravenhill was a man of powerful conviction, and quite intolerant of unholy compromising in the pulpit. I agreed with everything he said, so that was my way of seeing things. I was unwilling to compromise myself for someone else's lower standards.

So after the third night, I spoke to the Pastor, and told him that I felt that he and I were just too far apart on several issues, and that it would be best for both of us if I just moved on down the road. So we did.

Incidentally, during the 1960s, a significant number of Assembly of God Churches (and many others) began to accept the change in women's apparel. It would be dishonest to deny that that change came very much as a result of the spirit of rebellion that was saturating American culture at that time.

> **Observation:** Rebellion and anti-Christian social upheavals, especially among the hippies, began to dramatically affect the youth of that day. Social liberalism was rising like a beast from out of the sea, bringing with it a pandemic of drug and substance abuse, sexual immorality, and general rebellion against all traditional, Judeo-Christian social mores. From the bohemian

counterculture that sprang up in the Haight Ashbury district of San Francisco, to the Free Speech Movement at U.C. - Berkeley, to the "Beat" generation hedonists at Greenwich Village in NYC, to the half-million "Aquarians" who attended the Woodstock Festival in 1969, and ultimately around the world, ancient social and moral values were being dumped recklessly and forever into the sewer.

Music, theater, movies, schools, universities, and every other social venue became mouthpieces for the new counterculture. It was the day of the Beatles, the Rolling Stones, Janis Joplin, Jimmy Hendrix and more. Those were days of world-changing social revolution, and we saw it with our own eyes.

There can be no denying that this cultural revolution had a profound and dramatic effect on Christianity at large. Those of us who rejected the new social consensus found ourselves fighting hard to protect and preserve our long-held Biblical beliefs. It was only the beginning of what the Apostle Paul called a "falling away," 2 Thessalonians 2:3.

Observing Changes in the Church - Ecumenism

After we conducted several more revival meetings, we ended up in Charlotte, NC at Pastor Howard Fortenberry's Church. It was a strong, old-fashioned Assembly of God Church with about 200 members in an attractive new building. We had a great revival there for two weeks.

Pastor Fortenberry wanted to take us to the studios of a new Christian Television ministry that was based in Charlotte, so we could meet Jim Bakker, the Director of that ministry. Two years earlier, Jim and his wife, Tammy Faye had launched the Trinity Broadcasting Network in California with Paul and Jan Crouch. But when conflicts arose, the Bakkers departed TBN in January of 1974, and went to Charlotte to pioneer the PTL (Praise The Lord) Network (now called The Inspiration Network).

Jim had taken over the studios of WRET, Channel 36. I had been in that station a couple of years earlier when Pastor Clendennen and I held a crusade in a High School auditorium in Charlotte. We had been on the air on Channel 36 for more than a year. Already, Jim had a bright red Cadillac El Dorado Convertible with a white top sitting in front under the entrance.

He was dressed to kill, and wearing an enormous diamond ring on his finger.

Jim invited us to be on the next PTL show. Dixie and I would sing, and Jim would interview me. I played the white grand piano, and Dixie stood at her microphone playing her tambourine as we sang together on national television.

After we sang a couple of songs, I sat with Jim at his desk, and we got into a discussion about the Baptism of the Holy Ghost. When I mentioned speaking in other tongues, he began to back off the subject. I observed first-hand that day that Jim Bakker was being careful not to get crossways with his Baptist, Methodist and Roman Catholic partners. He dropped the subject of speaking in tongues like a hot potato and moved on to another subject.

(The truth is that speaking in tongues has ALWAYS been a dividing line between those who literally believe that the Book of Acts is the model for modern Christianity, and those who make excuses about why it is irrelevant to modern Christianity. THAT is also why I have been compelled to stand rock-solid firm on the doctrine of the Baptism of the Holy Ghost with the evidence of speaking in other tongues.)

That little episode at PTL was a real eye-opener to me. I suddenly realized that Christianity was already taking a dramatic change of direction backward. It was my first real exposure to hardcore ECUMENICAL thinking in what I thought was going to be a "Pentecostal" forum. I could not grasp, at that early stage in the game, what a profound revolution this medium would provoke. Not only would the Assemblies of God and Pentecostals in general be changed, but literally all of Christianity. Bakker and his kind would redefine Christianity by leveling the playing field for a thousand different, even opposing theologies.

Although Jim was an ordained Assemblies of God minister, he breached every traditional protocol by giving equal voice to every kind of doctrine and heresy. I was shocked to see him give an equal platform to Baptists, Methodists, Catholics, and a menagerie of other "Christian" groups.

Ecumenism would ultimately wash away virtually all the doctrinal and holiness distinctives that had always defined Pentecostals.

It was also while we were there that I discovered that Vestal Goodman (the famous Gospel singer), who had always been an icon of holiness Pentecostals, had finally cut off her long hair, and began wearing slacks, makeup, and jewelry. I was utterly shocked and deeply disappointed. I had played the piano for her on a few occasions, and never expected to see her abandon her holiness roots.

The sad reality is that Christian Television has done more damage than good to the Gospel message. The all-things-equal strategy of men like Jim Bakker, Paul Crouch, Pat Robertson, and other multi-denominational ministries accommodates non-Pentecostal Christianity on an equal par with Pentecostals. The end result of that strategy is that people are convinced that Christianity WITHOUT the Holy Ghost is equal to or better than Christianity WITH the Holy Ghost baptism. The problem with that conclusion is that the entire early Church was Pentecostal. The entire early Church spoke in tongues.

"Lord, I Need You Now, More Than Ever"

After the revival in Charlotte, Dixie was scheduled to fly to Beaumont for her last pre-natal doctor's appointment. I loaded up her luggage and took her to the Charlotte airport. When she got to Beaumont, her luggage did not arrive. She waited and waited. No luggage. ALL of her maternity clothes were in that luggage, and she was really up a creek. We had planned for her to return to Charlotte, but the loss of her clothes really changed our plans. She stayed in Beaumont, and I drove home by myself with the trailer in tow.

Dixie was almost nine months pregnant and would soon have our first baby. I had a two-week revival scheduled in Corpus Christi, Texas, so we agreed that I should go alone. She would stay with her parents in Beaumont, just in case she went into labor.

It was while I was alone in Corpus Christi that I stayed up all night in the Church one night writing the song, "Lord, I Need You Now More Than Ever." That song has always been one of my most-requested songs. More importantly, I think it reflected the disturbances in my own spirit due to the fundamental changes that were beginning to take place in Christianity.

Long Winding Road

I had been there preaching and singing from Sunday morning through Wednesday night. On Thursday morning, the pastor knocked on the door of my trailer to tell me that Dixie had called to let me know that she was having contractions and was on her way to the hospital in Beaumont to have the baby.

I panicked. I ran inside the Church, broke down all the sound equipment, hauled it out and loaded it in the trailer. I packed up all the records, tapes, Bibles and books and loaded them in the car. I broke down the trailer jacks and disconnected the utility hookups. I connected the trailer hitch and load levelers. I threw the car in gear and hit the freeway, driving as hard and fast as I could drive. Normally, it takes about five hours to drive from Corpus to Beaumont, including slow traffic in Houston. I got lost in Houston trying to find a shortcut somewhere along the Old Spanish Trail, yet I STILL made it to Beaumont in a record-breaking time!

Unfortunately, I was still about 30 minutes too late to see my first child born. Dixie had been in labor all morning, but Dr. Edgar Sarrafian decided that she would not be able to deliver him naturally. So he went ahead and performed a Caesarian section shortly after noon. It was a boy, weighing in at 7 pounds 14 ounces.

Dixie was still unconscious in the recovery room when I arrived. In those days, Daddies were not allowed in surgical suites, so I had to wait outside until they brought my little boy into the hospital nursery.

An Epiphany - The Wonder Of Having Of A Son

I stood alone in the hallway, looking through the nursery window at the first sight of my baby boy. I had an epiphany - "a sudden manifestation of the essence or meaning of something." Tears came to my eyes as I realized that I was a Daddy. Suddenly, I felt like I knew some of the meaning of God creating His own Son. I contemplated how that Jesus Christ was the creation of His Father. Jesus was the human version of God. I wondered if this baby would be a little version of me.

The marvel of having brought a new life into existence left me feeling awestruck. For a moment I trembled as I thought about the new, huge responsibility that had just been thrust upon me. A few minutes later, they allowed me into the recovery room to see Dixie as she began to awaken from the anesthesia. She looked exhausted but absolutely beautiful. I was so proud of my girl and my boy. I felt much regret for arriving late, and not being there when Dixie went into labor, and I apologized to her. She was very understanding and did not have any complaint against me. We were both very happy that he was born healthy and strong.

We had considered many names for a boy, but had not yet decided on one. We had seriously considered Brian Keith, which means "Strong Warrior," so when the nurse finally put me on the spot for a name, I said, "Brian Keith." Brian is now grown and married, with children of his own, active in music and ministry in his home Church, and has shown many, many times the evidence of the meaning of his name - "Strong Warrior."

Dixie and I bought a portable bassinet that folded up like a briefcase. In each Church where we went, she unfolded the portable bassinet and placed it on the floor beside her feet on the front row of pews. Brian was pretty faithful to sleep through our singing and my preaching. It was characteristic of Dixie to keep Brian on a strict schedule. She timed his daily regimen so that he would be ready for sleep at Church time. When Dixie came up to sing, she always enlisted one of the girls in the Church to sit by and watch Brian for us. Dixie sang and played her tambourine while I sang and pounded on the piano. I never thought to put a microphone on the piano, so all our tapes from those days feature lots of vocals with very little piano in the background. But you could always hear Dixie's tambourine.

"There's A Star In The Darkest Night"

Right away, we hit the road again, en route to North Carolina to preach in several Churches around the state. In Williamston, Pastor Johnny Bryant was a local Gospel radio personality on the Rocky Mount station. I preached on the radio every day and did interviews with him on his Gospel music show. I distinctly remember his IGA grocery store commercials with his HEAVY tar-heel accent, slick hairdo, and flashy sport coats. The services at his Church each night were well-attended. He always featured a lot of special music, including a trio of ladies called the Mizelle Sisters. They were awesome singers. I will never forget one of the songs they sang - "There's a Star in the Darkest Night." The lyrics to the chorus of that song were...

> There's a star in the darkest night, just to give us a ray of light.
> It will guide you through the night when hope seems gone.
> Soon the darkness fades away, and there breaks a golden day.
> Just remember the darkness comes before the dawn.

We held a revival in Havelock, where the Cherry Point Marine Base is. The Church consisted primarily of military families. We had a lot of conversions in that revival. The Marines loved straight-shooting preaching.

For months, we traveled around the state of North Carolina, holding revivals in Morganton, Asheville, Boone, Franklin, Highlands, Lexington, Hendersonville, Salisbury, Charlotte, Mount Holley, Jacksonville, Manteo, Wanchese, Avon, Buxton, Cape Hatteras, Colerain, Wilmington, Williamston, Windsor, Spartanburg, S.C., and several other cities. We also preached and sang in three state Camp Meetings at the two District Campgrounds in Franklin and Windsor.

My First Prophecy Conference

In Wanchese, I preached a 15-minute daily radio broadcast for fourteen consecutive days on the local radio station. On the last night of the revival, the place was packed with standing room only - about 250 people in attendance. I preached on "The Antichrist." This was 1974, and I spoke of the coming New World Order, its connections to the Rockefeller-Rothschild families, the C.F.R., Illuminati, Masonic roots, the subversive plans of the Federal Reserve Bank, Chase Bank, and so many precursors to the Mark of the Beast. I sold cases of books that night by Gary Allen called, "None Dare Call It Conspiracy." We sold a large number of records and tapes during that meeting, and had a lot of conversions. I had my cassette duplicator, and many people bought copies of those sermons every night.

Trying To Convert Souls, While Satan Hinders

Then we went to Avon, which is a fishing village on the north end of Cape Hatteras Island. We parked in a travel trailer park on the Atlantic beach and held a three week revival there. Attendance was good every night. Some of the old guys there who had been fishermen all their lives loved the straight, hard preaching.

I fought devils in that meeting. I had a bad case of the flu, with high fever for about three days and nights, but I went to the pulpit every night anyway. I spent a long, long time trying to get some teen-age boys into the altar to pray through, but they just resisted to the end. I was very troubled about them when I went to bed late that night.

At about 1 AM, I heard sirens screaming up and down the beach highway. The next morning, I learned that the boy I had tried so hard to reach the night before had been killed in a car wreck after Church. It had a profound effect on that revival, and many more responded in the following nights.

A Word From God: Forty Weeks

At some point in our travels, I got a feeling that we would be in North Carolina for forty weeks. I don't know why I felt that, but it seemed to be a spiritual impression - a word from the Lord. I told Dixie that I felt like God was going to make a big change in the direction of our ministry after we had spent forty weeks ministering in North Carolina.

In March of 1975, we parked our trailer on the District Campgrounds of the Assemblies of God while we held revivals in several Churches in the vicinity of Franklin, in the foothills of the Smoky Mountains.

The Dream

One night, between three and four o'clock in the morning, I had a dream. In the dream, I was in a morning prayer meeting at the Tabernacle on the Campgrounds, walking up and down the sawdust aisles as I prayed. I stopped to look out a large open window that had a view across the Cullasaja River. I felt a tap on my shoulder. When I turned to see who it was, Pastor Clendennen was standing there. He asked me to come back to Beaumont and be his Associate Pastor at Victory Temple.

Then I woke up. I roused Dixie from her sleep and told her what I had just dreamed. It was very vivid, and I felt very strongly that it was from God. But at four in the morning, Dixie was understandably more interested in going back to sleep. Still, I could not shake that dream from my thoughts.

The Dream's Fulfillment

Several months later, in July, Pastor Clendennen was in North Carolina preaching their summer Camp Meetings. Dixie and I were the featured singers nightly, and I preached the weekend services.

One morning at 7 AM, I was in the morning prayer meeting with several other ministers and campers, and I was walking up and down the sawdust aisles of the old tabernacle, praying. I stopped at an open window, and was looking out across the Cullasaja River when I felt a tap on my shoulder. Instantly, I knew what was happening. I turned around to see Pastor Clendennen standing there, exactly as I had seen him in that dream, four months earlier!

I looked at him and said, "I already know what you are going to say, because I saw this in a dream months ago!" With no other reaction, he said, "I want you to pray about coming back to Beaumont and being my Associate." I told him that I didn't think I needed to pray about it, because it seemed that the Lord had already showed me that it was going to happen.

My big question was, "WHEN?" I had two more revivals scheduled before the next Camp Meeting to be held in Windsor, NC, and then several revivals scheduled afterward. In my mind, I thought that I should at least fulfill my commitment to the next Camp Meeting before going home.

That night, I got down to pray about it, and something said, "Count the weeks." I thought about that, then decided to pull out my calendar and count HOW MANY WEEKS Dixie and I had preached in North Carolina alone.

Want to guess? The up-coming Camp Meeting in Windsor would be the FORTIETH WEEK. That satisfied me. I announced to Dixie and to Pastor Clendennen that at the end of the Windsor Camp, we would head back to Beaumont to work at Victory Temple.

Miracles and Signs Confirmed the Dream

I had three weeks to prepare for a radical change in my ministry. For instance, everything we had and did was geared for evangelistic travels.

Long Winding Road

The travel trailer, the sound system, the records, tapes, books, Bibles, concordances, etc. were all tools (and expenses) that I used on the road, but would not need at all when we settled down in the home Church.

I did not know how I would manage to pay for all the overhead I had. I prayed, and on the first day of the Windsor Camp Meeting, a pastor friend of mine came to me and said, "My wife and I have just resigned our Church, and are going on the evangelistic field. Would you be interested in selling your trailer?" I was ecstatic! God sent a buyer for my trailer at the perfect time! When I told him that I would sell it, he then offered to buy my sound system also. We made a deal on the spot. Before the camp was over, he produced cash money for all of it.

Then I had another dilemma. We didn't have a way to get all our belongings back to Texas, now that our trailer and living quarters was sold. Amazingly, another preacher came to me in one of the night services and wanted to know if I needed a utility trailer. He DONATED that trailer to us!

The third dilemma was the matter of selling out the cases and cases of records, tapes, books, Bibles and Concordances that I carried in my bookstore. All my unsold inventory would just be a financial loss, and I did not want to take all those unsold items back to Texas. But on Friday night, the last night of the Camp Meeting, out of the blue, a man approached me from Virginia Beach, and introduced himself as a Christian bookseller and distributor. He ASKED me if I wanted to sell all my record and book inventory! I was flabbergasted! He made a good offer, and I sold everything I had to him on the spot - several hundred dollars worth.

Dixie and I were totally convinced that this move was the will of God! Brian was one year old, and had hardly seen his grandparents, since we were always on the road. It would be nice to be back home.

It was comforting to believe that we were being miraculously led by the Spirit into a new place of ministry. The word from the Lord and the dream had been confirmed by several amazing miracles.

Chapter 7

Planting A Church

It was the summer of 1975. Married less than three years, we had traveled the country, preaching and singing. It was a big deal to be leaving the field and returning to Beaumont. We rented a nice three-bedroom apartment and moved in. I was 23 and had become the Associate Pastor at Victory Temple in Beaumont, a congregation of several hundred people at that time.

Years earlier, while attending Central Bible College in Springfield, Missouri, I had given myself to a three-day prayer and fasting vigil to seek the will of God for my ministry. I holed up in a large prayer room on the fourth floor of Welch Hall for three days. Except for the hours I had to be in classes, I stayed in prayer and Bible study.

I asked God to show me exactly what He wanted me to do. At the end of the third day, I got my answer while reading in 2 Timothy 4:5, "But watch thou in all things, endure afflictions, do the work of an evangelist, make full proof of thy ministry."

Do The Work Of An Evangelist

That verse had been my foundational stone ever since that day. I believed that God wanted me to be an evangelist. And that is the ministry that I had devoted myself to.

But the DREAM had dramatically changed my course. It was putting me into Pastoral Ministry.

I questioned God about that. "If it is your will for me to go back to Beaumont to be Pastor Clendennen's associate, then what am I supposed to do with this calling that I have to be an evangelist?"

As I prayed and studied the Word, I found what seemed to be my answer in Titus 1:5, "For this cause left I thee in Crete, that thou shouldest set in order the things that are wanting."

I also took note of several verses in which Paul spoke of "ministering to the saints," (Hebrews 6:10; Romans 15:25; I Corinthians 16:15; 2 Corinthians 8:4; 9:2 and others). I concluded that God wanted me to go to Beaumont and "set in order the things that were wanting, and minister to the saints."

Set In Order The Things That Are Wanting, And Minister To The Saints

With Pastor Clendennen building the television ministry and traveling around the country several days every week, the local Church needed a lot of attention. I took that as my project - to focus my attention on the building of the local congregation. That included pulpit ministry in Pastor Clendennen's absence, a great deal of pastoral calling and visitation, updating membership lists, initiating phone calls and letter writing, hospital visitation, etc.

Dixie and I threw ourselves into that ministry. I ended up taking over the choir again. I either played the piano or led the worship in every service. When the Pastor was out of town, I filled the pulpit. But within a few months, the demands of the rapidly expanding television ministry began to pull me away from the pastoral duties. Instead of ministering directly to the saints, I was spending enormous amounts of time in the office of the television ministry, working on audio and video material for radio and television, editing and remastering sermon tapes, and drifting further and further from a direct ministry to the people. That was very disillusioning, since before that time, I had been preaching nearly seven nights a week for almost three years.

Then, the Pastor's daughter and son-in-law returned to Beaumont from their evangelistic travels. They had been traveling for several years, but decided to settle down in Beaumont and join the ministerial staff. I could see my preaching opportunities evaporating, and simply lost my desire to stay there. I had to get back to preaching the Gospel. Someone else could do the editorial and office work that I was spending so much time with.

Again, I went to prayer and fasting, looking for a solution. After about six months, Dixie and I found ourselves looking for other options. I informed the Pastor that we were praying for another open door for ministry, and would be leaving as soon as God showed us what to do. He knew and understood how the circumstances had changed, and understood our desire to move on at that time.

Long Winding Road

Considering Our First Pastoral Position

During that period of time, the Pastor of the Church in Groves (my home town) resigned, and that congregation was searching for a new pastor. Attendance had dwindled, and they were barely keeping the doors open. Nevertheless, I decided to submit my name for consideration. Dixie and I went to Groves, preached, and sang. In all, eleven candidates submitted their names for a vote. The tiny group voted on all eleven names on one ballot. Not surprisingly, no minister received a majority. They started the process over, but I withdrew my name. That was not our destiny.

Meanwhile, to generate an additional income, I sat down and wrote a script for a series of lessons on "How to Play the Piano by Ear." Late one night, I went to the Church and recorded twelve five-minute lessons on tape. I designed a nice package label for that product, along with a professional-looking newspaper ad, and went to a local advertising agency and had them produce them for me. I bought a five-place cassette duplicator and started making copies. Then I began running ads in newspapers around the area to advertise the product. I sold about 500 copies of that tape before other priorities took me away from the project. Years later, I met people who actually learned how to play the piano from my lessons on that tape.

Then, I learned that another Assembly of God Church in Mid-County had gone out of business. They had an all-brick Church building on Highway 365 in Nederland - between Beaumont and Groves. I had preached in that Church several years earlier. But it had never had a large enough congregation to support it adequately, so the small congregation voted to close it, and the property was turned over to the South Texas District of the Assemblies of God. Since I had grown up in that area, I knew many, many people there, and felt that I could build a successful Church there where others had failed. So I went to the District office in Houston and talked to the District Superintendent and the District Secretary about the building.

First, I asked them for permission to re-open the Church and start a new work in it. They told me that they didn't want to do that. They had already had a board meeting and had voted to sell the property, and had decided to allocate the income from that property to another project. I then asked them to sell the property to me. They didn't want to do that either. The South Texas District did not want to revive that work in Nederland.

Putting A "Fleece" Before The Lord

Dixie and I had little to go by, except fervent fasting and prayer, which we committed ourselves to. We asked God to show us what to do. We wondered if we could succeed in starting a new Church from scratch in Mid-County. There was no strong Assembly of God Church anywhere in the Mid-County area at that time, but after appealing to the District concerning the defunct Church, I knew that they did not think a Church could be built in that area. But I did. It was my home.

I still believed that the area had potential, and I believed that we could make a go of it. So we put out a "fleece" and a prayer with certain conditions before God. Like Gideon's fleeces, we proposed that if God gave us certain signs, we would know that we should start a new Church. Well, the signs came to pass, so I went to Pastor Clendennen and told him my plans, and resigned.

If all this seems to be a convoluted way for a man to find the will of God, I will assure you that there are plenty of cases in the Bible when men sought after the will of God with just as much toil and exasperation. In our case, the process led me from being an evangelist, to an Associate Pastor, to Pastoring a Church of my own in little more than six months. While we were traveling, it never entered my mind to go home and start a Church. But that is what happened as we sought desperately to do the will of God.

You will often find that God uses incomprehensible, even troubling processes to move you from one place to another, either physically or spiritually. There is no point in trying to figure out all that God does. You will never understand them on this side of Heaven. That is why He repeatedly tells us to TRUST and HAVE FAITH in Him. The JUST shall live by faith.

So Dixie and I rented a three-bedroom house in Groves, and we immediately moved in. Brian was almost 20 months old.

It was time for me to renew my ministerial credentials with the Assemblies of God, which I had held for eight years. Instead of renewing them, I chose to let them expire. Many denominational preachers were going non-denominational in those days. I didn't know if I would regret it later, but at that time, it seemed the right choice. I was only 24 years old and believed that I could accomplish anything.

Gospel Outreach Ministries

I hired an accountant to create a non-profit organization called "Gospel Outreach Ministries." That enabled me to accept donations that would be tax-deductible.

I called around to find a place to meet. For the first three weeks, we met in a conference room at a local hotel. Then I found a store-front for rent on Lincoln Avenue in the commercial district of Groves. We met in that building for about three months and grew to a congregation of about forty.

The Hour Of Revival Radio Broadcast

I went to the local Christian FM radio station and purchased radio time and began a fifteen-minute program called "The Hour of Revival." It aired twice daily, Monday through Friday during prime "drive time" (7:10 AM and 4:10 PM). KTRM was a powerful Gospel station that dominated the Christian market throughout Jefferson County, and I had a large audience.

I borrowed Jimmy Swaggart's format; a prerecorded intro and outro, opening with one Gospel song, then announcements, and an eight-minute message. I created a professional logo, which was an hour-glass with a fire behind it, representing "The Hour of Revival." I advertised the radio program in newspaper ads, direct mail flyers and radio spot ads. I built an audio production console at home that had a reel-to-reel recorder, turntables, mixers, amps, headphones and microphone, and produced five programs for each week. Each program aired twice daily.

The Gospel Lighthouse

I also created a logo for the Church, which we named "The Gospel Lighthouse." The art featured the Cape Hatteras Lighthouse which Dixie and I loved so much. For several years, I had used an ad agency to produce art, graphics and typesetting. I knew the owner well, so had her create all our artwork and logos. We created an excellent-looking brochure entitled, "Why Go to Church?" with an eight-point lesson from the Bible. We printed them by the thousands and handed them out from door-to-door in Groves, Port Neches and Nederland.

Meanwhile, a local real estate investor purchased the same brick Church building I had enquired about earlier. As soon as I learned he had purchased it, I gave him a call and told him I wanted to buy it. We made an appointment, and I bought that property with nothing down, on a contract for deed for $75,000, my signature only. The notes started at $350 month, and went up $100 a month until it leveled off at $750 monthly. The year was 1976, and that was an enormous amount of money. But I believed in walking by faith and trusting God to meet our needs, and this was no time to change strategies. From the first week in the storefront, I told the members that we had a $600 weekly budget. I never failed to get the necessary $600 a week out of that small group of people.

We moved the congregation into that building, and we bought a nice mobile home for a parsonage and set it up behind the Church. I had good credit at two local credit unions and used my resources to totally outfit that building. I bought a Hammond Porta-B organ with a portable Leslie, along with a complete sound system with Cerwin-Vega speakers, and I bought a nice riding lawnmower.

Printing and Publishing

A local printer who printed several jobs for me decided to go out of business and offered to sell all his equipment for a good price, so I bought it and moved it into the Church. I had an AB Dick offset press, two letter presses, a metal platemaker, a folding machine, a commercial paper cutter, an Addressograph-Multigraph direct-mail addressing machine, and two photographic-process typesetters, and a large supply of papers and inks.

I had considerable printing and graphic arts experience. In my college days, I had worked for an international company producing their weekly national newsletter on an offset press. Then, for two years at Victory Temple, I had edited and produced a monthly 16-page magazine for Pastor Clendennen, as well as weekly newsletters to thousands, plus numerous other direct-mail pieces. We operated two large offset presses there.

I believed that the future of my ministry required the use of the printed page. Every month, I published a newsletter with a sermon in it, and sent it by bulk-rate mail to 1200+ households, which included the names of people who had responded to the radio programs and who had visited in our services. I also published a monthly Calendar of Events. We kept a very busy schedule.

Occasionally, I submitted my articles to the Port Arthur News for publication. They gladly published them on the Religion page as a guest columnist.

Jimmy Swaggart Crusade

Early on, I received a letter from Jimmy Swaggart. He planned to come to Beaumont for a crusade, and was inviting local pastors to sponsor the event. I signed on immediately. I helped organize Swaggart's crusade, which was to be held at the Beaumont City Auditorium. Of course, he had a ready-made following. The auditorium was packed to the top balcony - about 2500 people. I sat with about a dozen local pastors on stage. At the conclusion of the service, Swaggart gave an altar call, and hundreds of seekers responded. He instructed the sponsoring pastors to move to the edge of the stage and pray for as many as we could. In all, it seemed a profitable effort and good to be associated with such a successful crusade. It gave our new Church valuable exposure.

The Gospel Lighthouse averaged about sixty in attendance by the end of the first year, and within two years, the attendance averaged about one hundred. Our ministry there was typical of everything I had learned and believed and preached in my first 25 years of life. My message was relatively old-fashioned, my convictions were old-fashioned, but my methods were progressive and aggressive. I led the worship from the Hammond organ, and Dixie and I sang specials in every service. We used lots of material by Lanny Wolfe, Dottie Rambo and Andrae' Crouch.

An Old-Fashioned Gospel Ministry

I have always preached heavily and frequently on the subject of the Baptism of the Holy Ghost. I received the Holy Ghost at the age of 11, speaking in tongues as the Spirit gave the utterance. I have always believed that everybody ought to have the Holy Ghost. I didn't know it was such a strong doctrinal case until many years later, but nevertheless, I preached it very fervently.

Our standards of living were conservative. I believed and preached that a woman should have long hair, but in those days I didn't necessarily think that meant "uncut." Dixie and I agreed that her hair should be at least shoulder length. Dixie never wore slacks - only dresses, and her makeup and jewelry were very minimal.

Some of the ladies who came to the Gospel Lighthouse criticized Dixie sternly in those days for being in "bondage" to out-dated thinking on her dress-code. They urged her to start wearing slacks, but she believed it was wrong for a woman to wear slacks, and I did too. She stood firm. She always dressed with dignity, even in casual settings.

I followed the convictions I had learned from my childhood. I continued to preach against going to the movies, going to sporting events, participating in organized sports, smoking, drinking, carousing, etc. In those days, those teachings were NOT considered radical or extreme. They were not unusual standards for Full-Gospel Churches in those days. In fact, ALL Evangelicals had embraced similar standards for centuries.

But a new wave of thinking was going to rattle my cage before I knew it.

Chapter 8

A Major Paradigm Shift

The Spirit Of Love

I was 25 years old in early 1977, when an old friend from 1969 popped back into my life - the Pastor I had assisted while attending college in Beaumont. My sister-in-law had stayed in touch with him after he left Beaumont, and she was aware of the amazing success he was having with his ministry in Waco, Texas. She wanted me to re-connect with him and let him tell me what he was doing in Waco.

I invited him to come speak for us at The Gospel Lighthouse. He came, and we spent a couple of days in intense discussion about "what God was doing."

He and his family had gone to Waco to assume the pastorate of his retiring elderly father-in-law. They had a fine older Church plant, but almost no people. It was an Assembly of God Church, but he renamed it "The Spirit of Love Church." In his first year there, the congregation of 35 exploded to over 350. He raided Baylor University and was harvesting Baptist college kids by the scores, making Charismatics out of them.

Ecumenicalism and the Charismatic Movement

You would have to understand some of the major forces at work in the religious world at that time to appreciate the major upheaval that was about to take place in my life.

Almost nobody in those days realized the impact that the Vatican II "Ecumenical" Council of 1962-1965 was having on the entire Christian community around the world just a little more than ten years after the fact. A part-stealth, part-celebrated Roman Catholic presence had invaded the Pentecostal-Charismatic arena and was working feverishly to dilute or silence all the distinctive doctrinal teachings of Protestant Fundamental Evangelical Christianity.

In its most technical terms, Vatican II was meant to reach out to all its departed "daughter" Churches (Protestants), and bring them back into the fold of the "Mother" Church in Rome. But that certainly was not evident on the face of the ecumenical movement. It merely appeared that all Christians of all denominations were finally becoming one. Everybody seemed to forget that "Mother" was "the Great Whore," the Harlot Church of Revelation 17.

Dismantling the Protestant Reformation

It would not be until 1994, in a historic declaration, that Evangelicals including Pat Robertson, Charles Colson (one of the chief originators), Jesse Miranda (Assemblies of God), Bill Bright (Campus Crusade for Christ), Mark Noll (Wheaton University) and several other notables, would officially join with Roman Catholic leaders to sign a "non-proselytization" pact. That move, more than anything else, effectively nullified the Reformation and abolished Protestantism. The great anti-Catholics from the past, like Martin Luther, John Calvin, John Knox, John Wesley, and even Charles Spurgeon, must have rolled over in their graves. Protestants would no longer object to the Roman Catholic Church, but would actually call them brothers and sisters in the Lord. No need for Protestants to convert Catholics any more. The Catholics had pulled off a major coup.

There were new faces and new voices breaking onto the religious scene that were introducing radical new concepts about how to have Church. One example of the homogenization of Pentecostalism with Catholicism was the fact that Jim Bakker, President of the *PTL Club*, and Pat Robertson, President of the *Christian Broadcasting Network*, both warmly welcomed Mother Angelica, a Roman Catholic nun, to their national satellite television audiences in the mid to late 1970s. Her popularity grew so quickly across America that by 1979, she began organizing her own Catholic television network - the *Eternal Word Television Network (EWTN)* in Irondale, Alabama. EWTN now reaches almost 150 million homes on more than 5000 cable systems in 127 countries, making it the LARGEST religious television network in the world. All of this began when those two Pentecostal ministers ignored the long-held objections to the Roman Catholic Church and began not only to consent to Roman Catholicism, but also to actually welcome it into Protestant Evangelical and Pentecostal circles. (EWTN offers a 24-hour fare of Masses, Rosaries, Catechisms, and

Papal events, along with Catholic-slanted international news reporting and other programming.)

Years later, Paul Crouch, President of the *Trinity Broadcasting Network* would declare, "I'm eradicating the word Protestant even out of my vocabulary... I'm not protesting anything... it's time for Catholics and non-Catholics to come together as one in the Spirit and one in the Lord." Robert Schuller, *Hour of Power* author, and Pastor of the Garden Grove Community Church said, "It's time for Protestants to go to the shepherd [the Pope] and say, 'What do we have to do to come home?'"

The net result of the new "non-denominationalism" (more accurately called "Ecumenicalism") was that thousands of Churches across America were abandoning their denominational ties AND their doctrinal identities, and joining up with countless para-Church organizations, often laity-led (and in many cases, forbidding the participation of the clergy).

It was the beginning of a new day for Christianity. It was an "anything goes" day for Christianity. The old-game rules became the worst taboo. Denominationalism became the scourge of religion, and preaching doctrine its greatest sin. People from every denomination were coming together in free-style worship and ministry. Anything that felt good, and anything that could pull a crowd was permissible. The denominations could not compete.

The contrast was glaringly obvious in my particular situation. I had spent two years building a congregation from zero to 100, following a traditional model. The Church in Waco, following a maverick, free-style approach, hit 350 in less than a year with an almost completely experimental model. I asked him what he was doing to have that kind of revival.

"You've Got To Quit Preaching Hell, Fire, and Damnation!"

He told me, "Ken, you've got to quit preaching Hell, fire and damnation. You've got to quit telling people they can't do this and can't do that. You've just got to LOVE THEM! People are starving for love!" He continued, "You know I used to preach Hell so hot that you could smell the flames, but I don't do that anymore. God doesn't care how you dress, or whether you go to the movies, or things like that. He loves you, and He wants to save you. That is the message."

I was skeptical. I argued dogmatically with him.

He proposed two things to convince me.

First, he said, "I want you to come to Waco and see what God is doing." He had a Youth Training Seminar scheduled with Winkey Pratney, an author and speaker from New Zealand. Winkey was internationally known for his powerful books on youth conflicts.

So, on August 16, 1977, Dixie and I packed up and went to Waco to hear Winkey. It was the same day that Elvis Presley died, because we heard the news of Elvis dying while listening to the car radio on the way to Waco. Dixie had just learned that she was pregnant with our second child.

We spent several days in Waco, and spent quality time one-on-one with Winkey. We had sessions with him at the Church, at restaurants, in his room back at the hotel, even played a table-tennis tournament with him.

What we saw and heard in Waco was definitely impressive. The Spirit of Love Church had an astonishing amount of talent. Kevin Gould was a Christian recording artist with Light Records in the UK, and he had moved from Wales, United Kingdom to work stateside with Word Records, which was headquartered in Waco. Kevin was heavily featured in the ministry there. Several influential local TV and Radio personalities attended that Church, along with several prominent businessmen and local citizens. The Spirit of Love Church had a large staff, including three other full-time ministers - young couples who provided truly incredible music, youth, and children's ministries.

"New Wineskins For New Wine"

The Church owned a huge old three-story mansion which they converted into a teen half-way house/coffee house. About a dozen kids from the streets lived in the house, and it was a cauldron of activities day and night: concerts, seminars, parties, activities, etc. Hundreds of kids came and went from "The Wine Cellar - home of New Wineskins" - incorporating some of the popular concepts in Howard Snyder's smash-hit book, "The Problem With Wineskins." The Church also had a day care center with about sixty children in it. The whole place was a beehive of activity and excitement.

Secondly, the Pastor had another big idea for me. "There is one more person I want you to meet. His name is F.E. Ward."

Ward had been a Full-Gospel missionary to South America for many years, but in recent years had joined forces with Demos Shakarian to form the *Full Gospel Business Men's Fellowship International*. Demos Shakarian was a wealthy dairyman from California who worked very closely with Oral Roberts, and at one time, with William Branham. Ward was a "front man" for the organization, which at that time was the primary engine behind the Charismatic movement in the United States, and in many other countries. Ward traveled all over the United States, meeting with ministers and business men, and forming new chapters of the F.G.B.M.F.I. At that point, he had already chartered over 200 chapters. Jim Bakker and Pat Robertson collaborated with the F.G.B.M.F.I. again and again in huge national and regional events. Shakarian and Oral Roberts were frequent guests on CBN and PTL.

A New Thing

Dixie and I met Ward in Waco at "Surf and Turf," a local fine-dining seafood-and-steak restaurant with live music. Ward was a huge man and had a commanding way about him. Ward leaned into my face and said, "Ken, you've got to see what God is doing. He's doing a new thing." He invited me to Houston to the upcoming F.G.B.M.F.I. conference at the Marriot near the Medical Center. I promised him I would be there.

A few days later, I was in Houston at the appointed time. I walked into that vast ballroom that had been set up banquet-style. I don't know how many were in that crowd; maybe 1500, maybe 2000, from virtually every conceivable denomination. There were preachers in clerical collars, some smoking pipes or cigars, some wearing beards, some in high fashion, and some in street clothes.

The featured speaker that day was Howard Conatser, a silver-tongued orator if ever there was one. He was tall and slender, with snow-white hair and a heavy Dallas drawl. Howard was the pastor of the Beverly Hills Baptist Church in Dallas.

He testified that day of his deep hunger for God, and how it had led him to receiving the Baptism of the Holy Ghost, speaking in other tongues while in his private office. He told of being so overwhelmed with his new-found experience that he could not resist taking it to his Baptist congregation. Amazingly, many of them accepted his testimony, and in short order, nearly the entire congregation had received the Baptism of the Holy Ghost as well. The Church went into a massive, explosive growth phase, and attendance shot from 400 to 4,000 so quickly they had no place to meet. They ended up leasing the Bronco Bowl in Dallas, and that is where their Church was then meeting.

The attendees at the F.G.B.M.F.I. convention were so moved by Howard's testimony that they responded en mass. I watched in absolute amazement as over 1000 ministers of every denomination received the Baptism of the Holy Ghost that day, speaking in other tongues!

"If You Can't Beat 'Em, Join 'Em!"

I told Ward later that I didn't see how I could fight this. As best as I could tell, this must be the big last-days revival. I didn't think I could beat them. I came to the conclusion that I really had no choice but to join them, or get left behind. I didn't understand it, because it broke every rule I had ever learned, but I did not know how to explain it away.

I invited Ward to come to The Gospel Lighthouse, and he came right away. He told my congregation so many amazing stories, that I was left reeling from the amazement of it all.

Looking For Role Models

I reflected back on everything I could think of to decide if this was a true move of God's Spirit. My upbringing in two small Assembly of God Churches did not provide much of a reference point. Neither of my childhood pastors had formal educations, nor did they have any keen sensitivity to what was going on in the world of religion outside the four walls of their local assemblies.

In the earliest days of our marriage, Dixie and I looked for mentors. I devoured the autobiographies and biographies of numerous highly-influential contemporary preachers. I had been fascinated from my childhood with Oral Roberts and A.A. Allen. I read many of Oral Robert's books, and was especially affected by his "Seed Faith" teaching.

Long Winding Road

I remember reading A.A. Allen's biography, "Born to Lose, Bound to Win" out loud to Dixie one day while driving down Interstate 10 East through the state of Louisiana. Allen had been an exceptionally influential tent revivalist, and despite the complaints of many of his detractors, and apparently a few real hoaxes, Allen nevertheless had left a trail of signs, wonders and miracles like nobody else in his day. He was raised in his mother's tavern on a bar stool, and ended up preaching to some of the largest crowds in American history, with multitudes receiving miraculous healings. In his early days, he was a very powerful Bible preacher. But he finally died infamously, alone in a hotel room - a drunken alcoholic.

I read "Ever Increasing Faith," and "Faith That Prevails," by Smith Wigglesworth. Wigglesworth, whose dramatic faith and miracle ministry (which included raising numerous people from the dead) was known around the world, and it set a fire in me. I wanted God to give me dynamic healing and miracle ministry like that.

Kathryn Kuhlman also had a biography written by Jamie Buckingham called "Daughter of Destiny" in which she was portrayed as a prophetess without peer. Kuhlman's nationally renowned ministry, with an incredible boost from her weekly special on the CBS television network, catapulted her into the limelight of ecumenical Christianity, with countless multitudes attending her miracle crusades. Amazingly, the nagging reports of her adulterous lifestyle seemed to have little negative effect on her ministry.

I carefully followed several other national ministries, including Rex Humbard, Jimmy Swaggart, Morris Cerullo, T.L. Osborn, Leonard Ravenhill, David Wilkerson, and R.W. Shambach. Shambach and Brother Clendennen often teamed up in crusades and tent meetings, but they had not yet bought into the Charismatic, F.G.B.M.F.I. mindset. Shambach did later. Clendennen never did.

Anyway, when F.E. Ward came to The Gospel Lighthouse, my life was forever altered by his influence. He became my de facto mentor. I started taking cues from him. He persuaded me that I had nothing to lose, and everything to gain by going with the flow of this new "move of God." For better or for worse, I jumped in. Time would tell.

Long Winding Road

Chapter 9

Which Way From Here?

Under Ward's tutelage, I would soon discover a cornucopia of new ministry resources, venues and methods.

The Full Gospel Businessmen's Fellowship and Women's Aglow

First thing, I became the principal sponsor of a new chapter of the *Full Gospel Businessmen's Fellowship* in Port Arthur. We rented the Wyatt's Cafeteria banquet room, and two quite influential local businessmen and I started talking it up among denominational people, including some that Ward already knew in the area. The FIRST NIGHT over 150 people attended to hear one of Ward's recommended speakers. Dixie and I provided the music and singing that night.

Secondly, I became a sponsor and organizer for a new Port Arthur Chapter of the *Women's Aglow International*. We rented a room at the Driftwood Hotel and packed it out for the first meeting.

Then we got with some people in Beaumont and started promoting a *Women's Aglow* Chapter in Beaumont. Within three months, the attendance at the Ramada Inn was over 250.

I bought a nice bus-coach to transport people to Charismatic events in Houston. It was a 25-passenger custom vehicle formerly owned by a limousine company that had transported celebrities. This bus had carried the blues-rock band *ZZ Top* while they were in Houston. It had high-back captain seats, carpeting, refreshment bar, stereo music, PA system, etc.

We began carrying folks to events at John Osteen's Lakewood Church, Kenneth Hagin seminars, and various F.G.B.M.F.I. and Women's Aglow events.

Christian Television Takes The Lead

Christian television was experiencing explosive growth. Jim and Tammy Faye Bakker and Pat Robertson started the *700 Club* in Virginia Beach, which evolved into the *Christian Broadcasting Network*. Jim left CBN to go to

California, where he and Paul Crouch started the *Trinity Broadcasting Network*. Then, Jim moved again, this time to Charlotte, NC, where he started the *PTL Club*. (Ultimately, Jim Bakker played the key role in the establishment of all three of the original Christian TV networks – CBN, TBN and PTL.) Every Christian of every denomination was being profoundly influenced by their multi-denominational, inter-denominational, non-denominational, (even anti-denominational) ecumenical approach. Bible doctrines became utterly impertinent. Nobody spoke of Bible doctrines. The worst thing any preacher could do was to speak of Bible doctrines. It was a death warrant for any ministry.

Both CBN and PTL had huge audiences in the Beaumont-Port Arthur Media Market. I contacted both networks and became a monthly sponsor. As a local Church, I was able to obtain a monthly computer-generated report of all the people in my area who had contacted their ministry in the previous thirty days. Those became valuable contact leads, and I sent personal letters to those prospects, inviting them to The Gospel Lighthouse. I also began to organize and advertise a week-long chartered bus trip to PTL.

The Agape Force

Through the Church in Waco, we also connected with Tony Salerno and *The Agape Force* ministries in Lindale, Texas. *The Agape Force* was a huge youth ranch not far from David Wilkerson's private ranch, and Leonard Ravenhill's home, just outside of Lindale. We arranged to have a van-load of teens from *The Agape Force* come and conduct a week-long crusade for the Gospel Lighthouse, doing door-to-door evangelism, street concerts, training sessions, etc.

We set up a flat-bed trailer off of an 18-wheeler for a sound-stage on the parking lot at Wyatt's Cafeteria in Port Arthur on a Saturday night. Gulfway Drive was "the drag," and thousands of teen-agers cruised up and down the drag all night long. We cranked the PA system up as loud as we could stand it and put on a Christian music concert to get the kids' attention. Hundreds of kids came around, and we preached and witnessed and prayed with them.

Then we took our Church kids to the *Agape Force* ranch in Lindale for a couple of big events/concerts with artists like newly-converted Barry

McGuire (former star of the hippy Broadway show "Hair"), Nancy Honeytree (popular with "Jesus People" and the "Jesus Movement"), and *2nd Chapter of Acts*. Their hippy-savvy ministry was creating a whole new genre of youth ministry, an eccentric knock-off of Wilkerson's *Teen Challenge* coffee-house street ministries.

A Laity-led Movement

IMMEDIATELY, everything in my local ministry began to take a radically new direction! That is no exaggeration. Ward began to effectively mentor me in my pastorate. He sent me a steady stream of "ministers" to fill my pulpit. Our monthly calendar was jam-packed with activities and events.

One fellow was a businessman from Houston, the multi-millionaire owner of a chain of carpet stores. Another was a police captain from Houston. One was a hillbilly Gospel singer. Another was an executive officer from International Harvester in Louisville, Kentucky. He was a Church of Christ layman turned miracle worker. His specialty was stretching legs. A fifth guy was a Dentist who had the gift of healing. He testified to my congregation that, "just last night, while I was sitting in my den drinking a beer, one of my dental patients called me and said, 'Doc, I'm sick! I need you to pray for me!' So I told him to come on over, and I would pray for him. He did, and God healed him instantly!"

If I tell you, "I've seen it all!" - go figure!

The Happy Hunters

I was literally reeling from this radical new version of Christianity and the ministry. But before I could catch my breath, Ward sent "The Happy Hunters" to me. Oh, my. Charles and Frances Hunter. If you have never heard of them, there is no way I can describe them to you here. He was the retired wealthy president of a large CPA firm in Houston, and she was the retired owner of a large printing company in Houston. Together, they billed themselves as "Charismatically yours!"

The Happy Hunters were taking the world by a storm. They were regulars on Jim Bakker's PTL Club, and of course had appeared on all the other Christian TV outlets, too. They operated out of Austin Wilkerson's Evangelistic Temple (A/G) Church in Houston. Wilkerson had always been on the progressive cutting edge. He had Andrae' Crouch and the Disciples there almost before anyone had heard of them.

Now the Hunters were like nothing you have ever seen before. In hindsight, I remember them as psychedelic old people. Gaudy. Flashy. Hyperactive. First of all, they required a guaranteed minimum for their appearance. I forget now what it was, but it was astronomical, and I agreed to pay it. I also had to guarantee a crowd. So I rented the Port Neches-Groves High School auditorium, which seated almost 1000. I bought large newspaper ads in Port Arthur and Beaumont. I bought radio spots and sent out thousands of direct mail pieces. I worked like a slave on that meeting.

They came in like a whirlwind. They rolled in with their bus and rolled out with considerably more money than I had guaranteed them. They set up book racks, record racks, tape racks, t-shirt racks, mailing list tables, etc. They brought their own musicians, band and singers. They took over.

The house was nearly full; about 900 people showed up. Frances and Charles put their fast-talking, professionally orchestrated service into high gear. In no time at all, they had 150 people standing behind a closed curtain backstage listening to Charles instruct them HOW TO SPEAK IN OTHER TONGUES. He literally said, "Say what I say," then gave them a sample of his tongues-speaking skills.

Looking back from here, I can't believe that I didn't react violently to what I was seeing. I can't believe that I fell for it. But that is exactly what I did. In fact, I was so enamored with the "success" of the whole thing, that I decided I would sponsor an event of this kind once every month. I called them, "Charismatic Praise Gatherings."

"Charismatic Praise Gatherings"

I immediately contracted with *The Singing Rambos* to come to the Beaumont City Auditorium for a Gospel concert the very next month. Dottie was riding high on several new hits, and again, I ran huge, expensive ads in the Port Arthur News and the Beaumont Enterprise. I went to KFDM-TV and produced a television commercial advertising the Rambos, and ran that ad on the local evening news all during that month. I promoted it on radio and by direct mail. "FREE CONCERT!" I said.

Long Winding Road

I had a live radio show every Sunday morning from 7 to 8:30 called, "Sunday Morning Sunrise." I spun Gospel records and promoted the Church. I promoted the Rambo concert on that show for a month.

Almost 1000 people showed up to hear the Rambos. Dottie and her other female vocalist showed up in tight blue jeans that afternoon at the City Auditorium. I remembered when she had preached at the United Pentecostal Church in Port Arthur when I was a kid. She and Buck called their group, "The Gospel Echoes." She had made her name in Gospel Music as an Acts 2:38, Oneness, Holiness, Pentecostal preacher. But those days were long gone. I had never believed that women should wear slacks, especially jeans, but everybody hated rules now, so I didn't say a thing.

I had a defining moment a few weeks earlier, when a woman walked into my Church on a Sunday morning, wearing a bright red pants suit. The red pants suit was not particularly offensive, because I always felt that any visitor should be welcome to come to Church dressed however they felt comfortable. But this lady wasn't just an ordinary visitor. She stood up in the middle of the service and began to prophesy. I was repelled by the sight and wanted to tell her to sit down and be quiet. But the people responded so powerfully to the things she was saying, it appeared that she really did have a word from the Lord for the people.

Then and there, I caved in. I let the circumstances overrule principle. I argued that if the Holy Ghost will use a woman in slacks to minister in the gift of prophecy, then who am I to disapprove of slacks on a woman?? In psychology, they call it situational ethics: the rules don't rule.

At the end of the Rambo concert, I preached a little watered-down sermon that everybody liked. A Catholic lady came to me afterward and asked me how much money I needed to cover the expenses. I had spent thousands of dollars on that meeting, and the free-will offering added up to about half of the cost. She wrote a large check on the spot to cover the balance.

My relationship with the local Catholic Charismatics began to flourish. The F.G.B.M.F.I. was well-known for featuring Catholic Priests and Nuns as their guest speakers (although ministers in particular were not allowed in its leadership – only laymen). In the Houston area, the Catholic Charismatic movement had become a major force, with thousands of adherents. I found that locally, they were among my most enthusiastic supporters, and certainly some of my largest contributors. In short order, I found myself attending Charismatic fellowships at St. Charles Catholic in Nederland, and for the first time in my life, I attended Mass and partook of the Eucharist, receiving my wafer at the hand of the local priest. It just seemed "the thing to do" at that point. HOW RADICALLY I HAD CHANGED, overnight!

Gene Mullenax

The third month, I had another "Charismatic Praise Gathering" at the Beaumont City Auditorium. The featured speaker was Gene Mullenax from North Little Rock, Arkansas.

Gene had one of the most sensational testimonies of anyone in the world. In the 1950s, he was a godless young man with a wife and small child, and he was down on his luck. Working for some kind of manufacturing shop, he fell ill with a respiratory problem. The doctors examined him and found his lungs diseased and his condition terminal. They decided to operate. He came out of surgery with his left lung and three ribs REMOVED. He had a huge cavity in his chest that was reluctant to heal. He was permanently disabled, crippled and so weak he could hardly get around.

The short version of his story is that he stumbled into an A.A. Allen tent revival, not having a clue what he was getting into. On the second night, he got in the prayer line. After praying for hundreds of others, Allen finally got to him. Moments earlier, Gene had watched a large, cancerous tumor fall off the lip of a baby being held by its father. He was greatly moved. Briefly, Allen looked at him and said, "What do you need?" to which Gene responded, "A LUNG AND THREE RIBS WILL DO!" With no further conversation, Allen pointed to him and screamed, "Be healed, in the name of Jesus!"

Gene testified that instantly, he felt as it were HOT OIL flowing from the top of his head to his feet. He said it felt like someone placed a hose down into his chest and blew out the cavity. He stood upright with an immediate surge of strength. A burly friend of his was standing out in the audience, and when he saw something happening to Gene, he ran down the aisle to see what was happening. Gene grabbed up this hulk of a man and danced all over the platform with him in his arms.

He went back to the doctor right away to have X-Rays made. The X-Rays showed that NOT ONLY did Gene now have a NEW LUNG and THREE NEW RIBS in place, but the new lung was also far healthier than his other remaining lung!

Allen published Gene's photo and testimony on the front cover of his "MIRACLE MAGAZINE" from Miracle Valley, Arizona to a worldwide circulation. Somewhere down the line, the story came to the attention of someone in the FBI. He picked up on the startling claim of a lung and ribs being recreated and decided that the story had to be fraudulent. The FBI decided to charge Allen with mail fraud over the story.

FBI agents knocked on Gene's door in North Little Rock asking to see his medical records. He sent them to his doctor, who verified that he did indeed have a new lung and three new ribs. After a complete and thorough investigation, and seeing the BEFORE and AFTER X-rays, the FBI closed the case, and recorded it as a "BONA FIDE MIRACLE"!

Gene spent the rest of his life telling that story. He built a Charismatic Church in North Little Rock, and for a while ran a television ministry from there.

Coping With Change - Hazards and Costs of A Major Paradigm Shift

So, for me, within months of making the connection with F. E. Ward and the Charismatic movement, my life was radically and unalterably changed.

Things were not quite the same, however for the little congregation of 100 that had followed me to this juncture. They were traditional, classical, old-fashioned, Full-Gospel types. Some of them were relatives and close friends from many years. As I began to make the transition into the Charismatic movement, they balked.

They weren't as profoundly impressed with it as I was. They weren't buying it at all. But for me, the course was set.

I Was Forced To Choose Between The Old Way And The New Way

I went back to the Pastor for counsel. He presented me with an offer to come to Waco, and join the staff at Spirit of Love Church. There, said he, we would put together a television ministry that would open unlimited doors of ministry for both of us. I would join the ministry staff and oversee the development of a television and media ministry. I imagined vast potential. There were so many incredibly gifted people in that Church - musicians, artists, singers, actors, media professionals, and more. And they had money and buildings.

I relished the thought. I was 26 years old. I felt that I was on the brink of a national ministry, maybe international. I knew that they had the resources, and I had the talent, and if it was God's will, nothing could stop it.

I could not have possibly comprehended at the time how many powerful and subversive dynamics were at work. Little did I know what would be the ramifications of being snared in the Charismatic net. I could have never guessed the eventual outcome.

Meanwhile, Dixie was eight months pregnant with our second child when I decided to close the Church in Nederland and move to Waco.

I didn't want the Church to go on. I no longer believed that the old direction was the right direction. I did not want somebody else to come in and perpetuate the wrong thing. I knew that the group that was there did not want to go in the new direction. It would be war, and I was unwilling to go to war with them. So it was the end of the line.

If I had been able to take them in the direction I felt it should go, I would have stayed. But I knew that it was not going to fly the new course. I could not support two opposing ministry models at once, and I didn't want anybody else to sustain a ministry that I had deemed to be out-dated, self-limiting and headed for obsolescence. In only three years, I had taken many risks and made plenty of mistakes, but I had pressed forward, always looking for a better way.

This was no small or easy decision. Gut-wrenching would scarcely describe it. I fasted and prayed for days. I locked myself in the Church building, and lying on the floor, I wept desperately and uncontrollably. I could see that the end was near for my dream. It was like a death. In my spirit, I surveyed Jefferson County from my pastoral vantage point, and yearned for the opportunity to reach it for the kingdom of God. No words could describe the affection I had for that place. It was the land of my nativity. I had countless lifelong friends and acquaintances. It was by far the biggest decision I had ever had to make. My heart was shattered and broken. But in my heart, I knew that for then and for there, it was over. And I had no one to confide in except Dixie, and she was miserable with child. Not a sympathetic friend to be had in that city.

It Was A Very Lonely Time.

I proposed to the people that we should sell the building, pay off all the bills and disband. I had formed a board of ten men who had refinanced the property when we made several improvements to it. We had installed a nice cement parking lot and a nice illuminated sign on the highway.

The ten men, including myself, were on the mortgage together. I hired a lawyer to meet with the board and work out a solution. As it turned out, each one of them wanted to do something different. In the end, the building was sold, and the equity was split evenly among the ten men who then donated their part to the ministries of their choice.

I personally took the responsibility for all the miscellaneous loans - every other debt that had been created over the past three years, and in time, I personally paid them off out of my own pocket.

On April 24th, 1978 at 8 PM, I headed to Waco in a large U-Haul truck loaded with everything we owned. I left Dixie in Beaumont because she was due to have the baby. My goal was to get to Waco, unpack, and return quickly to Beaumont before our baby was born. I drove all night, arriving around 4 am. At 7 am, a phone call came that Dixie was on the way to the hospital to have the baby.

Chapter 10

Catch The Spirit Of Love

Chad Allen, our second son, was on his way into the world. I had driven all night from Beaumont to Waco in the longest U-Haul truck available, arriving at 4 AM. At 7 AM, the call came that Dixie was on the way to Women and Children's Hospital in Beaumont. She had worked hard the day before, helping to pack and box our belongings, and that had apparently induced labor. She was ready to be delivered.

Dewey Shannon was a leading homebuilder in Waco, and he attended the Spirit of Love Church. He also owned a twin-engine Beechcraft airplane. He offered to fly me to Beaumont immediately. So without any delay, I hopped a flight to Jefferson County Airport and arrived at the hospital just minutes before Chad was born. At least I was on time for this one. Precious Dixie. She was a brave soul. And Chad Allen (meaning "protector-defender-warrior" and "precious") was the new light in our lives. Dixie would have to stay with her sister for a few weeks while she recovered from a Caesarean-section surgery. I returned to Waco to set up housekeeping and start tending to my new ministry responsibilities.

Starting A Television And Radio Ministry

I spent the remainder of that year strategizing and organizing a national television project. I flew to Louisville, Kentucky to spend several days with Waymon and Bob Rogers, pastors of the 2,000-member Evangel Temple A/G. They ran an extensive local television ministry, as well as a huge K-12 school, and a multi-million dollar building project was underway. I picked their brains for the best counsel for a start-up television ministry, and while I was there, was invited to preach at their annual Camp Meeting.

Then I flew to Ninth and O Baptist Church in Memphis, Tennessee, to research their successful television ministry. Next, I flew to Florida to take a close-up look at the ministries of Karl Strader, Quinton Edwards and Roy Harthern (Benny Hinn's father-in-law), and investigate the Christian radio and TV stations and ministries they operated in Lakeland, Tampa and Orlando.

We were also interested in starting our own Christian radio station. I drove to Central Texas to visit the headquarters of a Christian organization that operated both radio and cable TV networks. They helped me prepare the proper applications to the Federal Communications Commission for a license to own and operate our own station in Waco.

As soon as I returned to Waco, we purchased a television production bus that was formerly owned by ABC SPORTS. We began to remodel the Church gymnasium to make it a teleproduction facility. We created an in-house advertising agency called "Spirit of Love Media," which allowed us to save the 15% agency fees in purchasing radio and television time. We began to produce radio and television content, spots, commercials, and all kinds of print and audio content. I developed a set of branding logos and began packaging everything we did in print and audio products. We took our best singers and musicians into a local recording studio and produced a catchy jingle for our radio and TV applications. Our slogan was, "Come Catch The Spirit Of Love!" and we spread it all over town via radio, television, billboards, newspaper and other venues. We went to Channel 39 TV in Dallas and produced a pilot TV program. Then I met with executives of the local cable television company and negotiated for permission to obtain full programming rights for our own channel to reach the tri-cities of Waco, Temple and Killeen. They granted me access to an unused channel and gave me permission to program it 24 hours a day with my own choice of programming -- FREE! That meant that I would have to come up with enough Christian video programming to fill 168 hours a week.

Along with all the media projects, I was an Associate Minister, providing some of the teaching and preaching, and was involved heavily in the music ministry. Dixie and I recruited a third voice and formed a trio which sang regularly in services. I still owned my Hammond Porta-B Organ with Leslie, and played that in every service.

Hungry Preachers Clinic

We invited Waymon Rogers to come from his mega-Church in Louisville to participate in a three-day intensive workshop for Pastors. We called it the "Hungry Preachers Clinic." About 100 ministers of every kind and from every direction came to hear the new ministry concepts that were being implemented in the fastest-growing Churches around the country.

Of course, The Spirit of Love Church was held up as a glowing example of how things should be done. In a nutshell, it included many of the very concepts that I had been hearing from the Pastor and from Ward in the previous 6-8 months.

The Brazos River Jesus Festival

The City of Waco put on a major annual event called "The Brazos River Festival," in the park along the river. Concerts, carnivals and entertainment drew tens of thousands of people from around the region. Shortly thereafter, we decided that we would stage "The Brazos River JESUS Festival," in the same location. It would be an all-day Christian Concert-Crusade with music, preaching and teaching from morning until night. Our featured speaker was Larry Lea, the Youth Pastor at Howard Conatser's Beverly Hills Baptist Church in Dallas. He had over 1,000 kids in his youth group and was in demand all around the country. We also booked a Contemporary Christian band called "Amplified Version," which was produced by Gary Paxton.

Paxton, the rock-and-roll star from the 1950s, and author of the hit song "Alley Oop," had been converted to Christianity and was a frequent guest on the PTL Club. (Paxton and Tammy Faye Bakker later became romantically linked, which provoked Jim's jealousy and furnished his excuse for the infamous fling with Jessica Hahn, which led to his downfall.) But just before that time, however, Paxton formed the group "Amplified Version" with about four guys and three girls. Simply put, they were Christian hippies. Paxton wrote and produced many of their songs, several of which became hits. "Jesus Keeps Taking Me Higher And Higher," "Jesus Is My Lawyer In Heaven," and Paxton's biggest Gospel hit, "He Was There All The Time."

The Brazos River Jesus Festival drew about 2500-3000 people. We set up two flat-bed trailers for stages and pitched huge tent-canopies over them. You cannot imagine how hip we were. Many of the men at Spirit of Love had full beards, including myself. Most of the younger guys had long hair, some down to their shoulders. Some of them wore enormous Afro-style hair. The dress code was... well, there was no dress code. When Amplified Version came out to sing, the girls wore tight blue jeans and braless halter-tops. The music was indistinguishable from popular rock-and-roll music.

Larry Lea's presentation that day was geared directly for the young audience.

Overdosing On "Liberty"

I had never been in this kind of environment. There were virtually no rules or regulations. This Church freely did so many things I had never believed Churches should do. No dress code whatsoever. Shorts, tank-tops, halter-tops, swim suits, etc. on Church-sponsored events. Practically everyone regularly attended the movie theaters, listened to rock-and-roll, and regularly attended sports and entertainment events. On one occasion, a group of more than a hundred young adults went white-water rafting in New Braunfels. ALL of these activities were quite contrary to the long-standing published beliefs of not only the Assemblies of God, but also just about every Fundamental Evangelical Church in existence before the 1960s. The A/G ministers' manual stated that the Assemblies of God disapproved of mixed-bathing (guys and girls swimming together), immodest apparel, attending movie theaters, organized sporting events, etc. But those rules meant absolutely nothing anymore. "GOD LOVES YOU! HE DOESN'T CARE ABOUT ALL THOSE THINGS!" they said.

I should have known better.

AMAZINGLY, every service seemed to be intensely spiritual. The music was phenomenal. The worship was lavish. The teaching was mesmerizing. The crowds continued to grow.

All around the country, this was the trend. Christianity was becoming POPULAR! Churches were exploding with growth! But although the crowds were growing, a troubling phenomenon was occurring. The saints appeared indistinguishable from the sinners. No wonder it was popular. You could have your cake and eat it too. You could have the world and the Church. You no longer had to make a radical change in your lifestyle to be a Christian. You could continue to entertain yourself with all the things you enjoyed in the world. Just add Jesus to the equation.

I had already seen that in the F.G.B.M.F.I. and in Women's Aglow circles, the same thing was true. Again and again, I met people who were professing great spiritual experiences, but they continued to smoke, and drink, and curse, and attend Churches which taught unbiblical teachings. And that was really only the tip of the iceberg.

It all brought one single verse to my mind again and again and again.

> **"This people draweth nigh unto me with their mouth,
> and honoureth me with their lips; but their heart is far from me."
> Matthew 15:8**

Ironically, historians now call this period of Christianity (1960s-1970s) the "Fourth Great Awakening." I wish they had asked me first. This was no awakening! This was only the opening salvos the Great Deception - the last great falling away! This was not revival, but declension!

At the first, it was exhilarating to be free of so many of the old inhibitions and restrictions. It felt good to "dress down," and be casual all the time. It seemed very liberating to freely go to the theaters. I had rarely ever listened to popular, secular music, especially rock-and-roll, and certainly no heavy metal. I had never dressed in sync with cultural fads. But now all those things were OK. No problem. I finally began to feel like I was one with the world.

But THAT was the problem. I wasn't SUPPOSED to be one with the world!

Unlike so many of the newcomers in that Church, I knew the Bible. I knew how many things were happening that just did not measure up to Biblical standards. I did not know what to do. I knew that I had already let down on many convictions that I had held so strongly. I was unhappy about my own personal backsliding. Dixie was too.

After a few months of all our new-found freedoms, Dixie and I realized that all these freedoms had not brought us closer to God, but closer to the world. I realized that I was lying to myself. I wanted to believe that God was really OK with all the carnal, worldly activities, but in my heart of hearts, I just knew better. When a thing feels so much like sin, it probably IS sin. And you can believe that there is an enormous amount of sin in the midst of such an environment.

I wondered out loud, "What is the big difference between a Christian lifestyle and that of a sinner?" There are only two directions a person can go - closer toward God, or farther away from God. We were moving away from God, and I knew that I had to do something about it.

Facing The Facts, Dealing With The Dilemma

In the seventh month of that tenure, I decided to give myself to prayer and fasting. I took three days off and told Dixie that I was going to lock myself in our spare bedroom for three days - no food, no interruptions - just prayer, Bible study, and fasting. I needed to hear from God. I needed a personal spiritual renewal. I was troubled about the condition of my own soul. I did not know if I could tolerate this new religion very much longer without completely melting down.

I laid out five things before the Lord that I desperately needed answers to. I wrote them down. I prayed over them. I asked God to clearly answer me on those five issues.

At the end of the third day of fasting, I came out of the room and broke my fast. Within one hour, I received a phone call from someone I hardly knew. Before I hung the phone up, all five of the requests I had put before the Lord had been answered explicitly. I was blown away.

As a result, I explained to Dixie that I felt we needed to be looking for some new direction for our lives and ministry. No sooner had I expressed that to her than another phone call came. It was an invitation to consider the pastorate of a Church in the suburbs of Atlanta, Georgia. I immediately accepted the invitation. The Church there purchased plane tickets for my entire family to fly to Atlanta for an upcoming weekend about two weeks before Christmas. They put us up in a nice hotel. We met with the people, Dixie and I ministered in music in both Sunday services, and I preached twice that day.

The people said, "We want you!" It looked like a dream-come-true. There were more than 300 members in their congregation. The building was brand-new and very beautiful. It was located on a major highway in the community. The pastor's office was plush and had massive bookshelves for my library. The Church had the distinction of having the #2 Church-Softball Team in the state of Georgia. They had a forty-voice choir directed by no less than James Goss of the famous Goss Brothers - the same musicians who had produced the record album for Dixie and me seven years earlier. And the parsonage was a magnificent, huge new brick home in a very nice neighborhood.

We flew back home and waited for them to conduct an election the following week. The phone call came. "We have elected you with 100% of the votes!" We were ecstatic! They ordered professional movers to haul all our belongings to Georgia. We moved in immediately - over the Christmas holidays. Suddenly, we were Georgians!

But there were some big surprises around the corner.

Chapter 11

Holy Ghost Or Nothing

We really hit the ground running as soon as we arrived in Georgia. Moving into the house was a major project at first, but in addition, baby Chad had contracted a bacterial infection that had persisted for six weeks. Because he became severely dehydrated, we had to put him in the hospital for treatments until he recuperated. So our first weeks in town were enormously stressful.

A most amazing sign appeared unexpectedly, making me believe that we were there in the will of God. I had dreamed a dream around the time that I was on the three-day fast back in Waco. I dreamed that I was walking the streets in an old, dark town. Many of the storefronts looked like old saloons. I had the feeling of an earlier century. I had never seen a place like that, had absolutely no clue about where it was, and never expected to see anything like it in real life.

An Amazing Sign

Shortly after moving into our new house, people began suggesting places and things in Atlanta that we needed to go see: the Coca-Cola Museum, the Varsity Drive-In restaurant across from Emory University, Stone Mountain, Underground Atlanta, and several other sights.

On a free day, Dixie and I took the boys to downtown Atlanta. We ate at the Varsity, and went to the Coca-Cola Museum. Then we discovered that Underground Atlanta was nearby. It was late in the evening, around dark.

When we walked into the entrance of Underground Atlanta, I froze. I stood there in near shock. This was the exact place I had seen in my dream about two months earlier. I had never heard of a place like this. Nothing I had ever seen or heard of would have prompted the dream. I told Dixie, "I saw this place in a dream about two months ago." "Are you sure?" she asked. "Absolutely!" I responded. I took her down the dark, underground streets and pointed out places I had seen in the dream; things like the gas lamps, and stone pavements, and swinging saloon doors. (It has since been dramatically reconstructed, and no longer looks the same.)

I had never heard that parts of historic Atlanta had been preserved from the Civil War days. In the same general proximity where Scarlett O'Hara and doctors treated wounded soldiers in the movie "Gone With The Wind," a bustling town of 10,000 had stood in the 1860s. In the 1920s, the city built viaducts which raised the streets to a second level. The old town fell into disuse until a restoration project revived it in the 1960s. And that is exactly what I had seen in my dreams.

"Well, God knows the end from the beginning," I told Dixie. "Apparently, He was showing me the place where we would be going next." Whatever it meant, I was impressed. I felt like it was a sign from God to let us know that we were following our divine destiny.

I went to work immediately, establishing contact with all the members of the Church. I wrote a weekly newsletter that was mailed to hundreds of households. I purchased a one-hour radio slot every Sunday morning on the local AM station and did a live show of music and preaching and promoting the Church. Within about 90 days, I purchased a half-hour television slot on Channel 17 in Atlanta and started producing video tapes for that Sunday morning program.

"Long Winding Road"

James Goss and I became fast friends immediately, meeting often for coffee. I was enthralled with his musical contributions to the Church. He and I took flying lessons together. It appeared that the sky was going to be the limit for that Church.

James came to Church one night with a brand-new song the Goss Brothers had just recorded at LeFevre Studios. He said, "We just did a session with a little gal from Louisiana named Mickey Mangun. She recorded this song, and I fell in love with it. It's called, 'Long Winding Road.'"

The Goss Brothers had also decided to record it themselves. He sang with the soundtrack of their own version. It was gorgeous. The studio was using a new Moog Synthesizer, and this song had some phenomenal synthesizer phrases.

But it was the words that captured me.

> *When I made my start for heaven, I could only find one way -*
> *a road that led me through the mountains and the valleys,*
> *a road not many take.*
> *But since I started traveling on my journey,*
> *I've traveled many miles behind me:*
> *miles of sun and rain, miles of smiles and pain.*
> *The road's been rough, but I again would choose the same.*

James' voice cracked and his eyes filled with tears as he sang the song. I knew his story. He had been enormously successful in the music business, but had experienced some devastating trials in recent years. He was struggling for survival. By the time he finished singing that song, there was hardly a dry eye in the house. That song burned hard into my soul. I picked it up and took it for my own. Since that night, I have sung that song more often than any other.

> *Long and winding road, keep on leading me.*
> *Up ahead, I see a sign*
> *and it points me straight ahead to victory.*
> *I know I must be traveling right,*
> *for I remember passing Calvary.*
> *And although it's dusty and it's old,*
> *for years it's borne this traveler's load,*
> *some day this road will turn to gold.*

That was New Years Eve, 1979. The house was packed.

We tried to engage the people with the local chapter of the Full Gospel Business Men that met monthly in a local cafeteria. I took several key members to Charismatic events in Atlanta. I hauled the youth group to an outdoor witnessing event with Brian Ruud. That was a hoot. Hippies and Corvettes and Rock and Roll music - all in Jesus' name. Lord, have mercy.

The 'JESUS '79 CELEBRATION' in Orlando

We took a major trip with fifteen teen-agers down to Orlando for the JESUS '79 CELEBRATION. 35,000 youth from all over America came to the week-long "Woodstock"-gone-Christian event. There were several Big Top tents set up in an enormous field near Disney World. All-day outdoor concerts were performed by Barry McGuire, Nancy Honeytree, 2nd

Chapter of Acts, and other extremely contemporary artists. Winkey Pratney headlined the event along with Tony Salerno, Alex Clattenburg and several of the hottest names in Christian youth ministry of that era. Thousands of kids sat around in their bell-bottoms and halter-tops "just cruisin' with Jesus," listening to hour after hour of lectures and music for days and nights. We added a couple of days at Disney World just to round out the spiritual experience.

The Welshman and The Scots

Back at home, I invited Kevin Gould of Cardiff, Wales to come and minister in music. His contemporary Christian ballads and acoustic guitar were well-received.

But I was ready for some more traditional Pentecostal-style preaching and singing. One of the most-beloved preachers in America in those days was a red-haired, red-faced Scotsman named Simon Peter Cameron. He came from Peterhead (near Aberdeen, in the Northeast of Scotland on the North Sea), where he pastored a thriving Full Gospel Church, was Overseer of several other Churches, and President of a Bible School for training young ministers. Simon Peter was a passionate and humble man whose preaching never failed to move his audiences to prayer and consecration. I had been in meetings with him in Kansas City and in Beaumont and loved his ministry.

The Cameron Family toured the United States each year, holding crusades and raising money for their Bible School. Simon's son, Philip, and his wife, Chrissie, formed a second evangelistic team.

I knew that Philip was in the states, so I tracked him down and scheduled a weekend of services with him. He came with his wife, his sister, and two other young people from the Bible School. His preaching and their Pentecostal-styled singing was like nothing that Church had ever heard.

They were all dressed in their red Scottish plaids, and Philip played the accordion while the others played tambourines. They sang a variety of songs they had written.

One of my favorite choruses said:

He's got the world in the palm of His hand
No need to fear, He's in command.
The days may come and go, but this one thing I know
He's got the world in the palm of His hand.

And another said:

The Holy Ghost will set your feet a-dancing.
The Holy Ghost will thrill you through and through.
The Holy Ghost will set your feet a-dancing,
And set your heart a-dancing, too.

And a third song said,

All over the world the Spirit is moving
All over the world as the prophet said it would be
All over the world there's a mighty revelation
Of the glory of the Lord, as the waters cover the sea

Pastor's Prayer Meeting

Dixie and I invited the adults in the Church to attend a "Pastor's Prayer Meeting" every Monday night at the parsonage. Usually, about 30 people attended that prayer meeting in our massive living room. For weeks, it was wonderful, and the attendance held steady.

Then, suddenly, one Monday night, the attendance more than doubled. Instead of 30, over 70 people showed up at prayer meeting. I didn't know what to think about it at first. But it didn't take long for their intentions to manifest. The newcomers had come with a complaint. They were a group of people who did not believe in speaking in other tongues. They had come to serve notice that they were opposed to my preaching about the Baptism of the Holy Ghost with the evidence of speaking in other tongues. I was shocked! I was literally broad-sided. It was a totally unexpected slam against the doctrine I believed so strongly.

They were clear in their statement. "We know there are a few people here who speak in tongues, but we do not want that to be a teaching of this congregation."

I told them that I had been speaking in tongues since I was eleven years old, and that it was one of my core beliefs, so I could never promise them that I would not preach about the Baptism of the Holy Ghost. Even though this was a non-denominational independent Church, the former pastor had been an Assemblies of God preacher who had once been a Methodist pastor in that town. Everyone knew that he made the change because he had received the Baptism of the Holy Ghost and spoke in unknown tongues. I presumed that he had already taught that congregation about the Baptism of the Holy Ghost, and that their beliefs were essentially the same as mine. But I was wrong.

When all the facts began to spill out, I discovered that the reason the former pastor had resigned was because he had committed adultery with a prominent businesswoman in that town, and it had been front-page news. He left in embarrassment and went to Texas. He assumed the Pastorate of a large Assembly of God Church and never looked back.

Since that time, the congregation had voted on seven different pastoral candidates, and none had received anything near a majority vote. I suddenly discovered that the Church had been deeply divided over many issues, including doctrinal issues, and it had almost completely fallen apart just before Dixie and I had arrived there. Ultimately, it appeared that the 100% vote that we received was a last-ditch effort on the part of the congregation to prevent the Church from going totally out of business.

A Forehead Of Flint

I spent the next twenty-four hours in prayer and fasting with my nose in the Bible. I was desperately looking for some wisdom from God. I read in the book of Ezekiel how God told Ezekiel that He sent the prophet into the midst of a "rebellious people."

> **"As an adamant harder than flint have I made thy forehead:**
> **fear them not, neither be dismayed at their looks,**
> **though they be a rebellious house,"**
> **Ezekiel 3:9.**

I thought that verse addressed my situation very well. He told Ezekiel that He had given him a forehead of flint to stand up to them and say, "Thus saith the Lord," so that "whether they hear or whether they forebear," yet they would know that there had been a man of God in the midst.

I decided that I would stand my ground on doctrinal matters, but I would let the people decide what they wanted to do. I called an emergency meeting of all the men of the Church to be held the very next night. Early that morning, my secretary called every member of the Church and announced that I wanted to have an emergency meeting with the men only.

That night, the fellowship hall was packed with men. I started right on time. It was not a long meeting at all. I simply explained to those who were unaware of the developments what was going on. I told them that my teachings about the Baptism of the Holy Ghost and speaking in other tongues were being rejected by a group of people. I then asked those men to each make their positions known. I said, "I need to know how many of you do not want me to preach about speaking in tongues."

Exactly half of them raised their hands. Exactly half of them did not want me to preach about speaking in other tongues.

A House Divided

I looked at them for a moment, wondering what my response should be. Then I said, "The Bible says that a house divided cannot stand. It also says that if a man's ministry is not being received in a city, that he should shake the dust off his feet and leave." With that said, I tendered my resignation to them on the spot. We would be leaving immediately.

The next morning, I called the movers and they came and packed all our belongings. When the 18-wheeler finally drove off, Dixie and our two little boys got into our Pontiac Bonneville with me, and we drove out to the edge of the city. I stopped the car on the shoulder of Interstate 75 heading toward Chattanooga, and got out, took off my shoes, and clapped them together as though I was removing the dust from them. Then I sat them on the ground, slid them back on my feet, got in the car and drove away.

I didn't have a clue what would happen after that.

I kept on praying and reading my Bible. I listed three things that I thought God was speaking to me from His word. I showed them to Dixie and told her what my plan was.

"Arise, Go Forth Into The Plain"

Most of my counsel that week had come from the Book of Ezekiel. The morning we left town, I read in 3:22 where God told the prophet, "Arise, go forth into the plain, and I will there talk with thee." I hoped that was a sign I should return to the Central Plains of Texas where we had just left. I decided I would at least drive back to Waco and consult with the Pastor.

We took a round-about trip through North Little Rock where we looked up Gene Mullenax (the guy with the miraculous lung). Gene was pastoring a large Charismatic Church at the time. They owned an entire shopping center, and he had started a television ministry next door to the Church. They had a satellite uplink to PTL and were feeding their programs live to PTL. Gene showed us around his studios, and invited me to preach in the next night service. We hung out with him and his wife in their home for a day or so. I tried to solicit his best counsel for my situation. He didn't know what to tell me. He invited me to come on staff in the ministry there, but I felt that I had permanently graduated from any more "second-fiddle" roles. I was looking for a position as a Lead Pastor.

We headed to Waco. That effort pretty much came to naught as soon as I got there. I told the Pastor all about what we had just experienced and asked him if he had any wisdom to share with me. He replied, "All I can tell you is that God's not through with you yet." I stayed less than an hour, and we were finished with Waco for the second and last time.

"God's Not Through With You Yet"

Gene had told me that there was a Full-Gospel Church in Temple, Texas that was looking for a pastor. He gave me the name of the Church, and the name of a man who attended the Church, but that was all the information he had. We drove to Temple in an attempt to find it. I couldn't locate the address. I saw a local police woman sitting in her cruiser at a convenience store. I drove up beside her and asked if she had ever heard of that particular Church. She reacted quite excitedly and said, "Yes. We were out there last night. They tried to kill the preacher!"

I pretended not to be astonished at that tidbit of information. We drove by the address she gave me, and we saw that it was a fairly large Church facility, but no one was there. So I went to another convenience store and asked for a telephone directory, and looked up the man whose name was given to me. He was supposed to be the head deacon.

I found him running a paint and body shop. When I walked into the shop, he was busy painting a nude woman on the side of a street van. Another bad sign. I asked him some general questions about the Church situation and quickly came to the conclusion that I wasn't interested in learning anything else about that Church. We checked out of town.

My third and last lead was an old minister who had been somewhat of a mentor to me many years earlier. He was retired and living in a small town near Temple. I decided to drive there and visit him and ask him for some counsel. When we finally located his home, I drove into the driveway, got out, and knocked on the door.

His wife came to the door and was overjoyed to see us. I asked if her husband was at home and if we could visit with him for a while. She invited us in, asked us to have a seat, and went to a back room to get him.

When he came out, something was desperately wrong. He didn't recognize us. In fact, he couldn't talk. He sat down in a chair as his wife offered us a cup of coffee. We accepted, and she went to prepare it. I tried to make conversation with my old friend. Actually, he was only in his late sixties, but he was in very poor health. He seemed to be in a daze. His eyes were glazed, and he was not responding to our attempts to make conversation with him. He picked up the cup of coffee she served him and poured it down the front of his shirt.

Then I realized that he was not in his right mind at all. His wife was embarrassed as she explained that he had just had a total mental breakdown and she didn't know what to do for him. Their situation was utterly depressing.

That was the last straw for me. Dixie and the boys and I headed home to Beaumont. We didn't know what would be next.

Chapter 12

Crash and Burn

We had not expected to return to Beaumont, but there seemed to be no choice. We rented a house and moved in, not knowing exactly what the next move would be.

We had to decide where we would attend Church while we waited on another open door for ministry. Since we had been so involved with the Charismatic movement, returning to Pastor Clendennen was out of the question. He never approved of any of that stuff. So we decided to visit the largest Assembly of God Church in Beaumont. For several years, they had been involved with many of the best-known Charismatic ministries, and I expected to find a Charismatic environment.

The auditorium was packed the first time we visited on a Sunday morning. In sharp contrast to what I expected, the service was actually very formal and dry. During the time of worship, someone stood to deliver a message in tongues, something which was not an uncommon occurrence in Spirit-filled Churches. I was astonished when, instead of waiting for an interpretation, the pastor nodded at one of the ushers, and the usher promptly walked down the aisle and escorted the person out of the building.

I looked at Dixie with a quizzical squint. What was that all about? The pastor had completely vetoed the operation of the gifts of the Spirit in a Pentecostal-Charismatic Church. Why? That really disturbed me.

Strike one.

We attended several more services. One of the members of the Church staff was an old friend. He invited Dixie and me to attend a banquet being held for all the Church leaders. I estimate that there were about forty or fifty leaders at that meal. It was at a fine restaurant. When the meal began, I was shocked to see that wine was being served all around the room! I could not believe my eyes.

I had never in my life been around people drinking alcoholic beverages, and the last place on earth I expected to see people drinking was at a banquet for Church leaders. All the Bible verses I could think of were racing through my head. And there are plenty.

> "Wine is a mocker, strong drink is raging: and whosoever is deceived thereby is not wise," Proverbs 20:1.
>
> "Look not thou upon the wine when it is red, when it giveth his colour in the cup, when it moveth itself aright," Proverbs 23:31.
>
> "And be not drunk with wine, wherein is excess; but be filled with the Spirit," Ephesians 5:18.
>
> "Woe unto him that giveth his neighbour drink, that puttest thy bottle to him, and makest him drunken also," Habakkuk 2:15.
>
> "Do not drink wine nor strong drink, thou, nor thy sons with thee, when ye go into the tabernacle of the congregation, lest ye die: it shall be a statute for ever throughout your generations," Leviticus 10:9.
>
> "It is not for kings to drink wine; nor for princes strong drink: Lest they drink, and forget the law, and pervert the judgment of any of the afflicted," Proverbs 31:4-5.
>
> "Woe unto them that are mighty to drink wine, and men of strength to mingle strong drink," Isaiah 5:22.
>
> "They also have erred through wine, and through strong drink are out of the way; the priest and the prophet have erred through strong drink, they are swallowed up of wine, they are out of the way through strong drink; they err in vision, they stumble in judgment," Isaiah 28:7.

That was strike two.

I didn't need three strikes. I was outta there. It was a very simple decision for us to make. Drinking alcohol is a primary sin. I saw no reason to go to a Church whose leaders drank, or who did not think that drinking was a sin. If the Church doesn't denounce sin, then who will?

We never went back after that.

A few of my old minister friends invited me to preach in their Churches, and I did. But we needed an open door for full-time, permanent ministry, and it was nowhere to be found. For the first time in thirteen years of ministry, I did not have a place to preach.

We needed a Church home. I was acquainted with just about every pastor and every kind of Full Gospel Church within a sixty-mile radius. We should have had plenty of choices, but having been in full-time ministry for my entire life, it was extremely difficult to imagine sitting on a pew in a small Church somewhere. It was a psychological barrier.

Disillusionment

I began to feel very disillusioned. I was twenty-seven years old, had been preaching for thirteen years, and had been in full-time ministry for more than ten years. In the few years since I had become a Charismatic minister, everything I was raised to believe had been severely challenged. Most of my old-fashioned convictions about right and wrong had been condemned as legalistic bondage. I had severed all my old ties and tried to play the new game as best I could, but I knew the Bible too well.

The further I went with the Charismatic-Ecumenical thinking, the more skeptical I became. I had forced myself to believe that all these people were really saved, even though it did not appear to me that their lives were truly being changed.

I was constantly reminded that I had no right to judge anybody about the way they lived. The youth group could party all weekend at the lake in skimpy bathing suits, the couples could go to R-rated movies on Sunday afternoons after Church, and I could take communion at the Roman Catholic Church with the Catholic Charismatics. One of my (married) minister friends who was then pastoring a Church of several hundred admitted confidentially to me that he kept a separate apartment in another city for his trysts with female friends. And this was still several years before the big scandals like Jim Bakker and Jimmy Swaggart occurred.

I watched all my new Christian acquaintances live just like everybody else who was in the world. In the old days, Christians didn't drink, smoke, chew tobacco, cuss or tell dirty jokes. In the old days, we didn't go to worldly amusements, engage in organized sports, go to the movies, ball games, mixed swimming or a lot of other questionable things. Women wore dresses, and men wore short hair. But now we could do anything we wanted to do, go anywhere we wanted to go, dress any way we wanted to dress. For a while, I had worn a full beard and long hair that completely covered my ears.

In the new "anything goes" environment, I could no longer distinguish a Christian from a sinner. I felt like many of my own peers in the ministry were complete space aliens. I could see the laity taking over the Church, and I could see the ministry abdicating all their responsibility for preaching Truth, Righteousness and Holiness. Chaos was pulverizing Christianity.

I finally overdosed on the "liberty" mantra. I told Dixie,

> **"If these are the people who are going to rule the world with Jesus Christ for a thousand years, it is going to be total ANARCHY!!"**

And I absolutely meant it. The thought of spending eternity with that kind had no appeal to me whatsoever.

I didn't want any part of it anymore. It was all just phony baloney. If preachers could smoke and drink and commit adultery, and if Christians could curse and swear and party and play around, then I didn't see any point in being a Christian.

Going Secular

Regardless of all these issues, I still had to support my family. Since nothing was developing in the ministry, I started looking for a secular job. Somebody told me I could make really good money as a longshoreman at the Port of Beaumont. I didn't know anything about that kind of work, but I checked into it. They told me to show up at the Union Hall at 5:30 in the morning.

Every day, the union boss would pick a crew for the day's shipments coming into the port. Some days there was work. Most days there was no work. When I did get work, it was grueling. They dropped us down into the hole of a ship, 20-30 feet down, while a crane on the dock lowered pallets of flour sacks to be stacked ceiling-high in the hole. The sacks weighed 110 pounds each, and they were burlap. Flour dust filled the hole. After throwing those sacks for twelve hours a day, the sweat and the flour made a cake of white glue over me from head to toe. I worked that job as often as I could get work, until after a few months, it plainly fizzled out.

I got a job in a refinery, doing a turn-around/shut-down as a boilermaker. I worked seven midnight shifts per week for about three months before the job ended. I made good money and caught up on the bills temporarily. When that job ran out, I had to look for more work.

Success Motivation

I decided to bury myself in success motivation teachings. I read Earl Nightingale's classic, "Think and Grow Rich." One of his famous quotes was, "Man, alone, has the power to transform his thoughts into physical reality; man, alone, can dream and make his dreams come true."

I read W. Clement Stone and Napoleon Hill's "Success through a Positive Mental Attitude;" and learned the mantra, "Whatever the mind of man can conceive and believe, it can achieve."

I read Dale Carnegie's "How to Win Friends And Influence People;" Norman Vincent Peale's "The Power of Positive Thinking;" subscribed to "Success" magazine, and grabbed virtually everything I could get my hands on – books or recordings - about success and how to get rich. I owned literally hundreds of audio cassettes about success principles.

Paul J. Meyer was a leading guru who owned the multimillion-dollar "Success Motivation Institute." I traveled to his headquarters in Waco, Texas and paid $700 for an intensive Success Motivation course with him, and learned his mantra, "Whatever you vividly imagine, ardently desire and enthusiastically act upon must inevitably come to pass."

I practiced elaborate goal-setting, making positive affirmations, used neurolinguistic programming, self-talk, subliminal messaging, and taught myself to believe in my "infinite human potential."

It never occurred to me that those were the very tactics that Lucifer himself used in both his own downfall, and in the overthrow of Adam and Eve. Lucifer had boasted repeatedly, "I will…, I will…, I will…" He had convinced Adam and Eve that if they disobeyed God, "your eyes shall be opened, and ye shall be as gods, knowing good and evil."

I did not know or understand at the time the devious spiritual influence of such teachings. Most of those men were high-degreed in Freemasonry and Scottish Rites, and their teachings were esoteric human-potential teachings from ancient times. They were the same arrogant, godless ambitions that built the Tower of Babel – which God angrily confounded and scattered.

I was brainwashing myself to trust in myself, to believe in my own unlimited human potential, and to function without God's direction or assistance. I don't have time or space to say the things that need to be said here, but I may write on the subject later.

Just believe me when I say that there are SPIRITS – yes, devils – that lurk in those teachings. They will draw you into the worst kind of materialism, selfishness, and godlessness, and before they are through, you will believe that you have no need of God.

Lest you forget, the Bible explicitly warns:

> "The love of money is the root of all evil:
> which while some coveted after, they have erred from the faith,
> and pierced themselves through with many sorrows.
> But thou, O man of God, **flee these things**; and follow after righteousness,
> godliness, faith, love, patience, meekness,"
> 1 Timothy 6:10-11.

Furthermore, Jesus also warned, "Ye cannot serve God and mammon [money]," Matthew 6:24; Luke 16:13.

Pursuing A Professional Career

I decided to try selling insurance. A new company had just come on the national scene, A.L. Williams. They were competing heavily with Prudential, Mutual of New York, and some of the real heavyweights in the insurance industry. Art Williams, a former football coach from Atlanta, was creating a sensation by replacing an entire generation of whole-life insurance policies with term-life insurance. The rates were vastly cheaper, and Williams was selling a high-yield annuity as a savings and investment side-product. The best part was that they were paying enormous advance commissions to their agents.

As soon as I went to work for A.L. Williams, things began to steam-roll. They trained me to be a Division Manager. Within four months, I hired and trained 75 new agents. We created a new-agent training program in Beaumont that was adopted at the national level. Locally, I produced a video training school that fast-tracked agents into the field. The Beaumont office was out-performing offices all over the country. We were in the top two percent of producers. Art Williams came to see us. He spent several days studying our operation, and we promoted several agents to managerial positions while he was there.

They asked me to go to San Antonio and start a new office. I took one partner and in one week, we hired and trained another 75 agents in San Antonio. We sent one of our top men from Beaumont to take over that office, and it soon became a top producing agency. The last time I saw that manager, he had become a millionaire.

Then our local manager was promoted to a Regional Vice Presidency. I became one of two Division Managers left to run the Beaumont office. We rented enormous second floor offices of a local shopping center, and were experiencing explosive growth. About 150 full and part-time agents were licensed through that office.

Then the unthinkable happened.

At the national level, the company was growing at almost the speed of light. Their mainframe computer systems were understaffed. The data processors and underwriters were not able to keep up with the thousands of new applications what were being submitted to them, and they began to be seriously backlogged. New business was sitting in stacks for weeks at a time in Atlanta, and policies were not being issued on a timely basis.

In about the sixth month of our project, we started receiving shipments of large boxes from the national office. In those boxes were literally HUNDREDS of policy applications that had been returned to us because they had expired. Due to backlogs in Atlanta, these policies had never been issued. We were told that we would have to go back into the field and re-write all those policies. The clients were furious, and the save-rate was minuscule. Most people didn't want to give us a second chance.

The real killer in that scenario is that I had been paid tens of thousands of dollars in advanced commissions on all that business as soon as it was received in Atlanta. When they finally returned the applications to us, they CHARGED BACK all those commissions to me. Suddenly, I found myself drowning in charge-backs. I was splitting all the overhead in the office with the other division manager - the rent, the utilities, secretaries, office equipment and supplies. Overnight, our cash-flow went into the red. I was in no position to survive the reversal. I had no reserves, no alternative game plan. I didn't feel like we could turn the situation around fast enough to survive.

As a peace offering, they offered to promote me to a Regional Vice-Presidency if I would immediately move to Los Angeles and start a new office there. I said no.

I had just turned 28 years old. I was completely exhausted from the events of that year.

I bailed.

Those were most stressful times. It had been about eight or nine months since we had been to Church by now. Several of my new friends were people who were burn-outs from various local Churches and religions. One of my agents was a Baptist guy who was also a Gospel music concert promoter. Several times a year, he put on gospel concerts with well-known singing groups. As a side-line, he also sold drugs. Pot. Acid. You know.

In the heat of my stress, he came to me with a joint of marijuana. "Man, this stuff will help you take the edge off." I was resistant, but he was undaunted. I had never done any drugs. I had never even smoked a cigarette. I had never drunk alcohol. But he prevailed on me to take the joint home with me. Little did I realize that the joint was laced with acid – LSD!

At home that night, I decided to try it. He had carefully instructed me to be sure to inhale it for the full effect. Unlike Bill Clinton, I inhaled. That was around 10 PM.

Timothy Leary would have been proud of me, as would the devil himself. For the next six hours, I embarked on the most mind-numbing, freaked-out, horrifying experience of my life.

I journeyed into worlds unknown.

I explored the mysteries of the universe. It was like writing a dual PhD dissertation on quantum physics and metaphysics while a fireworks factory was blowing up inside my brain. I theorized on the origins of the universe, and effectively explained away the existence of God to myself that night. I experienced episodes of heart palpitations, hyperventilation and anxiety attacks for about six hours. At four o'clock in the morning, I announced to Dixie, "From now on, I am an atheist."

After that night, nothing was the same for me. I suppose that Hell had a barn dance over my soul that night. Every kind of bitterness, rebellion, and evil intention filled my mind. I awoke the next day Hell-bent on avenging all the failed dreams and religious disappointments I had ever had.

It was Sunday. I bought a carton of Marlboro cigarettes and went to the office. No one was there. I worked all day and smoked cigarettes until I literally puked.

In short order, I took up with one of the older agents who was an alcoholic. He ordered a round of martinis. Two of my agents were backslidden Pentecostals who had sour attitudes about God and religion. They became drinking buddies. One had married a Buddhist woman and was practicing the Buddhist religion. I attended some of their Buddhist encounters and smoked pot and chanted mantras with them.

Within days, I crossed all the thresholds.

I was initiated and confirmed into the society of the damned. Smoking, drinking and doing drugs. With my obsessive-compulsive tendencies, and a full-throttle, no-holds-barred attitude, it took me no time at all to plunge into a quagmire of self-destructive behaviors.

Long Winding Road

Still, I had to make a living. I followed one of my leads to an insurance company in Houston. Through a series of interviews, I ended up being hired by a hundred-million-dollar Savings and Loan company in downtown Houston as the Assistant Vice President of Advertising, Marketing and Public Relations. They gave me a $250,000 annual marketing budget, and a handsome office on Allan Parkway.

I moved my family to Baytown, where we lived for almost two years. Dixie and I had no religion and no God. We were so turned-off to religion that we both made a pact with each other that even if one of us decided to get religion again, the other would not return. We became God-haters. We were vicious around Christians and attacked them mercilessly. I collected everything in my house that had any connection to religion: my Bibles, religious books, tapes, records, sermon notes, and everything else connected to the ministry - and threw them in a dumpster.

We gave ourselves to partying. We smoked dope day and night, chain-smoked cigarettes, and became foul-mouthed, intolerable people for any but the most misbehaved. A party was a party, whether it was line-dancing at a cowboy dance-hall in Kemah or disco dancing on the top floor at the Westin-Galleria. We became almost completely estranged from all our families and old friends.

On the job, I tended to massive direct-mail campaigns that generated millions of dollars in new deposits for the company. I produced radio and television advertising. I schmoozed with River Oaks executives and city officials and business leaders in towns where we had branch offices. I conducted Grand-Opening campaigns and threw country-club parties. Then, I learned that corporate parties go better with cocaine. My supplier furnished it to me in a gold pill box with a gold powder straw. That was the beginning of the end.

In all my socializing, I picked up several free-lance advertising projects for various clients. One was the owner of a chain of restaurants in East Houston. I created an advertising campaign for his restaurants that was successful. He offered to sell one of his restaurants to me on a verbal agreement. It was a troubled store that had seen a major decline in business since opening two years earlier. The owner had neglected it, and the manager he hired had embezzled heavily from him. Nevertheless, it had enormous potential.

I contemplated the offer, and decided to take it. I tendered my resignation to the Savings and Loan after about eighteen months there, and went into the restaurant business. I jumped in with both feet.

Dixie and I went to Richmond, Virginia to attend a week-long school in restaurant management. When I came home, I started working 12-14 hour days at the restaurant, seven days a week. No days off.

Despite the work-load, I maintained my addictions well.

I smoked three packs of cigarettes a day. I smoked pot day and night, 3-6 joints a day. My employees at the restaurant had access to a variety of drugs, and I quickly hooked up with a steady supply of amphetamines - speed. And just about every time I stepped out of the restaurant, I had a mixed drink - usually rum and coke.

In spite of my addictions, in short order, I had the restaurant back into profit, and was grossing several thousand dollars per week.

I did not have a contract on the business. I was leasing the building from the owner on a "gentlemen's agreement" with the intention of getting my own financing on the business as soon as I had established a profitable track record.

After a little over three months, the owner walked in one night at about 10 PM. His lawyer was with him. He came to notify me that he was entering his entire business into a Chapter 7 bankruptcy and he was going to close down this restaurant. The property I was leasing would be liquidated (lost) in the bankruptcy. I was instantly out of business. I didn't have a leg to stand on. I didn't figure I had any legal recourse. I cursed him madly and threw the keys in his face and walked out of the building.

I went to the home of some friends nearby who had lots of drugs. I sat down to ventilate all the events of the evening. I was enraged! Before long, I felt myself begin to black out. My heart was racing out of my chest, and I was having unbearable chest pains.

I knew that I was going to die.

I ordered somebody to take me home immediately. On the way home, drifting in and out of consciousness, I told someone to tell Dixie where my life insurance policies were filed. I knew that I was going to die that night. Going to the hospital was not an option because I was pumped full of illegal drugs and alcohol.

Miraculously, I survived the night. But when I awoke the next morning, a horrifying reality began to set in. I was out of business! Then a worse reality occurred. I had just mailed many thousands of dollars of checks in the mail on Friday, depending on the weekend receipts to cover them. In my rage, I had left the building without making the largest bank deposit of the week. I went to the restaurant, not expecting to find the money still there. Surely enough, the owner had raided the vault. Almost twelve thousand dollars were missing.

Not only was I out of work, out of business, out of income -- I had big, big trouble with those checks. They were not going to clear the bank, and I was not going to be able to cover them. It occurred to me that was just a matter of time before I would be contacted by the District Attorney. I could already imagine myself locked up in the Harris County Jail.

I was thirty years old.

I was a chain-smoking, God-hating, drug-abusing shipwreck, and I had finally come to the end of my rope. I had played all my cards and had no moves left.

For seven days, I hyperventilated for hours at a time. Prolonged, breath-taking panic attacks. Desperate attempts to find logic and solutions to my dilemma. I couldn't find any. I didn't know what I would do. If I even happened to say something like, "Maybe I need to get right with God," Dixie would remind me that we had already discussed all that before, and this was no time to be adding another round of religious confusion to an already complicated situation.

But at the end of seven days, I could no longer bear it. After pacing the floors, lighting one cigarette off another through an entire night, I was still pacing the floor when the sun came up.

I finally woke Dixie up at 5:30 AM. "I'm afraid that ALL this mess is because I have turned my back on God. I'm going to pray."

Dixie got up and got dressed. "What are you going to do?" I asked.

"I don't know," she said. But when she finished getting dressed, she took the keys and walked out of the house.

"Where are you going?" I asked again.

"I don't know."

"When are you coming back?"

"I don't know." And she was gone.

I fell on my face on the bedroom carpet.

It had been nearly three years since I had been to Church, read a Bible, or prayed.

I started to pray, but before I ever got the first word out of my mouth, a Bible verse pounded my head. "He that cometh to God must believe that He is, and that He is a rewarder of them that diligently seek Him." God was talking to me.

I listened to that verse in my head. I thought about it. If I come to God, I really have to believe that He is. He is not going to pay any attention to me if I don't really admit that He exists – if I don't have faith in Him.

I said, "God, I don't know who you are. I don't know what you are. I don't know where you are. I don't know what your name is. I just know that YOU ARE. And I know that I have offended you. I have sinned against you. I have been a very, very evil man, and I know now that I have been wrong. I don't know if you will forgive me. I have tried to blaspheme you, but I was a fool. I beg your forgiveness, in Jesus' name."

I don't know how long I prayed and wept and begged God's forgiveness. Hours passed before I got up off the floor.

At about 10:30 that morning, Dixie came back into the house. Her eyes were red and swollen from crying. She never really told me where all she had been, but she had just come from a pay phone at a convenience store. She said, "I called my mother and told her what was going on with us."

"Mother asked me if I would let her pray for me. I said, 'yes,' so she did. Ken, I FELT AN ANGEL PUT HIS ARMS AROUND ME at that phone booth!"

That's all I needed to hear. God was going to help us.

I knew it in my soul. We laughed and cried and hugged and wondered what was next.

The phone began to ring - calls from family and friends. The little Assembly of God Church that Dixie's parents attended offered to provide us a place to stay if we decided to move back to the Beaumont area. They had an old parsonage that was empty, next door to the Church.

We drove from Houston to Beaumont that evening to see the house and talk to the people. We did a quick walk-through of the old empty house, and I told the pastor, "I want to go next door to that Church and have a prayer meeting." They agreed that was a good idea.

Shortly before 7:00 PM that night, Dixie, our two small boys, and I walked into that building with the Pastor and my in-laws to pray. As I walked into the back of the auditorium, I looked down the center aisle and saw the pulpit where I had preached several times many years before. I was stricken again with conviction for the mess I had made of my life.

Dixie and I went down the aisle and knelt in the altars and began to pray.

The others found a place to pray as well. It was an old-fashioned prayer meeting.

Within about thirty minutes, other people started showing up to pray with us. By 8:00 o'clock, there were about 35-40 people in that little Church praying with us, and we all prayed like an inferno until eleven o'clock that night. Relatives and old friends came from all over the area. The word had spread like wild-fire: Ken and Dixie were coming back to God!

I laid down under an altar bench near the platform and buried my face in the carpet. I wept and cried and repented of just about everything except breathing. I begged God to forgive all my foolish, foolish ways. Dixie was nearby in her own world of prayer. God's Spirit enveloped the place, and it seemed as if time stood still for those four hours.

In the midst of that prayer time, I saw a Bible nearby, and opened it randomly. It fell open to Isaiah 54. I read the entire chapter.

Verse 4 said, "Fear not; for thou shalt not be ashamed: neither be thou confounded; for thou shalt not be put to shame: for thou shalt forget the shame of thy youth, and shalt not remember the reproach of thy widowhood any more."

Verses 7 and 8 said, "For a small moment have I forsaken thee; but with great mercies will I gather thee. In a little wrath I hid my face from thee for a moment; but with everlasting kindness will I have mercy on thee, saith the LORD thy Redeemer."

God promised a new beginning.

In the middle of the chapter, He said,

"And all thy children shall be taught of the LORD; and great shall be the peace of thy children. In righteousness shalt thou be established: thou shalt be far from oppression; for thou shalt not fear: and from terror; for it shall not come near thee."

He promised that "great shall be the peace of thy children." That verse hammered me like a sledge hammer. I was so afraid that all the garbage my children had seen in me would have a long-term effect on them. They were still small - eight and four years old, but they had seen far too much, and I was ashamed. I needed that promise from God. I took it instantly into my heart, and have claimed it in perpetuity.

That night, darkness lifted. God poured His Spirit out on Dixie and me. He renewed our hearts, our minds and our hopes. Driving down Interstate 10 the next day, between Beaumont and Houston, I was utterly amazed at how bright and beautiful the sky and the trees were. There was light!

I had actually been worried that I would never be able to cope with life without drugs. Instantly, for both of us, those days were over. Both of us completely abandoned all those habits immediately, and never resumed them. We were completely and instantly delivered. I carried out trash bags filled with cartons of cigarettes, booze, drugs and drug paraphernalia.

That nightmare chapter of our lives would soon be closed forever.

The godless period of our lives began in the fall of 1979 and ended in the fall of 1982. I had been determined to make it on my own and never look back at God or religion. I was convinced that God did not exist and made up my mind never to allow religion to interfere with my life again. Those three years had been a living hell, tainted by much bitterness, anger, frustration, disillusionment and rage offset by an obsession to party our way into happiness. It never worked.

God never allowed me to succeed on my own. Every rocket I launched crashed and burned. It took a parade of humiliating defeats to force me to realize that I could never beat God at His game. Every time I got close to success, He pulled the rug out from under me.

It is best to fail when you are doing the wrong thing.

All these many years later, it is easy to see that what seemed like grievous curses in those days were really blessings in disguise. One of the greatest lessons in life is this: It is best to fail when you are doing the wrong thing.

People who succeed while doing the wrong thing rarely get back to God. Many great men will never find the Truth about God because their success holds them in captivity.

If I had achieved my driving ambitions to get rich and make it on my own, I would certainly be lost today, and it is very likely that I would already be in Hell, considering how riotous I was.

At any rate, the big financial loss of losing the restaurant had to be overcome before Dixie and I could really move forward with our lives.

As I mentioned earlier, the man I was buying the restaurant from brought me the shocking news that he was filing corporate bankruptcy, and the property that I was operating in was being immediately foreclosed. I had worked 12-16 hour days for months, turning that restaurant into a quite profitable venture. The restaurant was finally operating in the black after paying off massive bills that were outstanding when I took it over. I had just started earning some very nice paydays.

But I did not foresee the calamity that suddenly walked in the door. The owner came in with his lawyer at closing time, and my world was completely destroyed in one five-minute conversation. Enraged, I cursed him and threw the keys to the building in his face and stormed out into the night. BIG mistake. In my fury, I did not think to retrieve almost $12,000 in the safe which should have been taken to the night depository at the bank that night!

When I realized first thing the next morning what a horrible mistake I had made, I jumped into my car and drove back to the restaurant. But just as I expected, the vault was empty. He had raided it the night before. I had no legal recourse. It was still (legally) his business. Quite unfortunately, I had already mailed several large checks to vendors that day, and now they were going to bounce.

Ten days passed. I consulted with a lawyer, hoping to find some recourse against the owner, as well as some way to deflect the checks to his account. But the lawyer could offer no helpful solutions. One way or the other, I had to cover all those checks immediately. Otherwise, I would soon be hearing from the District Attorney in Houston and facing criminal charges. The checks were pretty large, and by this time, they had already bounced, and the vendors had begun collection proceedings.

Dixie and I both began fasting and praying. We asked God for help.

My parents, Dixie's parents, and others voluntarily made financial sacrifices to help us. Because of their helpfulness, and by the grace of God, we were able to obtain enough money to settle the matter before a month had passed. It really was a miraculous salvation from a sickening disaster. There are no words to describe the relief we felt when the whole ordeal in Houston was finally put to rest.

But the biggest reality was that our lives had been turned around by the nightmarish ordeal. God was making a new beginning out of an ending. God had to pulverize me to get my attention and force me to pay attention to Him again. Up to that point, I had been harder than steel against God. He broke that resistance. Mercifully.

Chapter 13

Truth or Consequences

I knew and believed that if I would adhere to Bible **TRUTH**, God would bless me and my family.

But if I followed a man-made Christianity, I would still be on my own. God would not guarantee a man-made religion. Somewhere down the road, we would again suffer the worst possible **CONSEQUENCES,** if not here, then certainly on Judgment Day.

Dixie and I had suffered too many painful consequences over the previous years, and we were desperate to do the right thing this time. It would not be easy, but with God's help, we were determined to reject anything that did not fit the Bible description of a true Christian and a true Church. We wanted to be EXACTLY what God wanted us to be. And that meant carefully sorting through all the rights and wrongs of modern Christianity, identifying things that we MUST do to be saved, and eliminating the things that we absolutely MUST NOT do.

The Atheism Factor

Remember that for almost three years, I had been a hard-core atheist. A lot of people doubt me when I say that, but it was true. During that time, I frequently contemplated God and religion while spaced out on drugs, and was unequivocally persuaded that God never existed. I even wrote extensive papers on my new theories and kept them in a notebook.

I did, however, at one point, confess to Dixie, "If there really is a God, some day I will find Him." I felt like my pursuit of knowledge and truth had been genuine and sincere enough that if God really did exist, someday I would break through whatever barriers that kept me from Him.

Early on, I had been completely mesmerized by a thirteen-part PBS video series called "COSMOS," produced by astronomer Carl Sagan, Professor at Cornell University, visiting scientist at Jet Propulsion Labs in California, and consultant to NASA. As an astrophysicist and evolutionist, Sagan made the most convincing arguments for the origins of the universe and the origins of life that utterly precluded any notion of God. He was an atheist Jew. I was very deeply entrenched for some time in Sagan's scientific theories and postulations.

So, coming back to Church after those years of malicious cynicism was a major and unexpected change in my heart.

There was NO WAY I was going to buy into anybody's cheap religion. NO WAY would I go after any charlatan preacher. NO WAY would I join anybody's phony theological circus.

Having been so thoroughly devoid of any faith in God for that period, you can hardly imagine how adamant I was to NEVER buy into a FALSE religion. NO PREACHER impressed me yet. NO CHURCH and NO DENOMINATION had me convinced.

The only thing I really believed at that point was that the Bible was the inspired, infallible Word of God. I believed that EVERYTHING pertaining to me and my family's future resided in that Book.

So it is a gross understatement when I say that I was still skeptical of Christians, preachers, Churches and religious movements.

My mind was made up. If I am going to believe in God again, it will ONLY be in the true and living God. I must NEVER follow a mutated Gospel. I must never again believe in anybody who does not go strictly by the Bible.

As far as I was concerned, if it was not purely Biblical, it was from Hell.

I know that the Bible is entirely miraculous. It is entirely divine. Every jot and tittle of it is meticulously inspired by God. Not one stroke of a pen of it will ever fail.

So when men treat the Bible recklessly or carelessly, they are effectively mutating the Word of God. When it is misquoted, mis-preached, or mis-taught, it loses its supernatural power and authority.

A misquoted scripture or a false doctrine is not merely wrong. Not only is it powerless to do what God intended, but contrariwise, it is actually diabolical. Truth is truth. A lie is a lie. And every lie is Satan's offspring. A lie is pernicious. It is the spiritual equivalent of HIV/AIDs. It wreaks havoc on the spiritual immune system, and eventually destroys all spiritual immunity to error. It inevitably leads to death.

I told Dixie and several others who were close to us that I utterly refused to make commitments of any kind to anybody or anything until I first got back into the Bible and found an absolutely Biblical course of action. I did not then, nor do I now, have one whit of confidence in religious movements. I do not trust religious trends or fads. They are almost always categorically wrong. I do not trust men whose influence is predicated on their charisma or winsome ways.

Only sincere men of God who carefully and diligently follow the teachings of the Word of God with prayer and fasting have any bona fide legitimacy. A true man of God HAS to get His instructions first-hand from God. I was absolutely determined to be that kind of man from that time forward.

Dixie and I were not like a typical couple coming out of the world for the first time, ignorant of the Bible or of God's will. We were not naïve or uninformed about the core teachings of the Bible. We knew that we had a long, long way to go to be what God wanted us to be. We knew there were a lot of changes that had to be made.

That led us to do a whole lot of soul-searching. It was like digging through the rubble of a home that has been blown to bits by a Category 5 tornado. The biggest part of our lives had been left in splintered ruins, but there were sacred things in our younger years that we knew God wanted us to salvage. Not everything in our past had been wrong. Some things had been absolutely right, and had to be resurrected, reinstated, and re-assimilated back into our lives.

There HAD to be a will of God for me and my family, and once and for all, I intended to find it. I was concretely determined NOT to carelessly go back to anything that I came from. I refused to take up with anybody or anything just because it looked good or felt good. Religion had left a very bitter taste in my mouth. I only wanted God this time.

"This time," I said, "I am going to study until I find the perfect will of God. I am not going to follow anybody or anything unless I know with absolute certainty that they are preaching and believing and doing things according to the Bible. No more following people with bright ideas. If it is not in the

Bible, and if I cannot see it for myself, I am not going to buy into it." It was the same premise that I had sung in the old hymn:

"On Christ the solid rock I stand, all other ground is sinking sand."

That was based on Jesus' teachings about building on the Rock of Truth.

> "Therefore whosoever heareth these sayings of mine, and doeth them,
> I will liken him unto a wise man, which built his house upon a rock:
> And the rain descended, and the floods came, and the winds blew,
> and beat upon that house; and it fell not: for it was founded upon a rock.
>
> And every one that heareth these sayings of mine, and doeth them not,
> shall be likened unto a foolish man, which built his house upon the sand:
> And the rain descended, and the floods came, and the winds blew,
> and beat upon that house; and it fell: and great was the fall of it,"
> Matthew 7:24-27.

I turned thirty-one years old that September. I had lived my life in a very fast lane. I felt like I had already lived several lifetimes, like "a cat with nine lives." I felt like I had already spent up eight of my nine lives. I had already made both the rounds of religion and the rounds of atheism. I did not want to waste another single day of my life heading in the wrong direction. There was only one way to survive.

"This time, we are going by the Book."

From the day that we moved into that old house, Dixie and I made up our minds that we would both go on an extensive vigil of prayer, fasting, and Bible study. We both wanted to seek God diligently in prayer and fasting for as long as our bodies would hold out. We fasted days and weeks at a time. When we had to, we ate just a few meals and then returned to our fast. That went on for four months.

Two years earlier, I had thrown away all my old Bibles and religious books, so we needed new Bibles just to get started. Grandma Raggio gave me a new Dake Bible and Commentary. Granny Thompson gave me a new KJV Thompson Chain Reference Bible, and a Strong's Concordance that I had given to her many years earlier. We bought Dixie a new Thompson Chain Reference Bible.

During those four months, I spent my days in the Church next-door with my Bibles, the concordance, a dictionary and a large three-ring notebook. Dixie spent as much time as she possibly could (beside housekeeping and tending the children) in prayer and studying the Word.

I read almost the entire Bible during those four months and made hundreds of pages of handwritten notes on what I was learning. It was an intense period of spiritual reorientation and regimentation, much like a boot camp.

Every day around noon, the local postman came by the Church and sat down on the porch to eat his sack lunch. He did not know that I was in the building, or that I saw him on the porch, but while I was inside the Church praying, I could hear him outside praying, too. He was praying in tongues. I learned months later that he was an Apostolic Pentecostal preacher. I didn't know the significance of it at that time, but I sensed that God was sending him by there, because while he was praying, I felt as if an angel had come to strengthen me.

Someone offered to send Dixie and me to a Bill Gothard seminar in Austin. It would be a week-long intensive study in basic life principles. Thousands would be in attendance. We would have all our expenses paid, including a luxury car for the trip.

But I was skeptical. I knew that Gothard was not a Pentecostal, and that turned me off. I really believed, and still believe, that God intends for His Church to be led by Holy Ghost-baptized men of God, men who speak in other tongues, and are supernaturally led by the Holy Ghost. All of the Apostles spoke in tongues, all the New Testament writers spoke in tongues, and all of the Early Church was baptized in the Holy Ghost. Even the Deacons were required to have the Holy Ghost. I just could not see why I should follow anybody who did not have the Holy Ghost.

I prayed for several days about whether I should go to the seminar. One day, I was arrested by some verses in 2 Timothy 4:3-4.

> "For the time will come when they will not endure sound doctrine; but after their own lusts shall they **heap to themselves teachers, having itching ears**; And they shall **turn away their ears from the truth**, and shall be turned unto **fables**."

I was drawn to the word FABLES. I looked it up in Strong's Concordance. The Greek word "muthos" was derived from a root word "mueo," which meant **"teaching for tuition."** So, when this verse said that they "shall be turned unto FABLES," the context implied that people would be turning to those who charge tuitions to teach [myths] about God. Was God saying that some of the great deceivers of the last days would be men who turned the Gospel into a money-making teaching enterprise? (We have certainly lived to see that occur!)

Now, I know that in most cases, the word FABLE is synonymous with MYTH, but in this particular instance, it impressed me that there are no Biblical precedents for charging tuition to learn the Word of God. Jesus said, "freely ye have received, freely give," Matthew 10:8. God already has a plan for the support of the ministry, via tithes and offerings.

I simply was not ready or willing at that point to submit my thought processes to a non-Pentecostal teacher, because I was absolutely determined not to succumb to any more false religion. After much prayerful deliberation, I declined the invitation. We did not go.

As I studied the Word, it spoke powerfully to me.

I began my studies in Genesis 1, and had worked my way up to the Book of 2 Chronicles when I was arrested by a story in chapter 20 about the righteous King of Judah, Jehoshaphat.

Jerusalem was completely surrounded by three murderous armies; the Moabites, the Ammonites and the people of Mount Seir. They laid siege on Jerusalem, meaning to destroy the people of God and take the holy city. There seemed to be no way out alive. Jehoshaphat and his people were facing a certain death.

In fear and desperation, King Jehoshaphat stood among the people of Judah in the court of the Holy Temple and prayed aloud to God.

"O our God, wilt thou not judge them?
for **we have no might against this great company** that cometh against us; neither know we what to do: but our eyes are upon thee."
2 Chronicles 20:12.

As I read Jehoshaphat's prayer, **that was EXACTLY how I felt!**

I felt as though I was trapped just like Jehoshaphat, surrounded by "Christian" enemies who had all the wrong ideas about God and the Bible. Jehoshaphat's enemies were physical armies. My enemies were false Christians and false ministries.

How can a man who seeks Truth protect himself from the powerful voices and movements that preach popular false doctrines and false teachings? How can a man stand firm, when false religionists surround him, fighting viciously day and night to take complete ownership of Christianity and the Church, and push lovers of Truth to the fringe, or out the door, or even to a bitter end?

I knew from first-hand experience that Christianity was becoming so ecumenical, so ambiguous, so misguided and misled, and its leaders so deceived and so deceiving, that if I did not keep a careful watch over my soul, I was in mortal danger of being forced right back into the same quicksand of non-descript, conviction-less, ecumenical Christianity that had nearly destroyed us earlier.

I could not and would not allow that to happen to me and my family.

I refused to pursue anything that I already knew was heresy or deception, for fear of losing my eternal soul. I begged God to show me the perfect way. I wanted to know what our next move should be. Where should we go from here? What should I do?

I knew that the hand of God was on me, or I would not have survived so many ordeals. God had called me to Himself at the age of eleven, and it was my business to make my calling and election sure. I could never again give myself to a secular way of life. I knew that I had to do the will of God from that time forward.

But I did not know at all what Dixie and I should do with our lives at that point. I felt like Jehoshaphat's prayer was my prayer, "We have no might against this great company... neither know we what to do!"

I was extremely eager to find out the details of how God would deliver Jehoshaphat from this siege.

I continued reading.

The Spirit of the Lord came upon a man named Jahaziel. He said,

> "Thus saith the LORD unto you, Be not afraid nor dismayed
> by reason of this great multitude; for the battle is not yours, but God's.
> ...**Ye shall not need to fight in this battle**: set yourselves,
> **stand ye still, and see the salvation of the LORD** with you,
> O Judah and Jerusalem: fear not, nor be dismayed;
> to morrow go out against them: for the LORD will be with you."

So Jehoshaphat bowed his face to the ground, and all the people worshipped and praised the Lord with loud voices.

The next morning, they rose up early and began to move toward the wilderness of Tekoa, southeast of Jerusalem. As they did, Jehoshaphat stood and admonished the people to believe in God and His prophets. Then,

> "he appointed singers unto the LORD,
> and that should **praise the beauty of holiness,**
> as they went out before the army,"
> 2 Chronicles 20:21

When they began to **praise the beauty of holiness,**

> "**the LORD set ambushments** against the children of Ammon, Moab, and mount Seir, which were come against Judah; and **they were smitten.**"

So, in a nutshell, Jehoshaphat told the people to **"PRAISE THE BEAUTY OF HOLINESS!"** When they did, God smote their enemies!

I was glued to that phrase: "Praise the beauty of holiness."

As they praised the beauty of holiness, God miraculously turned their enemies against each other, and they were smitten!

It all seemed very magical to me. Does that mean that if I will praise the beauty of holiness, God will deliver me from my enemies? If so, WHY?

What does it mean, to "Praise the beauty of holiness"?

WHY is holiness so important that if I praise its beauty, God will deliver me from my enemies?

I did not know the answer to that question, but I made up my mind that I would find out the answer.

Those words lodged in my mind like a splinter in my finger.

PRAISE THE BEAUTY OF HOLINESS!

That story sent me on a quest to know and understand what is so important about holiness.

I studied the etymology of the word HOLY. In its most ancient context, it means, "that which must be preserved whole or intact without being transgressed or violated; consecrated; sacred; godly."

Therefore, to be HOLY, one must not be transgressed or violated. That requires separation from things that violate. Hence, to be holy, one must be "set apart, sanctified, consecrated, dedicated, peculiar."

> **Set Apart:** This calls for SEPARATION from things that are contrary to the will of God: The world. The flesh. The devil. To be holy, there must be a GAP between the saint and the world. Not touching. NOT OVERLAPPING!
>
> **Sanctified:** Set apart; made clean or holy; purified; hallowed; sacred. This indicates a lifestyle that maintains continuous **abstinence from** things which defile.
>
> **Consecrated:** Designated to be holy, devoted, dedicated, ordained, set apart, held in highest religious regard.
>
> **Peculiar:** Having unique properties, exclusive to its type. As a one-of-a-kind jewel having great value because of its uniqueness.

I was impressed that God wants His people to be SEPARATE from all things that are not His will. He wants us to isolate or quarantine ourselves spiritually from unclean things and evil influences that defile and profane us. He wants us to be PRECIOUS in His sight. He wants our bodies and our minds to be distinctly different – identifiably different - from the rest of the people in the world. Unique. One of a kind.

There is nothing else in this world like the true Church of Jesus Christ. The true Church does not look, act, walk or talk like the world. We are not the same as the world.

We are called to be different. We are called to be HOLY.

> "Sanctify yourselves therefore, and **be ye holy**:
> for I am the LORD your God,"
> Leviticus 20:7.

> "As he which hath called you is holy,
> so **be ye holy** in all manner of conversation;
> Because it is written, **Be ye holy**; for I am holy,"
> 1 Peter 1:15-16.

It wasn't just the story of Jehoshaphat that was speaking to me. It was everything I was reading in the Bible. In verse after verse, story after story, I saw that HOLINESS was the universally-prescribed state for important things pertaining to God. The doctrine of SEPARATING UNTO HOLINESS is not an obscure platitude in the Bible. It is clearly articulated from Genesis to Revelation in countless examples. For instance:

FROM all iniquity. UNTO Himself.

> "[Jesus] gave himself for us, that he might redeem us
> FROM ALL INIQUITY, and purify UNTO HIMSELF
> a peculiar [treasured] people, zealous of good works."
> Titus 2:14.

OUT OF darkness. INTO His marvelous light.

> "Ye are a chosen generation, a royal priesthood, an holy nation,
> a peculiar people; that ye should shew forth the praises of him
> who hath called you OUT OF DARKNESS into his marvelous light,"
> 1 Peter 2:9.

Adam and Eve had been created holy. But the moment they touched the forbidden fruit, they became unholy. Anytime we touch something God has forbidden, we become unholy. It was time to get away from all forbidden fruit, both physical and spiritual. When God says, "Don't touch the fruit," all of paradise is at stake. I do not want to go to the Judgment bar with forbidden fruit in my hand. To even desire the fruit that God forbids is insanity. It means that I can never stay in paradise.

Dixie and I were ready to make whatever changes that God wanted us to make. Getting rid of drugs, cigarettes and booze was only the beginning.

"Know ye not that ye are the temple of God,
and that the Spirit of God dwelleth in you?
If any man defile the temple of God, him shall God destroy;
for the temple of God is holy, which temple ye are,"
1 Corinthians 3:16-17.

"Know ye not that **your body is the temple of the Holy Ghost**
which is in you, which ye have of God, and ye are not your own?
For ye are bought with a price: therefore **glorify God in your body,
and in your spirit, which are God's,**"
1 Corinthians 6:19-20.

I read Hebrews 12:13 which said, "Follow peace with all men, and **holiness, without which no man shall see the Lord."**

I could not see any loophole in that verse.

Without holiness, I'm not going to see God.

If I don't figure out what holiness is and get some of it, I'm not going to be saved.

Holiness alone cannot save you, but you cannot be saved without holiness. No matter what your other beliefs or doctrines are, if you are not living a holy life, you are not going to see God.

Chapter 14

House-Cleaning Time

Dixie and I talked about holiness constantly.

She said to me, "I've been reading theses verses that say that a woman should not be adorned with gold or pearls or costly array."

> "That women adorn themselves in **modest apparel**,
> with **shamefacedness** and **sobriety**;
> **not with broided hair**, or **gold**, or **pearls**, or **costly array**;
> But (which becometh women professing godliness) with **good works**,"
> 1 Timothy 2:9-10.

She said, "I can't see how that verse means anything but that a woman must be **shame**faced. Women wear makeup because they are **ashamed** of their faces, and they want to be attractive. So if you are **trying to get rid of your shame**... **How can you be shamefaced** wearing makeup and jewelry?"

She threw away all her makeup. I never asked her or told her to do those things. She never wore makeup again.

"Do you think I should get rid of my jewelry?" Dixie wore a valuable, full-carat solitaire diamond on her wedding ring, and she owned a lot of costume jewelry.

"What do YOU think?" I threw the ball back into her court.

"I believe that I ought to get rid of my jewelry," she said without any hesitation. She didn't wait. She went into the bedroom right then and gathered up all her jewelry, including rings, earrings and bracelets, and took them outside to the trash can. A jeweler bought her diamond, and that was the end of that. Neither of us were reluctant about making that decision. I got rid of the little bit of jewelry that I had, too.

To be honest, this was not the first time we had ever faced these choices. Both Dixie and I had been exposed to a certain amount of holiness preaching all of our lives. She, in Sabine Tabernacle under Harry Hodge, and later at Victory Temple under Pastor Clendennen, and I, in several Assemblies of God Churches.

The Jezebel Spirit

From our childhood, we had heard preachers preach against women **"decked"** out like Jezebel. Jezebel is one of the few women in the Bible who wore makeup and jewelry, and she was a despicable, evil woman. Jezebel hated God and set out to kill Elijah the prophet. God smote and killed her for her wickedness, and dogs ate her carcass.

For thousands of years, preachers and Churches all over the world had associated makeup, jewelry, immorality and rebellion with the evil spirit of Jezebel.

There are no less than five significant Bible condemnations referring to women who were "decked" with jewelry, including the great harlot church of the last days. And we knew there were other proof texts in scriptures that showed God's expressed displeasure with jewelry.

When Moses came down from the Mount and found Aaron's Golden Calf, and the people in idolatry, "The LORD had said unto Moses, Say unto the children of Israel, Ye are a stiffnecked people: I will come up into the midst of thee in a moment, and consume thee: therefore now **put off thy ornaments from thee**, that I may know what to do unto thee. And the children of Israel **stripped themselves of their ornaments** by the mount Horeb," Exodus 33:5-6. **God threatened to destroy Israel if they did not give up their jewelry.**

Subsequently, God demanded that the people of Israel could not keep any jewelry that they might gain from the spoils of war. If they conquered an enemy at war, God said, "Thou shalt not **desire** the silver or gold that is on them, **nor take it** unto thee, lest thou be snared therein: for **it is an abomination** to the Lord thy God. Neither shalt thou bring an abomination into thine house, lest thou be a cursed thing like it: but **thou shalt utterly detest it, and thou shalt utterly abhor it; for it is a cursed thing**," Deuteronomy 7:25-26. **God said, "DETEST IT ...ABHOR IT." It is cursed.**

We had heard sermons in our youth about Achan, and the need for having a "house-cleaning" to get rid of accursed things. In Joshua 7, "the anger of the LORD was kindled against the children of Israel," and thirty-six men died in a war, because a man named Achan had hidden away in his tent a **costly Babylonian garment, a wedge of gold, and much silver** that he had found among the spoils of war. Because he had kept the very things that God had commanded them not to take, Achan and his family were stoned to death and burned in fire that day. THAT is a compelling reason for anybody to have a house-cleaning!

In Judges 8, Gideon, the man who had once led a great deliverance, later caused the people to sin when **he coveted the earrings, ornaments, collars and chains** of their prey. Gideon's heroic, Godly legacy was reproached.

In Isaiah 3, God condemned the women of Israel for their **"wanton [painted] eyes,"** and their **chains, bracelets, earrings, rings, nose jewels, crisping pins**, etc., promising to smite them with plagues and put them to shame.

In Ezekiel 16 and Hosea 2, God again condemned the women of Israel for using enticing clothes, **ornaments, bracelets, chains, jewels, earrings**, and other **gold and silver** to deck themselves, to "play the harlot," "commit whoredoms," and "lewdness." He swore to destroy them in humiliation at the hands of their enemies – their former lovers.

It was impossible to ignore what Dixie and I knew was in the Word.

The Bible was very clear about jewelry. From one scriptural case to the next, the **wearing of makeup and jewelry** was almost always associated with **pride, vanity, haughtiness, idolatry, or immorality**, and ultimately, many other lusts and sins of the flesh. Possessing and loving jewelry opens the heart to many unclean and evil spirits.

Even in the New Testament, Jesus told his disciples not to take gold and silver with them. Peter said, "Silver and gold have I none." Paul said, "I have coveted no man's gold or silver."

Finally, Paul (in 1 Timothy 2) and Peter (in 1 Peter 3) instructed women not to wear ornaments in their hair, nor to wear **gold, pearls, or costly array**. How can anyone fail to see that the Apostles were telling those who WERE wearing ornaments that they should NOT wear them?

Instead, they taught them to adorn themselves **"in modest apparel," with "shamefacedness and sobriety,"** and **with "a meek and quiet spirit."** That demeanor is the extreme opposite of the demeanor of one who wears makeup, jewelry, or skimpy clothes.

We just wanted to do the will of God.

It did not matter at that point what God wanted. If we could be convinced of it, we were ready to do it. So, if God had a problem with gold, and pearls and costly array, then we did, too. Such things added nothing spiritual whatsoever to our lives, but only encouraged fleshly vanities which led to more and more carnality and worldliness.

And there was more.

Dixie asked, "What about the verse in the Bible that says a man should not wear that which pertains to a woman, or a woman that which pertains to a man," (Deuteronomy 22:5)?

"What do YOU think?" I knew that I did not have to answer. She already knew. It was not a new issue. It was an ancient precept that people around the world had clearly held to for more than three thousand years (i.e., In 1431, Joan of Arc was burned at the stake by the Catholic Church for wearing men's clothing.)

Dixie was not asking out of stupidity or ignorance. She had spent her life in Church and in the Bible. She knew the Bible better than many preachers. Hers was not an act of "legalism," or of being intimidated or pressured by a controlling preacher. She was not trying to be "holier than thou." She was not enslaved to anybody's "bondage," except to God Himself. She had faced all those accusations from her detractors many years earlier, and had stood her ground. She knew that God wanted her to look feminine, not masculine, and godly, not worldly. It just did not matter what anybody but God thought.

Dixie boxed up every pair of slacks and jeans she owned, plus a lot of other clothes that she knew were not as modest as they should be, and threw them all in a garbage dumpster. She could have given them away, but if they really were wrong, she didn't want anybody else to have them either.

Everything that was too short, too tight, too low-cut, or sleeveless went into the trash. She figured that they were not merely wrong for her; they were also wrong for any other woman to wear in public. So she disposed of them, and that was the end of that matter. She never put on another pair of slacks as long as she lived.

Now, I know that a lot of people vehemently contest this issue, but from Genesis to Revelation, God defined and emphasized distinct gender-specific roles and identities for men and women. God made it clear that He passionately abhors the mixing or confusing of male traits with female traits. He forbids males from female roles and female apparel, and He forbids females from male roles and male apparel.

Under God's design, men and women are supposed to be as different as daylight from dark. Men are to be distinctly masculine. Women are to be distinctly feminine.

(The entire modern gay/lesbian/bisexual lifestyle is a morbid contradiction to these very Biblical commandments. Not only does God utterly forbid men to lie with men for sexual purposes as with a woman [Leviticus 18:22; 20:13; Deuteronomy 23:17; Romans 1:27], but men are also warned not to be effeminate. The Word declares that God will send effeminate men to Hell [1 Corinthians 6:9].

Women are warned not to invade the masculine role - forbidden to usurp the role of a man [1 Timothy 2:12]. Women must not wear masculine apparel, and men must not wear feminine apparel. The modern, nearly-universal UNISEX look, where men and women dress very much alike is clearly something that God did NOT want to happen!

When the last word is said, there is simply no reason why a woman cannot wear modest, exclusively-feminine clothes, or a man wear modest, exclusively-masculine clothes. It is not a difficult task, regardless of the excuses that are made. It is a spirit and an attitude: right or wrong.

The same is true of modesty. There is simply no legitimate reason why anyone should expose their thighs, their shoulders, or their midriff in public. Such standards of modesty are thousands of years old, and we cannot show any justification for lowering those standards today.

We just wanted to go by the Book.

Now in the Church we were attending, most of those things were not considered wrong at all. Most of the ladies wore slacks. Most of them wore makeup and jewelry. So Dixie's decision not to dress like that anymore put her in a conspicuous and peculiar position. But that did not deter her in any way. She was not ashamed or embarrassed in any way about being more modest, more sober and less flamboyant. She was determined to stand for what she believed God wanted, and she felt very bold to do it.

Both of us were on fire. The longer we prayed and studied the Word, the more our spirits were strengthened to do the will of God. We knew that God's hand was on our lives, and that He had called us to do His will above all else. We looked to Him daily for direction, and He spoke to us again and again.

We were not concerned about other people's disagreements or objections to the changes we were making. We knew that anytime a Christian makes a more-than-typical commitment to do the will of God, Christians-in-name-only are likely to demonize them for being "holier-than-thou," or "legalistic." But that did not matter to us. All that mattered was that we gave ourselves wholly to God without any reservations.

Along with all the other changes we were making, I began to be concerned about the effects that the television was having on our lives. One Wednesday evening, after I had been in the Church all day long praying. I came home for a while to change clothes for the Wednesday night Church service. As I walked through the living room, the television was on, and a program called "Charlie's Angels" was playing. Charlie's Angels were three female private investigators. It was a highly sexualized show that was enormously popular at that time, but after being in prayer all day long, I was shocked by how it offended my spiritual state of mind. It seemed very evil. I turned the television off and told Dixie that the television was full of junk.

The following Saturday morning, I saw some of the cartoons that our two boys were watching. Their entire story-lines were about witchcraft, goddesses and other supernatural powers. It occurred to me that the messages my boys were getting from those programs were not harmless. They were really subversive values that were against our Christian beliefs.

I could have ignored them again as I had a thousand times before. But having been alone with God in prayer and Bible study for several weeks, my senses were sharpened to the uncleanness of so many things.

Dixie and I had a discussion about the television. It was a very nice piece of furniture, a large entertainment center that we had spent a lot of money on. It had a radio, record player, a tape deck and extension speakers in other rooms. But there could be no denying that the television was working against the values we were trying to live by, and trying to teach our boys to live by. It was filling our house and our minds with a lot of perverse and evil things that we simply did not want in our lives anymore.

So, we decided that our home would be better off without a television. There were enough battles to fight without our minds being bombarded every single day with Hell's propaganda. We were really weary of sin and Satan's effects on our lives. We just wanted God. We wanted the devil out of our house.

We loaded the television in the trunk of the car and took it to the nearest dumpster and threw it away. That was the end of that. As a consequence, we raised both of our boys without a TV in our home. It did not hurt them. It did not hurt us. In fact, to this day, there is nothing that is more offensive or obnoxious than to sit down in a room where a television blares loudly, mindlessly, and endlessly by the hours. I don't know how anybody tolerates it without losing their mind. In fact, I think it causes more mental, emotional and behavioral malfunction and turmoil than anyone has ever admitted.

Now, I think it's important for me to put a disclaimer in right here, to make it abundantly clear to whoever may be reading this, that I am perfectly aware that we are not saved by the kind of works I have been referring to. I am perfectly aware that a person's clothes are not going to save him or her. **Don't even make the charge!** I know as clearly as anybody living that it is **only the grace of God that saves us from our sins.**

I hear some folks screaming, "That's salvation by works!!" Well, I've heard that argument too, read all about that argument, and argued both sides of that argument. But I don't believe it. Holiness teaching is NOT "salvation by works." Holiness teaching is NOT "LEGALISM!!" as so many charge.

Holiness and separation from carnal, worldly things is obedience to the Word of God.

> "I beseech you therefore, brethren, by the mercies of God,
> that ye **present your bodies a living sacrifice, holy**,
> acceptable unto God, which is your reasonable service.
> And **be not conformed to this world**: but be ye transformed
> by the renewing of your mind, that ye may prove what is that good,
> and acceptable, and perfect, will of God,"
> Romans 12:1-2.

This has nothing to do with somebody being "holier than thou." That topic is a cheap, overworked cop-out that has been used a million times by people who simply do not want to make the kind of changes that God requires of them. I refuse to dodge or evade issues like that anymore. I have dealt with every argument in the book on these issues over a period of several decades. I have had enough. Leonard Ravenhill said, "When there's something in the Bible that Churches don't like, they call it 'Legalism!'" Ravenhill was right.

> "Many a modern evangelist, usually a cheerful fellow,
> offering free pardons for mighty offences against a
> Holy, Righteous God, offers too much for too little.
> Now some people may charge us with demanding works for salvation.
> Well, if repentance preaching is offering works,
> lay the charge at John the Baptist's feet,
> lay it on Jesus (Luke 5:32),
> lay it against Peter for his Pentecost sermon,"
> Leonard Ravenhill.

I want to be saved, and I do not want to be unwilling to do whatever it takes to have a pure heart and pure mind before Almighty God. If that means throwing something away, or taking a financial loss, or losing a friend, so be it. To REPENT means to PUT AWAY the forbidden things.

I do not believe that any of us are going to be saved by works. But IN EXCHANGE for the priceless grace of God, God clearly expects us to abandon our worldly and sinful pursuits. Shall we continue in sin because grace abounds? God forbid! (Romans 6:1-2).

Think of it as letting your children go outside and play in the mud every day. If you want to let them do that, it is your prerogative. But God has something much better in mind for His children than playing in the mud every day.

And that's the way I feel about being a Christian. If you want to believe that God is satisfied with your playing with the world, the flesh and the devil every day of your life, that is your prerogative. But I don't believe it.

I believe my divine destiny is profoundly and dramatically impacted by my consecration – my willingness to pay the price of renouncing the world, the flesh and the devil. "**A double-minded man is unstable in all his ways,**" James 1:8.

Sooner or later, everybody is going to polarize to one side or the other of these issues. This is the side I'm on, and this is the side I am staying on. I got here by agonizing, thoughtful, **expensive**, painful choice, and I'm not going back.

If there is any value whatsoever in my telling this entire story, it is to say that I have been around the block with these issues just about as thoroughly as anybody I've ever heard of, and at as great a personal expense. Consequently, they are the most deeply-held convictions.

I did not get my convictions out of a box of Cracker Jacks. I got them out of the Bible. God has called us to holy living. Holy living means "set apart unto God."

Our compliance with God's wishes for our holy living is the least we can do to RECIPROCATE for God's lavish mercies toward us. We are debtors to God for His infinite mercies.

Of all people who have ever received abundant grace, Dixie and I had certainly received abundant mercy. I have been as evil and demon-possessed in my day as any other sinner. But when God forgave me and set me free from all those snares, I became forever indebted to Him.

To whom much is given, much will be required. That's what the Book says. JESUS said it in Luke 12:48. Because God was so merciful to receive us, we owe Him anything and everything He asks for.

It is a matter of branding – wearing God's brand.

My convictions about some of these issues were seriously fortified when I remembered an experience I had in the advertising business in Houston. I spent time working with a major ad agency in Houston - the Winius-Brandon Agency. They had all the McDonald's restaurant accounts in that area. I sat in an office with the account executive who was in charge of those local accounts. Behind her desk was an entire wall of bookshelves containing McDonald's manuals that defined, in thousands and thousands of pages, virtually every imaginable advertising scenario they would ever encounter.

I looked through some of those manuals. I saw tightly-controlled regulations that required all advertising to comply with their guidelines. Every item had to be within certain guidelines with regard to color, size, placement and a long list of eventualities. Every marketing piece ever produced had to be done in the strictest compliance with those regulations. You can do this. You can't do that.

There are many, many reasons why McDonald's demands compliance with their regulations. They have a very valuable brand to protect. They have enormous corporate liabilities. They need consistency in service, consistency in products, and consistency in everything. They want their customers to know who they are and what they stand for. They want every product ever sold to be consistently the same. They want their vendors to deliver consistent products. They want their marketing efforts to consistently deliver a pre-determined message that has been carefully thought-out and carefully planned.

What would you think if you ordered a McDonald's hamburger, and it came to you looking like a sloppy, piled-on concoction that a bunch of 10-year-old boys had thrown together on a camping trip? You would certainly think somebody must have lost their mind. And it would be VERY BAD for business!

This whole concept is interpolated into the entire world of commerce. Wendy's, Taco Bell, General Motors, Ford, Chase Bank, you name it, it's got rules.

And you can get fired if you don't comply with them.

Now, do you think that Almighty God has any LESS interest whatsoever in the identity, branding, appearance, behavior, or conversation of HIS HOLY PEOPLE?

Do you think that Almighty God doesn't really care if we throw around four-letter words, dress like a punk or a hippy, are immodestly exposed, or feed ourselves on an endless diet of Hollywood's swill?

Do you not think that God Almighty CARES if a man looks like a woman or a woman looks like a man? How about the tattoos and body piercings and vulgar artwork on clothes? So God doesn't care if we smoke or drink or tempt each other to commit perverted or immoral acts? He doesn't care that we stay home from Church to watch a football game or to attend a Little League practice?

You had better believe that He does! You and I are supposed to carry God's branding. Everywhere we go, and everything we do should bear witness to the fact that we are "bought with a price," and that we are not enslaved to our peers, or to the cultural and social values of the world.

Do you look like **God's brand** - or **the world's brand**? Do you look like someone who is submitted to the disciplines of God, or do you look like a completely self-made, self-designed, self-willed free spirit?

Why on earth did God ever micromanage the nation of Israel with such strictness for hundreds of years? He literally drenched them in rules and regulations. Why? To demonstrate to the entire world what kind of people He created us to be, and to make a people for His name's sake.

Should the New Testament Church be less holy, less set-apart, less identifiable, or less consistent than Israel was in its day? No, it should not be. Why should we be free to indulge in carnality, worldliness and selfishness when the early Church saints literally sacrificed their lives to stand for Jesus Christ? How can we justify divided allegiances? Why are so many of us torn between two lovers?

A lot of people will tell you that we don't have to keep commandments because God abolished the Law, but that is not true. The prophets said that God would PUT HIS LAWS IN OUR HEARTS! (Proverbs 3:3; 7:3; Jeremiah 31:33; 2 Corinthians 3:3) That is a whole new level of law-keeping!

Jesus said that He would build a Church that the gates of Hell would not prevail against. That's not a loose-knit, come-as-you-are, do-as-you-please mob He was talking about. It is a militant, highly-disciplined Church that is conceived, birthed and carefully led by the Holy Ghost and the Word of God. It is a mighty army that marches lock-step to the commands of its Captain.

Anarchy and Christianity are on opposite ends of the spectrum. Chaos and disorder belong to Hell. God is a God of order, structure, and orderliness.

He demands modesty, humility, unselfishness, sacrificial living, and self-denial as a body of evidence to the world that His people have seen Him, heard Him, know Him and love Him more than all of this corrupt, temporal world.

And that makes them 100% DIFFERENT.

PECULIAR. If we are not **PECULIAR** when compared to the rest of society, then we are not what Jesus redeemed us to be. God saves His people to stand out, to be identifiably different. God expects His people to renounce the world's ways, to refuse to be one of THEM anymore.

From ancient times, God warned His people not to practice the ways of the heathen. He did not even want them to LEARN the ways of the heathen (Jeremiah 10:2). Jesus wreaked havoc in the Temple because things were going on there that just didn't belong in the Temple. Maybe it's time that some of us have a tantrum about all the junk that has made its way into Christianity – and specifically into Christians!

I say that God absolutely cares. I don't just think that. I can prove it again and again in the scriptures!

Enough said. Next page.

Chapter 15

Eat No Bread, Drink No Water

While studying the Bible one day, I was again ARRESTED by a relatively obscure Bible story; obscure not because it was insignificant, but because most people would probably not remember the story. It is rarely told.

When I say that I was ARRESTED by the story, it is because it lodged in my mind and haunted me for literally MONTHS afterward. It was one of the most unshakable concepts I had ever had to deal with.

It was a lengthy story (1 Kings 11:28 through 14:20). It concerned **King Jeroboam of Israel (in Samaria)**, and an **idolatrous altar** that he had built to a **golden calf**. (He had built two golden calves, and set them in different cities.)

When the legendary **King Solomon** of Israel died, his kingdom fell into the hands of **his son, Rehoboam**. But Rehoboam was not wise like his father had once been. **Rehoboam was a cold-blooded, evil despot who oppressed the people**, and the people hated him. Before long, there was an uprising and revolution, led by **one of Solomon's mighty men, Jeroboam**.

Tragically, most of Israel had already fallen into idolatry before Solomon died. Many Jews were already worshipping false gods and idols.

Before Solomon died, **a prophet of Israel had called out Jeroboam**, and prophesied that **God would divide the twelve tribes** of Israel after Solomon died.

The prophet said that **two tribes (Benjamin and Judah)** would remain with their king [Rehoboam] in Jerusalem, but that **the remaining [northern] ten tribes** would eventually follow **Jeroboam, and he would become their king**.

And that is exactly what came to pass. Ten tribes revolted against Rehoboam at Jerusalem, and Jeroboam took them to Samaria and formed a new kingdom of Israel, with ten tribes under his leadership.

Long Winding Road

Tragically and unfortunately, Jeroboam failed to reform Israel, or lead them back to right relationship with their Holy God. As their new king, Jeroboam should have denounced their idolatries, and led them back to true worship of Jehovah, but treacherously, he did not.

Instead, Jeroboam added sin to sin by committing outrageous, pagan abominations, including building two golden calves, and altars to their false gods (idols).

It was inevitable that God would judge Jeroboam and the ten tribes for their outrageous abominations.

Surely enough, one day, God sent an unnamed prophet to Samaria, where Jeroboam, the King of Israel, was standing beside his altar at that very moment, burning incense to his golden calf.

It was a cataclysmic moment - the prophet of God facing down the reprobate King of Israel. The prophet condemned the evil altar.

"And **he cried against the altar** in the word of the LORD,
and said, O altar, altar, thus saith the LORD;
Behold, a child shall be born unto the house of David, Josiah by name;
and upon thee shall he offer the priests of the high places
that burn incense upon thee, and men's bones shall be burnt upon thee.
And **he gave a sign** the same day, saying,
This is the sign which the LORD hath spoken;
Behold, **the altar shall be rent**,
and the ashes that are upon it shall be poured out.
...when king Jeroboam heard the saying of the man of God,
...he put forth his hand from the altar, saying, Lay hold on him.
And **his hand**, which he put forth against him, **dried up**,
so that **he could not pull it in again** to him.
The **altar also was rent**, and the **ashes poured out from the altar**,
according to the sign which
the man of God had given by the word of the LORD.
And the king answered and said unto the man of God,
Intreat now the face of the LORD thy God, and **pray for me,
that my hand may be restored me again**.
And the man of God besought the LORD,
and the king's hand was restored him again, and became as it was before.

Long Winding Road

      And the king said unto the man of God,
Come home with me, and refresh thyself, and I will give thee a reward.
      And the man of God said unto the king,
**If thou wilt give me half thine house, I will not go in with thee,
neither will I eat bread nor drink water in this place:**
For so was it charged me by the word of the LORD, saying,
**Eat no bread, nor drink water,
nor turn again by the same way that thou camest.**
So he went another way,
and returned not by the way that he came to Bethel,"
1 Kings 13:2-10.

Eat no bread. Drink no water. Do not return by the same way you came.

Here is the short version:

The prophet condemned the altar.
The King reached out to seize him.
The King's hand instantly became withered and paralyzed.
He begged the prophet to pray for him.
The prophet prayed, and he was healed.
The King asked the prophet to come home with him, saying,
"I will give thee a reward."

      "And the man of God said unto the king,
**If thou wilt give me half thine house, I will not go in with thee,
neither will I eat bread nor drink water in this place:**
For so was it charged me by the word of the LORD, saying,
Eat no bread, nor drink water,
nor turn again by the same way that thou camest."

I was stricken by the high anxiety in this showdown. What did it mean?

At the very least, I could see that there were two powerful but opposing forces at work: the **abominable idolatry of Jeroboam** versus **the Word of the Lord**. It was an **evil king** versus a **true prophet of God**.

Now any Bible-believing person would automatically know at the outset who the winner would be. The Word of the LORD will ALWAYS prevail over any evil situation.

But there was a secondary lesson that seemed to be as important as the first, and here it is:

When God sends a man with Truth, he must not allow himself to be influenced in any way by outside powers. No bribes. No deceptions. No false voices. No competing voices. Nothing.

God had commanded the prophet, "Eat no bread, nor drink water, nor turn again by the same way that thou camest."

So the prophet concretely refused to even entertain Jeroboam's offer to come home with him. He concretely ignored the offer of a reward. He concretely refused to be influenced in any way by Jeroboam.

> "So he went another way,
> and returned not by the way that he came to Bethel."

But that was by no means the end of the story! The man of God was tested the SECOND TIME on the very same command.

In the next episode, there was an old prophet living in Bethel who heard about the younger prophet's dramatic exploits with Jeroboam, and he quickly chased him down. He found the man of God sitting under a tree.

> **Then he said unto him, Come home with me, and eat bread.**
> And he said, **I may not return with thee**, nor go in with thee: neither will I eat bread nor drink water with thee in this place:
> For it was said to me by the word of the LORD,
> Thou shalt eat no bread nor drink water there,
> nor turn again to go by the way that thou camest.
>
> He said unto him, I am a prophet also as thou art;
> and an angel spake unto me by the word of the LORD, saying,
> Bring him back with thee into thine house,
> that he may eat bread and drink water.
> **But he lied unto him.**
>
> So he went back with him,
> and did eat bread in his house, and drank water,"
> 1 Kings 13:14-19.

This was a very disturbing development. The man of God had obeyed the LORD on the first test. But on the second test, he failed.

> "And it came to pass, **as they sat at the table,**
> that **the word of the LORD came** unto the prophet that brought him back:
> And he **cried** unto the man of God that came from Judah, saying,
> Thus saith the LORD,
> Forasmuch as **thou hast disobeyed the mouth of the LORD, and hast not kept the commandment** which the LORD thy God commanded thee,
> But camest back, and hast eaten bread and drunk water in the place,
> of the which the LORD did say to thee, **Eat no bread, and drink no water;
> thy carcase shall not come unto the sepulchre of thy fathers.**
>
> …**And when he was gone, a lion met him by the way, and slew him:**
> and his carcase was cast in the way, and the ass stood by it,
> the lion also stood by the carcase."

When the old prophet heard rumors of it, he said,

> **"It is the man of God, who was disobedient unto the word of the LORD:
> therefore the LORD hath delivered him unto the lion,
> which hath torn him, and slain him,
> according to the word of the LORD, which he spake unto him.**

The old prophet took the body of the dead man of God and took it back to the city and buried it in his own grave, and mourned over him, saying,

> "Alas, my brother!"

He told his sons that the word of the LORD against the altar in Bethel and all the other high places would certainly come to pass. (Certainly enough, the prophecy DID come to pass in the days of King Josiah, 323 years later!)

This story took my breath away.

Why? Because I could plainly see how DEAD SERIOUS God is when He tells a man of God to handle His message in a particular way, and he fails to handle it according to the Word of the Lord.

Consider the key elements of this story.

1. Israel and their King were in gross idolatry.
2. God sent a man of God to pronounce judgment on them.
3. The man of God was instructed to EAT NO BREAD, and DRINK NO WATER with anyone on his journey, and to return home by a different way than he came.
4. The man of God did exactly as he was told at first, and God confirmed his word with signs following.
5. THEN – another prophet came into the picture, enticing the man of God to eat bread and drink water with him.

The last point was all too poignant for me. I had personally been enticed by other "men of God" to follow after things that I already knew contradicted the Word of God. And I had suffered great agony (and great losses) for following them.

To be honest, the whole story stoked the fear of God in my soul. It was terrifying to think that I could be trying really hard to do the will of God, and even doing a pretty good job of it, only to be undermined and destroyed because I allowed some other man of God to convince me of something that I already knew was not Biblical.

This whole concept was a giant pill to swallow, but it HAD to be swallowed if I wanted to survive spiritually.

It was a screaming reminder that we must ALWAYS be spiritually alert! We must NEVER assume that ANYBODY is ALWAYS right about the things of God. It does not matter how long any preacher or prophet has been in the ministry, there is ALWAYS the possibility that a man of God can go wrong.

The man of God was TRICKED by the old prophet. The old prophet told him that an ANGEL had instructed him to come home with him. But verse 18 says, **"He LIED unto him."**

I have never met a preacher (or any Christian) that was 100% immune to a deception. The Apostle Peter himself tried to prevent Jesus from dying, and Jesus said to him, "Get thee behind me, Satan." Satan was using Peter to tempt Jesus to avoid Calvary.

That does not mean that I cannot trust preachers. Jesus used Peter, even after calling him the devil. It was an isolated situation. Still, He rebuked him. And we must absolutely have enough fortitude and force-of-will to look at a preacher who is telling us something that is contrary to the Word of God and say, "I don't buy it, and I won't do it, because it is contrary to the Word of God."

God meant for us to trust and reverence preachers, but we must never fail to try the spirits, AND be discerning about whether we are hearing Truth or error. There are many deceivers in the world. We must always be aware that Satan could be slipping his vile hand into a situation.

Failure to put a situation like that to the test can be FATAL! And that is no exaggeration.

So HOW can we be sure? We must ALWAYS put the pure and true WORD OF GOD on trial. What did GOD say? We must always obey the Word of God first. Anytime anybody contradicts the Word of God, trouble is brewing.

Tragically, the man of God yielded to the convincing lie of the old prophet. And more tragically, he DIED an early death for his error. His sin was not substantially different from the sin of Adam and Eve. God said one thing, and the Devil said another. **We have to be concretely determined to obey the voice of God** and reject every other contrary voice.

The Acid Test

From the moment I read that story, I began to put everything I was personally hearing and seeing to the acid test. In metallurgy, if you pour acid on GOLD, it does not affect it whatsoever. But if a metal is not pure GOLD, it will corrode under the acid. That is what we need to do with all the preaching and teaching that we hear. Put it to the acid test. Everything we hear must be put to the acid test of the Word of God. If the preaching and teaching is Biblical, it will come forth like GOLD. But if the preaching and teaching cannot pass the acid test, it will corrode.

In the end, no preacher has the last word over the Word of God.

I am not teaching skepticism. I am not teaching rebellion against authority. I am not telling you to give your preacher a hard time.

I am telling you that if you know that something is in the Word of God, and you start following ANY doctrine that disagrees with the Word of God, you are putting yourself at the very same risk that the man of God did when he ATE BREAD and DRANK WATER with the old prophet.

Just don't do it!

There were actually THREE elements to God's instruction.

1. Eat no bread.
2. Drink no water.
3. Do not return the way you came.

The third element means that when God sends you to do a job, you will be growing in the will of God as you do it. You will be a better person when that task is completed. You will know and understand more about how God operates after you have obeyed Him. Now, do not backslide. Do not go back the way you came. Continue to move forward, "from faith to faith," (Romans 1:17).

> "Now the just shall live by faith: but **if any man draw back, my soul shall have no pleasure in him**,"
> Hebrews 10:38.

Learn from that experience and stand steadfastly on what you have learned. Do not return or regress to less wisdom, knowledge or understanding. Never backslide. Never go backward from where God has matured you to. Don't let your spiritual muscles atrophy.

Always continue to follow the voice of God in a continuing revelation of Truth. Many people do not maintain the revelation that God gave them earlier in their lives. They have backslidden. They went back the way they came. They disobeyed God.

I did not know exactly how I was supposed to apply this lesson of "**Eat no bread, drink no water**," but I was adamantly determined that I was not going to let another preacher, Church, or denomination deceive me.

My eyes were peeled, my ears were tuned, and I was on high alert for Satan's tricks and deceptions. As I studied my way through the entire New Testament, literally hundreds of verses jumped out at me, warning me about great spiritual perils that all Christians would face in the Last Days. I saw the **warnings about a coming great "falling away."**

Again and again, I saw Bible verses warning me that in the Last Days, Christianity would fall into the hands of **evil men and seducers, deceivers and deception, strong delusions, false prophets, false doctrines, false ministers, wolves in sheep clothing, even false Christs**, and much more.

Those verses were like giant signs on a beach warning swimmers to stay clear of rip tides, lethal undertows, and other drowning hazards.

I had seen every one of those prophesied beguilers with my own eyes. I had been on stage with them. I had rubbed shoulders with them; been in their offices and in their TV and radio studios; read their books; listened to their tapes and radio programs; and watched their videos and their TV broadcasts.

God said, "Let no man deceive you." Don't let them deceive you!

> "Now we beseech you, brethren,
> by **the coming of our Lord** Jesus Christ,
> and by **our gathering together unto him**,
> …**Let no man deceive you** by any means:
> for **that day shall not come**,
> except there come a **falling away first**…"
> 2 Thessalonians 2:1-3.

So the lesson of "Eat no bread, Drink no water" was simple:

"Let no man deceive you!"

The Apostle Paul expressed it this way,

> **"Have no fellowship with the unfruitful works of darkness,
> but rather reprove them,"**
> Ephesians 5:11.

Even Moses had warned of such dangers from the very beginning:

"**If thy brother**, the son of thy mother, **or thy son, or thy daughter**, or the **wife** of thy bosom, or thy **friend**, which is as thine own soul, **entice thee secretly, saying, Let us go and serve other gods,** which thou hast not known, thou, nor thy fathers, Namely, of the gods of the people which are round about you, nigh unto thee, or far off from thee, from the one end of the earth even unto the other end of the earth;

Thou shalt not consent unto him, nor hearken unto him; neither shall thine eye pity him, neither shalt thou spare, neither shalt thou conceal him," Deuteronomy 13:6-8.

Solomon taught,

"My son, **if sinners entice thee, consent thou not,**" Proverbs 1:10.

And to the Romans, Paul said,

"Now I beseech you, brethren, **mark them which cause divisions and offences contrary to the doctrine** which ye have learned; and **avoid them**. For they that are such serve not our Lord Jesus Christ, but their own belly; and **by good words and fair speeches deceive the hearts** of the simple," Romans 16:17-18.

I realized from the moment I came back to God that one of my biggest challenges would be to prevent myself from being pulled back into the influence of anybody like that.

Going BACKWARD would never take me FORWARD.

It was a very simple premise: "You cannot get to the North side while driving in the Southbound lane."

If the people I join with have less conviction today than they had yesterday, they are falling away. If they pray and study the Bible less now than they used to, they are falling away. If they are less interested in true doctrine and holiness than they once were, they are falling away.

Those who are falling away…

- They did not drink alcohol, but now they do.
- They did not use bad language, but now they do.
- They did not dress immodestly, but now they do.
- They did not watch inappropriate movies, but now they do.
- They did not approve of unbiblical preaching, but now they do.
- They did not attend questionable amusements, but now they do.
- They did not tolerate false doctrines, but now they do.
- They did not wear makeup, jewelry, or scanty clothes, but now they do.
- They did not miss Church for sports or games, but now they do.
- They once **enjoyed unfettered Bible preaching**, now they **don't**.
- They once desired to hear preaching that convicted them of sin, but now they **don't**.
- The list could go on and on…

I remembered hearing a preacher say, "If you were ever closer to God than you are today, to that degree, you are backslid." Now, most Christians do not believe that. They believe "once-saved, always-saved." They believe that no matter how you live, if you believe in Jesus, you will be saved.

A lethal syndrome has infested the spirits and minds of men. Nothing is wrong anymore. Nobody goes to Hell.

Open up today's newspaper to the obituaries column. Select one funeral announcement at random. Go to any funeral in your town. No matter what kind of life the person lived, the eulogies will say "He's in a better place," or "He's smiling down from Heaven," or "We'll see him again," ad infinitum. Nobody goes to Hell anymore.

But Jesus pointedly contradicted that.

> "**Not every one that saith unto me, Lord, Lord,**
> shall enter into the kingdom of heaven;
> but **he that doeth the will of my Father** which is in heaven,"
> Matthew 7:21.

Old convictions and the sense of guilt for sins committed have very nearly vanished. It is rare to find anyone who genuinely fears God. People love a feel-good religion, but they turn stone-deaf around inconvenient TRUTH. They do not study their Bibles seriously. They can quote almost no scriptures. They will not discuss important Bible doctrines. They do not know, or have forgotten many of the principal Bible stories, and cannot moralize or spiritualize their lessons with any depth or accuracy.

Apostates. That is what they are.

> "In the latter times **some shall depart from the faith,** giving heed to **seducing spirits,** and **doctrines of devils,"**
> 1 Timothy 4:1.

Apostasy is a weird thing. People can see it at a distance, but they can't see it up close. They can see other people falling away, but they can't see themselves falling away. That is probably one of the reasons why it is called a **"strong delusion,"** 2 Thessalonians 2:11. Satan deludes and captures men unaware.

> "And that they may recover themselves out of **the snare of the devil,** who are **taken captive by him at his will,"**
> 2 Timothy 2:26.

I had personally been taken in by so many false things. I had seen and been involved with so many versions and cheap imitations of the real New Testament Church.

I had kept company with many powerful preachers. Some had hearts that were as dry as a West Texas dust storm. Others were high-rolling, self-aggrandizing zealots, obsessed with building multi-million-dollar empires in the name of Jesus. We didn't need all kinds, but we had all kinds.

I listened to silly cheap-grace preaching. I listened to easy-believism. I heard the name-it-and-claim-it, prosperity-preachers, get-rich-in-Jesus'-name crowd; and the success motivation gurus. I suffered listening to the once-saved, always-saved crowd. I wearied of the Christian entertainment celebrities whose knowledge of God and the Bible was almost zip. All they knew how to do was sing, yet they had much larger followings than most preachers. That always irked me.

I saw so many hard-core phonies. Christians-in-name-only. Preachers who led double lives. Gospel musicians who were nauseating shams. Christians who were as carnal, worldly, lustful, materialistic, money-mongering, flamboyant and unspiritual as any godless person.

But the WORST part about it was that they continued to build larger and larger followings! Their crowds just kept on growing, and the money just kept on rolling in!

The SECULAR crowd could see through them, and openly mocked and ridiculed the phony religious crowd. But INSIDE Christianity, charlatans and phonies prospered virtually unopposed. Anybody could do anything they wanted and still have a huge following!

I did not want any more of any of it.

I absolutely refused to spend the rest of my life hanging around Christians who were like Diet Cokes. Zero calories. No nutrition. No food value. No eternal, spiritual essence. Deceivers. Seducers. Decoys!

But unfortunately, I knew that most people were not going to see it the way I saw it. They were not going to agree with my observations.

They refused to believe that these kind were hucksters. They were in total denial that all those roads lead to destruction.

Dixie and I could not and would not go back in that direction again. It was bridge-burning time - mentally, spiritually, emotionally, and doctrinally.

I was done with big-name celebrity preachers, Christian TV networks, and show-biz Gospel music. No more ecumenical junk. By the help of God, I would not be taken in by any more Christian imposters.

The time had come for us to make some concrete conclusions. We must Biblically define TRUE CHRISTIANITY and draw a line between it and false Christianity; a line which we absolutely refused to cross.

I must no longer be a part of - or victim of – the prophesied falling away. I intended to save myself, my family, and everyone I possibly could from its treachery.

The Apostle Paul issued a terse warning:

"Beware lest any man spoil you..."
Colossians 2:8.

I refused to do like so many do, and stick my head in the sand like an ostrich. I refused to deny that there was a general apostasy taking place, because there WAS.

I had personally experienced my own falling away, and it had been horrifying. I had taken myself, my wife and my children to the brink of Hell and very nearly fallen in.

I must never let that happen again. My heart was fixed.

Chapter 16

This Time, We Are Going By The Book

After some time had passed, the pastor of the little Assembly of God Church where we attended invited me to preach every Wednesday night, and I was happy to have that opportunity. Weeks and months of intense prayer, fasting and Bible study had set me on fire.

From Wednesday night to Wednesday night, one thing dominated my mind: knowing the Biblical differences between true Christianity and false Christianity.

I began with a precept that had been deeply ingrained in my soul from the earliest years of my ministry. I had preached a message in the North Carolina District A/G Western Camp Meeting in 1973 entitled, "What the Father Giveth."

"What the Father Giveth"

It had been an epiphany for me in those days. The followers of John the Baptist reported to John that all men were starting to follow Jesus. They were obviously wondering why John was being forsaken.

John the Baptist said, "A man can receive nothing, except it be GIVEN HIM FROM HEAVEN," John 3:27. He knew that the debut of Jesus' ministry had effectively ended his own personal ministry. In only a few days, Herod would take off John's head.

That told me that a man's calling and purpose is entirely under the sovereign control of Almighty God. No man can of his own initiative do a work for God that God did not call and ordain him to do.

That immediately disqualifies and nullifies all man-made religion.

If a man's ministry is not ordained of God – if it is not founded firmly on the WORD AND SPIRIT OF GOD, then God did not GIVE it to him. Therefore, that man is an interloper, an intruder, an invader, an alien, a charlatan, an impostor.

That is the bunker-busting truth.

If my ministry is not led by the Spirit and validated by the Word of God, I am a trespasser, an infringer, a fake, and a fraud.

That is not only true for me, but it is true for every professing Christian or minister.

In John 17, Jesus used the word "give," "given," "giveth," or "gavest" fifteen times in reference to one of two things:

1. What God had GIVEN to Him
2. What He had GIVEN to His saints

Jesus demonstrated that He was not concerned about things that the Father had not GIVEN Him to be concerned with, when He revealed His prayer list:

> **"I pray not for the world,**
> but for **them which thou hast given** me;"
> John 17:9

Our great task is to know WHAT THE FATHER HAS GIVEN, and tend to that.

I have, for most of my Christian life, been keenly aware that I only have a RIGHT to do what God has GIVEN me to do. I have no right to preach anything that is not purely Biblical, nor to assume any role in the Church that God has not ordained by His Spirit and that cannot be soundly validated by His Word.

Some people hang around influential preachers or denominational officials, hoping to advance themselves in the Church. They should hang around God instead, because real promotion comes from the Lord. Only God promotes at the right time and the right place.

> "Many seek the ruler's favour;
> but every man's judgment cometh from the LORD,"
> Proverbs 29:26

> "For promotion cometh neither from the east …the west …the south. But God is the judge: **he putteth down one, and setteth up another**," Psalms 75:6-7.

That reality wreaks havoc on ambition-driven, name-it-and-claim-it, dream your own dreams, "conceive it, believe it, receive it," heresies. We have no business concocting dreams and visions for ourselves (or for God).

Man-made dreams do not build the Kingdom of God. They build things that conflict with the Kingdom of God. Man-made dreams spend up resources and potential that should have been invested in the will of God and the Kingdom of God. Man-made dreams build sand castles. They have no eternal value. They only accomplish temporal goals for the gratification of the dreamer, not for the glory of God or His kingdom. Whatever man-made dreams build will be destroyed.

> "For as many as are **led by the Spirit** of God, they are the sons of God," Romans 8:14.

I have heard a ton of preachers draw from the story of Joseph as they preached, "Dream big dreams!" But there is a rudimentary problem with that kind of preaching.

Joseph did NOT dream His own dream.

God miraculously GAVE that dream to Joseph. Joseph had no agenda, no goals, and no ambitions of his own. Joseph's dream was totally from God, and God alone made it come to pass. Joseph was entirely led by the sovereign hand of God to his sacred destiny. Joseph did nothing of his own initiative to make God's dream come to pass.

Joseph's dream is an example of WHAT THE FATHER GIVETH.

Therefore, we must either walk in the GIVEN will of God, or we should just stand still until His Word speaks to us, GIVING us direction.

This is also true about every DOCTRINE, every STANDARD, and every MESSAGE that is not absolutely true to the Word of God. It is an abomination for us to borrow our message from the world's gurus, psychologists, sociologists, corporate trainers, coaches or anyone else.

If a doctrine or teaching cannot be firmly substantiated by the Word of God, it must not be preached. Nothing should come across a pulpit that cannot pass the most rigorous scriptural standards. If it obviously contradicts the Word of God, I cannot tell you how much God hates it.

> "Thus saith the Lord GOD; **Woe unto the foolish prophets, that follow their own spirit, and have seen nothing!**
> …Have ye not seen a **vain vision**,
> and have ye not spoken a **lying divination**,
> … saying, The LORD saith: and the LORD hath not sent them,"
> …whereas ye say, The LORD saith it; albeit I have not spoken?
> Ezekiel 13:3,6-7.

Ezekiel listed the divine judgments against ministers whose words, dreams and visions are not God-given:

- They shall not be in the assembly of my people.
- They shall not be written in the books of Israel.
- They shall not enter into the land of Israel.
- Their works will be destroyed.
- True saints will be delivered out of their hands.

God did not GIVE a flesh-pleasing sermon to a preacher. God did not GIVE a false doctrine to a teacher. God did not GIVE sensual, indulgent, carnal, worldly, comedic entertainment to anyone to use on a Church platform. Those things come from the carnal mind, and THAT was fathered by the Devil (John 8:44).

That same proposition is also a stabbing indictment against any person who speaks personal prophecies loosely in the name of the Lord. If those personal prophecies are not absolutely inspired by the Holy Ghost, that "prophet" is introducing chaotic lies into that person's life, and is heaping coals of judgment upon himself! Why? Because he falsely represents God.

Jesus said, "All that the Father GIVETH shall come unto me…" and then, "This is the Father's will… that of all which He hath GIVEN me, I should lose nothing, but should raise it up again at the last day," John 6:37,39.

The million-dollar question, then is, "What has God GIVEN ME?" Jesus answered that question in John 6.32:

"My Father GIVETH you the TRUE BREAD from heaven."

What IS the True Bread from heaven? Jesus Christ – the Word of God.

God has GIVEN us the man Jesus Christ and the Word of God.

The Word of God alone legitimizes any claim we make. If we cannot legitimize our claims by the Word of God, we have no claim.

I was determined to either prove or disprove every doctrine and every standard that I would be encountering. If I found something to be a false doctrine or a false teaching, I must of necessity reject it.

> "**Prove all things**; hold fast that which is good,"
> 1 Thessalonians 5:21

> "Beloved, **believe not every spirit**,
> but **try the spirits** whether they are of God:
> because many false prophets are gone out into the world,"
> 1 John 4:1.

I refused to build on sand. I intended to build on **BEDROCK,** no matter how deep I had to dig to find bedrock.

For Dixie and me, this was a process we adamantly refused to avoid or bypass. It was a mutual obsession. And for both of us, it was a fight – a fight against all kinds of unclean spirits that did not want to be silenced.

If we were going to build our lives on a rock-solid, Biblical foundation, we could only do so by carefully evaluating each and every Bible doctrine, and casting aside every Christian teaching, practice, or standard that did not meet the canon of scripture.

We were adamantly determined never to get involved with any Church, preacher or religion that we already KNEW would not teach so many important things that were speaking to us from the Bible.

I could see countless warnings in the Bible of the perils of false religion in the Last Days. I compiled so many of those verses and made sermons out of them, which I preached every Wednesday night for almost two months.

My weekly sermon titles came from those passages.

- **They Hold the Truth in Unrighteousness**

"For **the wrath of God is revealed** from heaven **against all ungodliness and unrighteousness of men, who hold the truth in unrighteousness**;
Because that which may be known of God is manifest in them;
for God hath shewed it unto them.
For the invisible things of him from the creation of the world
are clearly seen, being understood by the things that are made,
even his eternal power and Godhead; so that **they are without excuse**:
Because that, when **they knew God, they glorified him not as God**,
neither were thankful; but **became vain** in their imaginations,
and **their foolish heart was darkened.**
Professing themselves to be wise, **they became fools**,
And changed the glory of the uncorruptible God
into an image made like to corruptible man,
and to birds, and fourfooted beasts, and creeping things.
Wherefore **God also gave them** up to **uncleanness** through the **lusts of their own hearts, to dishonour their own bodies** between themselves:
Who **changed the truth of God into a lie**,
and **worshipped and served the creature** more than the Creator,
...For this cause **God gave them up unto vile affections**: for even their **women did change the natural use** into that which is **against nature**:
And likewise also **the men**, leaving the natural use of the woman,
burned in their lust one toward another;
men with men working that which is unseemly, and
receiving in themselves that recompence of their error which was meet.
And even as **they did not like to retain God in their knowledge,**
God gave them over to a reprobate mind,
to do those things which are **not convenient**;
Being filled with all unrighteousness, fornication, wickedness,
covetousness, maliciousness; full of envy, murder, debate, deceit,
malignity; whisperers, Backbiters, haters of God, despiteful, proud,
boasters, inventors of evil things, disobedient to parents,
Without understanding, covenantbreakers, without natural affection,
implacable, unmerciful: Who **knowing the judgment of God,**
that they which commit such things are worthy of death,
not only do the same, but have pleasure in them that do them,"
Romans 1:18-32.

Those were graphic, explicit warnings from the Apostle Paul to Christians who hold the TRUTH in UNRIGHTEOUSNESS.

That could be any Christian who forsakes the holy, godly lifestyle, or who corrupts pure Bible doctrine by embracing false doctrine.

God would literally GIVE THEM UP! God would give these Christians over to a reprobate mind – one that says good is evil and evil is good!

Why? Because they do not keep Him holy. Because they corrupt, contaminate and profane Christianity. They do not have the fear of God in their souls. God will give them over to their lusts, and they will become slaves to every kind of sin and abomination, including a scourge of homosexuality among both men and women!

Those verses scorched my soul and made me want to practice the utmost care NEVER to offend God, NEVER to treat Him carelessly or lightly.

It was all exceedingly obvious to me that Christianity was, at that very time, experiencing those pronounced judgments of God. With my own eyes, I had watched Christianity slide down the slippery slope of compromise, doctrinal deviance, irreverence, unholiness, hypocrisy, mockery and every kind of carnal, worldly thinking.

I knew, as surely as I lived, that the Titanic of fake Christianity was already taking on water. If I wanted to survive with my wife and my family, I absolutely had to abandon that ship!

In those verses in Romans, God promised to turn backsliding believers over to a reprobate mind. I did not want God to turn me over to a reprobate mind. It prophesied that God would give them over to homosexuality – not for their good, but for their ultimate destruction. He prophesied a generation gone wild, plunging into every unspeakable sin, debauchery and abomination.

These verses should terrify any Christian who is half-hearted or lukewarm about God. It should drive us to our knees to search our hearts and repent of even the smallest sins.

- **They Have No Root In Themselves**

Another glaring failure among neo-Christians that I could not ignore was their spiritual shallowness. "They have no root in themselves."

Jesus' parable about the Seed of the Word taught that the Word does not grow and bear fruit in most people, and for profound reasons. The sad truth is that most people who are exposed to the Word of God will not be saved. Here are the reasons Jesus gave in Matthew 13:3-23.

1. Some seed is sown by the **wayside**.

   > "Some **seeds fell by the way side**,
   > and the fowls came and devoured them up."

   People hear the Word of God, but if they are not genuinely interested – if they don't read, study or pray enough - Satan comes quickly, like birds stealing newly planted seed from a garden. Satan provides a distraction, or a change in the conversation, and they instantly forget that God was on their mind. Giving them the Word is like throwing seed away! Sadly, they will not be saved.

2. Some seed is sown in **stony places**.

   > "But he that received the **seed into stony places**,
   > the same is he that heareth the word,
   > and anon with joy receiveth it;
   > **Yet hath he not root in himself**, but dureth for a while:
   > for when tribulation or persecution ariseth because of the word,
   > by and by he is offended."

   Many joyously hear the Word, but they have "no deepness of earth." They do not really study the Word, or meditate on it. They do not pray as they read the Word. Their hearts do not cleave to the Word, or nourish it. Because the seed never grows a root in their soul, it cannot grow. "When the sun was up [when trials came], **they were scorched**, and because they had no root, **they withered away**," Matthew 13:6. "**These have no root**," Luke 8:13. And they will not be saved.

3. Some seed is sown **among thorns**.

> "And **some fell among thorns**;
> and the thorns sprung up, and choked them."

Jesus said these are those who hear the Word, BUT "the care of this world, and the deceitfulness of riches, **choke the Word**, and he becometh unfruitful." Cars, homes, vacations, sports, wealth-building, parties, heavy social schedules all **choke the Word of God**. What God WOULD have done in their lives never gets done, because they were so busy living for themselves. They will not be saved.

4. Some seed is sown in **good ground**.

> "But **other fell into good ground**,
> and brought forth fruit, some an hundredfold,
> some sixtyfold, some thirtyfold.

These are the true saints, the true Christians; "that heareth the word, and understandeth it; which also beareth fruit, and bringeth forth, some an hundredfold, some sixty, some thirty."

I am obsessed with being good ground for the precious seed of the Word of God. I am determined to pay close attention to it, to nurture it, to water it, and give the maximum heed to what it says. I believe it is the ONLY way to be fruitful, and to have life everlasting.

- **They Cause the Truth to be Evil Spoken Of** (2 Peter 2:1)

> "But there were **false prophets** also among the people,
> even as there shall be **false teachers** among you,
> who privily shall **bring in damnable heresies**,
> …and bring upon themselves swift destruction.

Peter said that the **false teachers** of the last days would be the equivalent of the **false prophets** of ancient times.

One of the biggest reasons why I had finally stopped going to Church years earlier was because I had become so disillusioned by the flood of false teachings that had pervaded the Church, and the near impossibility of standing up for Truth without being run over like a freight train by the majority of Christians who did not want to hear it or live it.

I had seen Catholicism strong-arming its way into Evangelicalism and Fundamentalism. Yes, Catholicism, with its Mariology, idolatry, false communion (transubstantiation), indulgences, confessionals, purgatory, prayers for the dead, false papal "apostolic succession," mass, rosary, infant baptism, apparitions, Bible censorship, catechism heresies, Inquisitions, Crusades, and so much more. With a following of over one billion deluded souls, Catholicism was far and away the largest perpetrator of false and abominable teachings put forth in the name of Jesus Christ.

There were obvious cults. The Mormons, Seventh-Day Adventists, Jehovah's Witnesses, Christian Scientists, Church of Christ, "Moonies," and others.

But the worst offenders were those who were closest to the real Truth. Of all the Christian religions, Evangelicals were those who purportedly believed in the doctrine of the New Birth - in being "born again."

I watched Evangelicalism going to the dogs.

As "Gospel Radio" and "Christian Television" proliferated, so did the opportunists and shysters.

> "And **many shall follow their pernicious ways;
> by reason of whom the way of truth shall be evil spoken of.**"

In the late years of his ministry, A.A. Allen had resorted to trickery in his crusades. People "miraculously" got up out of wheelchairs that had been furnished by the crusade staff. Peter Popoff was found to use earpieces and two-way radios with his wife who told him names and personal information about people he was "discerning by the Spirit." (I had been in one of Popoff's meetings, and it was pathetic.) W.V. Grant did similar tricks, using handwritten notes passed discreetly to him by his wife.

There were the carnival-barker preachers who hawked bottles of "holy water from the Jordan River," "holy anointing oil from the Garden of

Gethsemane," blessed coins, blessed bracelets, and blessed concoctions that defied the imagination.

Because of the high profiles of these preachers, the whole world saw and heard about all their shenanigans.

Dixie and I were still engaged to be married when "Marjoe" came on TV one night. It was a documentary-style story of Marjoe Gartner, a self-styled "Pentecostal" preacher. It was produced by Marjoe himself to expose his own phony "ministry," and was meant to discredit Christianity and Pentecostalism at large. It was the most upsetting thing I had ever seen.

Marjoe was named by his charlatan parents after "Mary" and "Joseph." They deviously groomed him to be a child preacher, and worked methodically to make him a child star in tent revivals all over the West Coast. By his own admission, he helped his dishonest parents raise over three million dollars in phony revival meetings before they divorced, and Marjoe went out on his own.

I watched in sickening horror as film crews followed him from revival to revival, filming his wild preaching antics, his hypnotic influence on unsuspecting crowds, his phenomenal money-raising tricks, and alas, his lewd, drunken and immoral lifestyle in local hotels and clubs, even while the revivals were still in progress.

I could not sleep that night, after I saw that documentary. I could not believe that anyone could be so diabolical. I could not understand why Almighty God did not instantly strike dead people like that. The movie "Marjoe" won the 1972 Academy Award for Best Documentary, but it left a bleeding scar on the face of Pentecostalism.

"And **many shall follow their pernicious ways;
by reason of whom the way of truth shall be evil spoken of.**"

"Elmer Gantry" was a similar film produced in 1960 that was based on a 1927 book that loosely told the story of evangelist Aimee Semple McPherson, founder of the Church of the Foursquare Gospel, and the famous 5,000-seat Angeles Temple in L.A.. That movie shined a spotlight on her duplicity and immorality in the ministry.

And many others brought shame and embarrassment to the name of Jesus.

- **Evil Men and Seducers Shall Wax Worse and Worse, Deceiving and Being Deceived** (2 Timothy 3:13)

Worse and worse? God, help us! In 1982, the dramatic declines in Christianity, and especially Pentecostalism, that Dixie and I had seen and experienced were enough to make unbelievers out of anybody. But that was only the beginning. The Bible said they would get "worse and worse."

- **Grievous Wolves Will Come In, Not Sparing the Flock**

> Jesus said, "**Beware of false prophets**,
> which come to you in **sheep's clothing**,
> but inwardly they are **ravening wolves**.
>
> ...Not every one that saith unto me, Lord, Lord,
> shall enter into the kingdom of heaven;
> but he that doeth the will of my Father which is in heaven.
> Many will say to me in that day,
> Lord, Lord, have we not prophesied in thy name?
> and in thy name have cast out devils?
> and in thy name done many wonderful works?
> And then will I profess unto them,
> **I never knew you: depart from me, ye that work iniquity**,"
> Matthew 7:15-23.
>
> Paul said, "For I know this, that after my departing
> shall **grievous wolves enter in among you, not sparing the flock**.
> Also of your own selves shall men arise,
> **speaking perverse things, to draw away disciples after them**,"
> Acts 20:29-30.

According to Jesus' own words, these WOLVES are men who have prophesied in His name, cast out devils, and done many wonderful works.

Paul added, "of YOUR OWN SELVES shall men arise." So, according to both Jesus and Paul, the WOLVES are men who work freely among us.

They look like us, talk like us, and act like us. They do the same works that the true Church is supposed to do. But they are frauds. Not merely frauds, but DEVOURING frauds. These men would utterly destroy the Church if left unopposed.

But Jesus warned that when these men and women come to the Judgment, He will declare,

> **"I NEVER KNEW YOU!**
> **DEPART FROM ME, YE THAT WORK INIQUITY,"**
> **Matthew 7:23.**

So, how in the world can we know who is a WOLF and who is a true man of God?

The WOLVES speak perverse things (Acts 20:30). That is very nearly the ONLY CLUE! And, they do so "to draw away disciples after them."

These WOLVES, these false preachers, have two notable trademarks. They preach perverse doctrines, and they draw men away from TRUE DOCTRINE unto themselves! They work feverishly to build their own following on their niche doctrines.

Now there are a lot of doctrines in the Bible, and most preachers never even touch on most of them. Sometimes, we do not even know how strange a man's beliefs are until we have gone a long way with him.

BUT – there is one thing that is imperative. We MUST BE DISCERNING. God requires that of us.

> "And we beseech you, brethren,
> **to know them which labour among you**,
> and are over you in the Lord,"
> 1 Thessalonians 5:12.

That admonition is not talking about **knowing** what football team they favor, or whether they hunt or fish or golf. That is talking about **knowing** what this man BELIEVES and PREACHES. Is it Biblical? Is it pure, unadulterated Truth?

I have one MAJOR RULE that quickly eliminates a vast number of preachers that I will not follow. "Have you received the Holy Ghost since you believed?"(Acts 19:2). If they have not been baptized in the Holy Ghost, and speak in other tongues, then they are not qualified to minister in the Church (Acts 6:3).

That rule quickly eliminates a multitude of preachers that I must not follow. There is not one writer, one Apostle, one Prophet, one Pastor, one Teacher, or one Evangelist in the New Testament who did not have the Holy Ghost and speak in tongues. Not one Church. Not one saint. The entire Early Church was full of the Holy Ghost and spoke in tongues.

KNOW THEM.

There are other qualifications that a man of God must fulfill.

> Blameless. Steward of God. Not self-willed. Not soon angry.
> Not given to wine. No striker. Not given to filthy lucre.
> A lover of hospitality. A lover of good men.
> Sober. Just. Holy. Temperate.
> Holding fast the faithful word as he hath been taught,
> that he may be able by sound doctrine
> both to exhort and to convince the gainsayers.
>
> For there are many unruly and vain talkers and deceivers,
> ...Whose mouths must be stopped, who subvert whole houses,
> teaching things which they ought not, for filthy lucre's sake.
> (From Titus 1:7-11)

Not given to wine.

I will not follow any man who drinks.

Sober.

I will not follow a man who is frivolous and comedic about holy things.

Holy.

A man of God must take this business of separation from the world seriously.

Sound doctrine.

This one requires something of ME. I must **know** the Word of God well enough to recognize when a preacher does not preach sound doctrine. If you do not personally know the Bible well, and do not have a mature understanding of fundamental Bible doctrines, then you cannot know for sure if the preacher you are following is a true man of God. You will also be dreadfully vulnerable to sneaky deceptions.

One thing is certain, however. When you finally realize that a preacher is preaching things that are contrary to the Bible, you HAVE to have the guts to admit to yourself that, "**This man is a wolf.** This man is speaking perverse things. This man is NOT teaching what God wants me to know. I must find a true man of God, and NOT follow this man astray."

Teaching things which they ought not, for filthy lucre's sake.

Of course, "filthy lucre" is talking about money. And here is where MOST MODERN WOLVES are exposed. They teach things they ought not for MONEY!!

As I see it, there are only two PREDOMINANT reasons why anybody is in the ministry.

1. To preach the Truth of God and do the will of God, or,

2. To make money and/or a name for themselves.

There are very few things that can motivate a ministry if it is not for a genuinely Godly purpose – except money. The love of money is the root of all evil. And the love of money is the root of most false ministries.

> "**They that will be rich** fall into temptation and a snare,
> and into many foolish and hurtful lusts,
> which drown men in destruction and perdition.
> For **the love of money is the root of all evil**:
> which while some coveted after, they have erred from the faith,
> and pierced themselves through with many sorrows.
> But thou, **O man of God, flee these things**;
> and follow after righteousness, godliness, faith, love, patience, meekness,"
> 1 Timothy 6:9-11.

Oral Roberts may well be the father of the modern "Prosperity Theology." His roots had been in the Pentecostal Holiness Church, but when his giant miracle tent crusades began to decline, Roberts began to suffer financial strains. The United Methodist Church, which had plenty of money but very little spiritual life, welcomed him to associate with them. Their financial support helped sustain him for a while.

Then Roberts took a perfectly scriptural concept (combining "faith as a grain of mustard seed," [Matthew 17:20] with "give and it shall be given unto you,"[Luke 6:38]), and coined the phrase "seeding a miracle." That teaching mushroomed into a turbo-powered money-making machine.

His "Seed Faith" doctrine was articulated in his 1977 book, "The Miracle of Seed Faith," and every month in his "Abundant Life" magazine and television broadcasts. Homogenizing seed-faith with "abundant life" teachings, Roberts lifted countless millions of dollars from his vast audience for TV, colleges, a hospital - and the lifestyle of a king.

As more and more preachers caught on to Robert's success, they copied his message and his methods. Before we could say, "who will give $100?" we had a tsunami of radio and TV preachers begging us to "plant a seed into this ministry."

Today, the prosperity message has become the stock-in-trade of just about every TV preacher and mega-Church pastor. "Plant a thousand-dollar seed in this ministry today!"they say. Pay for their palatial estates, their jets, and their lavish lifestyles.

Meanwhile, the REAL Gospel of Christ is long-forgotten in those venues.

> "And **through covetousness** shall they **with feigned words make merchandise of you**: whose **judgment** now of a long time lingereth not, and their **damnation** slumbereth not.
> ...God spared not the angels that sinned, but cast them down to **hell**, and delivered them into **chains of darkness**, to be reserved unto judgment; [these] shall **utterly perish in their corruption**,"
> 2 Peter 2:1-4,12.

I learned, at the age of 20, what it was like to catch the "red-eye," (a late night flight) carrying a briefcase containing over $10,000 in cash that had been donated in a single service that night. I also knew what it was like to produce a single fundraising letter that pulled in over $100,000 in contributions from one direct mailing.

And I knew that there were many other people in the ministry who could do the very same thing. But I also knew that it had virtually nothing to do with whether or not GOD was behind it. Charlatans are a dime a dozen.

The SUCCESS of a ministry RARELY proves its legitimacy. There are much more vital measures, more weighty measures that must be applied than merely the amount of money or the size of the crowds.

Think of it. Mormons are successful. They have a huge, world-wide following. Catholics? There are one billion of them. Muslims? 1.5 billion. Does that prove that they are Biblically correct? There are more than one billion NON-religious people on this planet, and almost a billion Hindus. Does that prove that atheism or Hinduism should be believed?

Why should we apply the same misleading metrics to our own ministry?

Anybody can put on a concert, a crusade, or a seminar. Anybody can rent an auditorium. Anybody can buy television time. Anybody can run newspaper ads and radio spots. Anybody can build a crowd if they have enough money and skills.

But that says NOTHING about the legitimacy of a ministry.

NOTHING – I said "NOTHING" – legitimizes a Church, a Preacher, or a Christian except the infallible Word of God, the Bible.

Christianity is marred by a disfiguring pox of carnality, worldliness, false prophets and false doctrines. You would think that there would be a screaming OUTCRY among God-fearing people to DUMP everything that is unholy and phony in Christianity, and call for a revival of the preaching of the pure, unadulterated Word of God; a revival of Truth, righteousness, and holiness!

Ask yourself…

How did phony Gospel musicians and wannabe rock stars come to have so much influence and take up so much time and budget in our Churches?

How did secular, corporate trainers, psychologists, success-motivation gurus and the like manage to invade our pulpits?

How did Hollywood, Branson, Las Vegas, Broadway and Nashville infiltrate our platforms and projection screens with their show business, entertainment and comedy routines?

How did the Church of the living God turn into a wealth-building and human-potential movement?

How did once-great preachers turn into pathetic, flesh-pleasing, give-them-what-they-want circus masters?

Why do preachers and Churches emulate Televangelists and celebrities?

Truth has fallen in the aisles of our Churches. Pulpits have vanished. Prayer meetings are nearly extinct.

The Bible has been replaced with "The Message" and a dozen other pseudo-Bibles that nobody recognizes as the authoritative Word of God anymore. Nobody can quote them. Nobody is afraid of what they say.

There are no altars in our Churches. Nobody knows what heart-felt conviction for sin is, or what mournful repentance looks or sounds like.

An entire generation of young people knows nothing whatsoever about the Church or its history. Their parents left the Church years ago, and the children have no clue as to WHO or WHAT Jesus is.

To the outside world, there is nothing holy, sacred or authentic about Christianity. It is almost universally perceived as commercialized, entertaining, and self-serving. More and more people now view Christianity as a complete fraud.

And Christianity has no one to blame but themselves. Eve tried to blame the serpent. Adam tried to blame Eve. But they were all three guilty.

Everything that is wrong with Christianity is our own fault, and we are the only ones who can fix it.

If we continue to tolerate and underwrite false doctrines, false prophets, deceptions, charlatans, and their kind, we make ourselves accomplices in their abominations, and we will have no one to blame for our plight but ourselves on Judgment Day.

I knew that I did not want to run with that crowd any more. That was one train I did not want to ride. It was a Hell-bound train.

But WHAT WERE MY OPTIONS?

I did not know. But on Wednesday nights, I just kept on preaching whatever I had uncovered that week in my on-going prayer and Bible studies.

I was still looking for answers.

Chapter 17

Beware the Leavening of Hypocrisy

For four months, I had pressed tenaciously through almost the entire Bible, making volumes of notes as I went. I was absolutely determined to get a fresh, thorough, and trustworthy understanding of what true Bible religion was all about. Those were profoundly defining moments for me, so I had to get it right this time. The rest of my life was at stake.

One thing, however, troubled me greatly.

As I studied carefully through the New Testament, intimately internalizing all their teachings, and contemplating the recorded experiences of the original saints and Apostles…

I could not convince myself that the modern Church that I had known was that kind of Church. The peg was SQUARE. The hole was ROUND.

It was like looking at a photo on a drivers license, and realizing that the person standing in front of me was not the same person in that photo. Something was (shall I say it?) criminally wrong.

One day, in my Bible studies, a verse I read jumped out at me.

Jesus said, "**Beware ye of the leaven of the Pharisees which is hypocrisy,**" Luke 12:1.

HYPOCRISY!!

I looked up the definition. Jesus used a Greek word, "hupokrisis." Strong's Concordance said it meant, "acting under a **feigned** part, **deceit**." The Greek word derived from its root, "hupokrinomai," which meant "to speak or act on a **false** part, to **feign**, **pretend**." So, what is a hypocrite?

A hypocrite is someone who is not who he represents himself to be.

I can put on a Santa Claus suit, but that does not make me Santa Claus. I can put on a military uniform, but that does not make me a soldier. I can preach a sermon, but that does not make me a man of God.

I can tell all my friends that I am a Christian, but if I am not living the way God's Word says to live, I am a hypocrite - a "Pharisee."

But most disturbing to me was that Christianity-at-large was suspect. Everywhere I looked, there were fakers. Phonies. Get-rich-quick types. Ego maniacs. Charlatans. Showmen. Starry-eyed celebrity wannabes. And much, much worse. There were crooks and perverts, too.

Hypocrites were the primary adversaries of Truth in Jesus' day. We should not be surprised that hypocrites are the primary adversaries of Truth in modern times!

The Pharisees in Jesus' time were known in public by their religious show. They wore specially-made garments with large decorative borders on their hemlines that exaggerated their priestly status. They wore "phylacteries," little custom-made boxes that were strapped to their wrists and foreheads, in which hand-written Bible verses were kept.

Those practices had originated in the ancient oral traditions, and were eventually written into the Talmud, the book of oral tradition. Phylacteries were not specifically prescribed in the Torah - the Bible itself - so the very things for which they were known the most were not even Biblical! They were extra-biblical teachings and habits. (Neither Jesus nor His disciples made use of any of those things.)

Their pompous look was comparable to what we now see on the Pope, Archbishops and Cardinals of the Roman Catholic Church. They wear expensive, lavish, custom-made wardrobes and symbolic jewelry that make them look like they are holy or sacred. But behind those impressive garments are men whose doctrines are abominable heresies; sending up a profane stench into the nostrils of God.

Many modern Gospel preachers, singers and musicians were beginning to emulate their silly pageantry, wearing expensive, lavish, custom-made robes, clerical vestments, or one-of-a-kind creations that look more like the stage-show outfits of Elvis Presley, Michael Jackson or another rock star.

Obviously, somebody thinks that ostentatious apparel projects an image of great religious value, but in hard, cold fact, they do not. Lavish, showy clothes only appeal to the lust of the eye, feed ego, pride and self-righteousness, and are on the opposite end of the spectrum from true Biblical holiness. Pink hair? Blue and purple eye-lids? $5,000 custom-made suits? Christians and ministers who wear such garments are just as hypocritical as the ancient Pharisees. They are their modern counterpart.

But their apparel was not the Pharisees' biggest problem. That was only the tip of the iceberg.

The Pharisees worked hard at maintaining celebrity status among the people. They made attention-getting, pretentious prayers in public.

They were in religious show business. They were national celebrities.

> **"They loved the praise of men** more than the praise of God,"
> John 12:43.

The Pharisees would have LOVED Christian television. Nothing in the history of the world has done more to feed the lust for the praise of men than Christian Television. The world had scarcely contemplated the possibility of such Christian celebrity, or Christian "stardom" before Christian TV came along.

The power of television is so enormous that one single appearance on a nationwide or worldwide program can instantly catapult a once-unknown preacher, singer or musician into extraordinary name-recognition, open countless doors of opportunity, and in time, create unimaginable wealth.

Unfortunately, there are no New Testament precedents for that kind of success and wealth among true ministers of the Gospel. Luxurious, flesh-pleasing lifestyles such as those people enjoy grossly contradict everything that Jesus and the Apostles practiced and taught concerning self-denial and the crucified life.

> "He that hath two coats, let him impart to him that hath none;
> and he that hath meat, let him do likewise,"
> Luke 3:11.

> "Whosoever will be chief among you, let him be your servant:
> Even as the Son of man came not to be ministered unto,
> but to minister, and to give his life a ransom for many,"
> Matthew 20:27-28.

> "A rich man shall hardly enter into the kingdom of heaven.
> ...It is easier for a camel to go through the eye of a needle,
> than for a rich man to enter into the kingdom of God,"
> Matthew 19:23-24.

In too many cases, such "success" only serves to ignite vanity, pride, ego, power-mongering and more. It also subsequently exposes or magnifies personal weaknesses and flaws that should have been in subjection to Christ. The majority of high-profile Christian television celebrities now live lifestyles of the rich and famous. They live in palaces, ride in limousines, and travel in their privately-owned jets and motor coaches. (That is no longer the exception, but the rule.)

In the end, celebrity Christianity is a repugnant perversion of true Christianity that reinforces and galvanizes the secular public's perception that all Christians are phony. **They cause the Truth to be evil spoken of**.

Hypocrisy is LEAVENING.

Jesus said that the Pharisees were LEAVENED by HYPOCRISY.

> **"Beware ye of the leaven of the Pharisees which is hypocrisy,"**
> Luke 12:1.

Leavening is the fermenting agent (yeast) that is placed in bread dough. Yeast is added to **agitate, excite,** and **exhilarate** the dough. It foments it, and makes it swell. That is what carnal, worldly activities do in a Church. They foment it, and make it swell, without the anointed Spirit and Truth.

Any time a **religion is excited and exhilarated** by anything other than God, the Bible, and unadulterated TRUTH, that is evil leavening.

That is what hypocrisy does to people. **Hypocrisy excites, agitates, and exhilarates people.** When they SHOULD be excited by Truth, Righteousness and Holiness, they are instead exhilarated by lights, cameras, sound stages, recording projects, cheering crowds, luxurious lifestyles, the praise of men, celebrity status, sports, ad nauseum.

The Pharisees loved their high visibility in the community. But if they had been **tested for the Biblical accuracy** of what they believed, practiced, and taught, **they would have made FAILING grades**.

They did not FOLLOW the Bible correctly, but that did not slow them down. The things they were most widely known for were not even in the Bible. They were religious shams. John the Baptist and Jesus Christ shined a bright light on their hypocrisies.

Such an outward pretense of religiosity, when the rest of a person's life is carnal, worldly and sensual, was a fraud, a sham, a shill. Hypocrisy!

God hates a religious performance, even enormously popular preaching, teaching, or musical performance, when the personal lives of those who minister are glaring contradictions of New Testament Christianity. Instead of self-sacrificing, devil-hating, Godly-minded people that He saved our sinful, selfish souls to become, Christians have by-and-large become self-indulgent gluttons for worldly, sinful entertainment and pleasures.

The Pharisees loved their high-profile leadership roles. That was their life. They were not in love with God, but with their esteemed positions. As such, they were worthless to God and His Kingdom.

If the Pharisees had truly loved God and the Bible, and the prophecies of the Bible, they should have recognized that their long-prophesied Savior and Messiah was standing right there in front of them. But they did NOT recognize Him. Their hearts were evil.

Consequently, the Pharisees played a relentless, antagonistic, adversarial role in the life and ministry of Jesus Christ. Those hypocrites were Jesus' worst nightmare. His entire adult life and ministry was tormented again and again by their cold-blooded trouble-making.

They hated Him! He had crashed their party. He was on "their" turf, "their" stage. They knew that their power and popularity was doomed if He stayed around very long, because Jesus was REAL and powerful; and they were phony. Their hatred and vitriol boiled higher and higher until, at last, they brought Him to trial, and rioted until the Romans killed Him. Jesus ultimately died in the hostile crossfire between THEIR hypocritical show-biz religion and HIS pure and holy Bible-based religion.

Jesus knew from the start what He was dealing with. When He was only 12-years-old, He had gone into the Temple alone. After three days, His parents found Jesus…

> "...sitting in the midst of the doctors,
> both hearing them, and asking them questions.
> And all that heard him were astonished at
> his understanding and answers,"
> Luke 2:46-47.

Jesus' understanding of the sacred scriptures at 12 years old already exceeded that of the Doctors of Religion. He obviously interacted with them at a high level of intelligence and spiritual perception. At 12, He was smarter and more discerning than they were.

But His first recorded encounters with the Pharisees in His adult life occurred at His baptism by John the Baptist at the Jordan River.

Earlier that day, John had called the Pharisees and Sadducees **VIPERS** (poisonous creatures). He charged them to bring forth fruit meet for repentance - indicting them for not being genuinely repentant.

John warned them not to claim legitimacy merely because they were sons of Abraham. He gave them a bold warning that God would chop down every tree that did not bear fruit unto Him. He clearly insinuated that the Pharisees were NOT bringing forth righteous fruit unto God.

In fact, they did not even KNOW God! John told the Pharisees,

> "there standeth **one among you, whom ye know not**;
> He it is, who coming after me is preferred before me,
> whose shoe's latchet I am not worthy to unloose,"
> John 1:26-27.

"One whom ye know not..."

The Pharisees, like professional actors, played the role of the spiritual leaders of Israel. But Jesus saw them as hypocrites, and said, **"They be blind leaders of the blind**. And if the blind lead the blind, both shall fall into the ditch," Matthew 15:14.

They were spiritually blind.

The Pharisees did not realize that the long-prophesied Messiah was standing in their face. They did not know that their God was embodied IN this man. Isaiah's prophesied Emmanuel, "God with us," had come to save them, but they wanted to kill Him. That is how blind they were.

But John knew who Jesus was.

Amazingly, John the Baptist clearly understood and declared who Jesus was. "Behold **the Lamb of God, which taketh away the sin of the world**," John 1:29.

From the very beginning, many other Galileans had also acknowledged that Jesus was the Messiah.

Andrew reported to Simon his brother, "**We have found the Messias, ...the Christ**," John 1:41.

Philip told Nathanael, "**We have found Him of whom Moses in the law, and the prophets, did write**, Jesus of Nazareth, the son of Joseph," John 1:45.

Within moments after meeting Jesus, Nathaniel told Jesus, "**Thou art the Son of God; thou art the King of Israel**," John 1:49.

In Samaria, the woman at the well confessed that she knew that Messiah (Christ) was coming. Jesus said, "I that speak unto thee am He." She believed Him!

Immediately, she went into the village and told everyone. After coming to meet Him, many of the Samaritans confessed that day, "**This is indeed Christ, the Savior of the world**," John 4:42.

Two days later, in Cana, many Galileans received Him, and a certain nobleman from Capernaum believed on Him with his whole household.

Later, Peter declared, "**Thou art the Christ, the Son of the living God.**"

At the last, it was Thomas who expressed the most profound claim, when he thrust his hands in Jesus' side and declared, "**My LORD, and my GOD!**"

Of course, there were many others who also knew who Jesus was.

Nevertheless, the false religious crowd either could not or would not recognize Jesus' true identity.

The Pharisees accused Jesus of casting out devils by Beelzebub, "**the prince of devils**," (Matthew 9:34; 12:24), when in fact, Jesus was the incarnation of the invisible God.

Jesus gave them the most fearful warning for likening Him to Beelzebub. He warned that they were dangerously close to committing BLASPHEMY!

> "All manner of sin and blasphemy shall be forgiven unto men: but the **blasphemy against the Holy Ghost** shall not be forgiven unto men," Matthew 12:31.

When Jesus returned to Jerusalem, He healed the lame man at the Pool of Bethesda. Still, the Jews persecuted Jesus, "and **sought to slay Him** because He had done these things on the Sabbath Day," John 5:16.

They would have killed God in flesh!

Jesus explained to them that the Father had sent Him, and that "**all men should honour the Son**. …He that honoureth not the Son, honoureth not the Father which hath sent Him," John 5:23.

> "…the Father himself …hath borne witness of me.
> Ye have neither heard his voice at any time, nor seen his shape.
> And **ye have not his word abiding in you**:
> for whom he hath sent, him ye believe not.
> Search the scriptures; for in them ye think ye have eternal life:
> and they are they which testify of me.
> And **ye will not come to me**, that ye might have life.
> …I know you, that **ye have not the love of God in you**.
> …How can ye believe, which **receive honour one of another**,
> and seek not the honour that cometh from God only?
> Do not think that I will accuse you to the Father:
> there is one that accuseth you, even Moses, in whom ye trust.
> For had ye believed Moses, ye would have believed me:
> for he wrote of me. But if **ye believe not his writings**,
> how shall ye believe my words?"
> John 5:36-47.

WOW! Jesus hammered them! The Father was Jesus' prime witness, and Jesus only did miracles because **He was the embodiment of their invisible God**. Yet they had no clue! NO CLUE.

- **Jesus told them they had never heard Him or seen Him.**
- **"Ye have not His word abiding in you."**
- They thought they had eternal life in the Old Testament scriptures, but the OT testified of Christ.
- **"Ye have not the love of God in you."**
- "Had ye believed Moses, ye would have believed me: for **he wrote of me**." They did not even believe Moses!

In these accusations, Jesus made felony indictments against the false religionists.

1. **They did not know God.**
2. **They did not know the Word.**
3. **They did not have the love of God in them.**
4. They did not even believe Moses and the Law!

They HATED Jesus. Jesus was an alien intruder into their selfish, carnal, falsely-programmed minds.

Now, if you had only seen and known the Pharisees by their presence in the community, you may not have perceived all the things that Jesus perceived about them.

They were the dominant religious teachers, leaders, and officials of their time.

Today, we have multitudes of teachers, leaders and officials in false Churches and false movements who dominate the religious scene.

1. **They did not know God.**

Today, we have many who love their high profile Christian roles when they are performing at events. But back-stage, and on their touring buses, and in their palatial homes, and in their jet-set lifestyles, they bear almost no resemblance whatsoever to New Testament Christians. They are worldly, carnal, sensual, and do not obey or live by Bible rules.

2. **They did not know the Word.**

In far too many cases, they have never thoroughly studied the Bible. They have no mastery of the great body of Biblical teachings. They have a few pet teachings (i.e., "prosperity," human potential, feminist empowerment, "pursue your dreams," etc.) that they rarely stray from. Their knowledge of God's Word is shallow, and tainted by false teachings borrowed from other phony teachers. They follow the latest popularity trends and not the hard-core Word of God.

3. **They did not have the love of God in them.**

These phony preachers preach what they practice. They practice wealth-building, so they preach wealth-building. They practice pursuing their man-made dreams, so they preach pursuing your dreams. They practice personal kingdom-building, so they preach personal kingdom-building. They PREACH WHAT THEY LOVE. Success. Wealth. Human potential. But NOT the Kingdom of God and His righteousness.

Hypocrisy was their leavening.

Hypocrisy was their lock, stock and barrel. Hypocrisy was their principle commodity. Hypocrisy was their life, their joy, their love. They were heartless religious play-actors.

NOW – consider the meaning of the doctrine of UNLEAVENED bread.

In the Old Testament, the children of Israel were commanded to eat **unleavened bread** in their Sabbath feasts. At the Last Supper, Jesus broke **unleavened bread**, and explained, "**this is my body**, which is broken for you." Jesus' body was **unleavened**. He was **sinless**. He was the **pure, unleavened** Word of God. **No carnality. No worldliness. No sin. No unclean spirits.**

Anything **carnal, worldly, or demonic** would have defiled – leavened - Jesus Christ. Adultery would have leavened Jesus. Love for money would have leavened Jesus. Greed would have. Dishonesty would have. Hatred.

But worst of all, HYPOCRISY, would have utterly spoiled Jesus. Let me remind you again of the meaning of hypocrisy:

A hypocrite is someone who is not who he represents himself to be.

A true, New Testament Christian is, at the very minimum:

1. Truly repentant, both by confession and by a changed life.
2. Born of the Water and of the Spirit.
3. Holy, Consecrated, Sanctified, Peculiar
4. A faithful follower of all the teachings of Jesus and the Apostles.

When Preachers or laymen are carnal, worldly, sensual, or evil, their hearts are not right with God. They instinctively make people **drunk** on the same deceptions they are drunk on so the people will be devoid of the Truth, Righteousness and Holiness that would indict their phony ministries.

If **hypocrisy** leavens the lump, so do **hypocrites**!

Hypocrites LEAVEN the Church.
Hypocrites SPOIL the Church.
Hypocrites RUIN the Church.

They LEAVEN the people – agitate them – inebriate them – with every kind of intoxicating lie and sham so that the people will NOT be able to convict them of their sins. **They make other people drunk** on carnal, worldly, sensual things. Sports. Music. Drama. Entertainment. Comedy. Secular stimulants of every kind.

They behave like King David did after he committed adultery with Bathsheba. When David discovered that Bathsheba was pregnant with his illegitimate child, he devised a scheme to cover his sins. He called for Bathsheba's husband, Uriah, to be brought in from the battlefield where he had been at war.

David had been drunk on lust. He tried to make Uriah drunk on liquor.

Animal control personnel routinely use a similar tactic to capture wild animals. They shoot **tranquilizer darts** into their prey to sedate them. Once the animal is sedated, they are easily captured.

Satan knows that trick. He will inebriate or sedate any unsuspecting Christian with ANYTHING that will dull their senses to the will of God.

David planned to get Uriah drunk, then send him to spend the night with his wife, Bathsheba, so that her pregnancy would appear to be Uriah's.

David, by LEAVENING, tried to disable and disarm the one righteous man who could expose his sins. Uriah could have brought down David's kingdom if he had wanted to. But David could not risk that, so he attempted to manipulate him into being an accomplice.

In the Apostle Paul's day, the sin of fornication was leavening the Church.

Paul had to rebuke the Corinthian Church, because a man in their congregation was committing the sin of fornication – namely incest with his father's wife. Paul rebuked the whole Church because they did not mourn that grievous situation and put that man out of the congregation.

Satan loves nothing better than to see the Church drunk on anything the world has to offer. ANYTHING, that is - but God.

Satan will make you or me drunk on ANYTHING that amuses us. Sports. Movies. Music. Television. Internet. Wealth. Drugs. Sex. ANYTHING. That is why we must forever be on our guard. We must be watchful, and pray that God will not allow us to be taken captive by Satan at his will.

> "And that they may **recover themselves out of the snare of the devil**, who are taken captive by him at his will,"
> 2 Timothy 2:26.

It is CRITICAL that you realize that **Satan is NOT obliged to give you any warning** as to when or where he plans to trap you. Satan's very specialty is taking men UNAWARES. Satan will happily broad-side you. If he has to, he will body-slam you into a drunken stupor.

Never doubt that Satan is a vicious, conniving adversary. If God won't let him kill you, he will resort to anything else to cripple or disable you. Be diligent to know what you are up against.

> "And beside this, **giving all diligence,**
> add to your faith virtue;
> and to virtue **knowledge**,"
> 2 Peter 1:5

Chapter 18

Purge Out The Old Leaven

Paul told the Corinthians, in effect, that tolerating one gross sin such as fornication would spoil the entire Church. He said it must be PUT AWAY.

> "Know ye not that **a little leaven leaveneth the whole lump? Purge out therefore the old leaven**, that ye may be a new lump, ...let us keep the feast, not with old leaven, ...but with the **unleavened bread of sincerity and truth**.
>
> ...I have written unto you not to keep company, if any man that is called a brother be a fornicator, or covetous, or an idolater, or a railer, or a drunkard, or an extortioner; **with such an one no not to eat.**
> ...Therefore **put away** from among yourselves **that wicked person,"**
> 1 Corinthians 5:6-13.

If fornication "leavens the whole lump," or spoils the whole Church, just imagine how spoiled the modern Church is, with its countless perversions!

There is much leavening in the modern Church.

During my High School years, a new genre of music was born, called "Christian Rock." A musician by the name of Larry Norman wrote a song about the rapture and Second Coming of Jesus, called, "I Wish We'd All Been Ready." It was the featured song in an enormously popular movie about the rapture, called, "A Thief In The Night." Over 300 million people saw that movie.

But Larry Norman himself was a highly controversial figure. A young rock star with no real Church background, he became one of the very first self-styled, Christian hippies. He had very long hair, lived in Hollywood, and wrote counter-culture type songs – some "Christian," and some about social issues. He was considered the father of Christian Rock music. He was denounced by Jerry Falwell, Bob Larson, Jimmy Swaggart and many other mainstream Christian leaders in those days, and his freaked-out looking and sounding albums were largely rejected by Christian bookstores and radio stations for years because of their non-conformity to long-held Christian teachings.

Significantly, Norman was a close personal friend of a guy named Lonnie Frisbee. Frisbee was a long-haired, flipped-out hippie, and a heavy LSD user from the San Francisco area. He was also a practicing homosexual. Frisbee was known to hold communal Bible studies while tripping on LSD. He called his followers "Jesus Freaks," and "Jesus People."

Frisbee was extremely Charismatic, utilized the "gifts of the Spirit," performed healings and miracles, and was generally a sensation among young people everywhere he went. His self-styled "Pentecostal" methods were characterized by massive numbers of people speaking in tongues and "falling out" under the power. Frisbee called his methods "power evangelism."

Lonnie Frisbee and Larry Norman worked together in many of the first "Jesus People" events in California, which quickly proliferated into hundreds of "Jesus communes" around the country. Frisbee's forte' was preaching all about "the love of Jesus." Hippies followed him and Norman en masse. Norman also mentored Randy Stonehill and Keith Green. All three headlined gigantic "Jesus Festivals" around the country, even around the world. Green eventually gravitated to the teachings of Leonard Ravenhill, David Wilkerson and Winkey Pratney. At the very last, Frisbee aligned himself with Derek Prince, Bob Mumford and the "Shepherding Movement."

But in the late 1960s and early 1970s, Christian Rock music was the hard-driving force behind the new "Jesus Movement." "Jesus Festivals" were held in various parts of the country, some of which were attended by as many as 150,000 youth, with Norman, Stonehill, Green, Barry McGuire, Second Chapter of Acts, and others on stage. (Dixie and I had attended Jesus '79 in Orlando, which was attended by about 35,000 youth.)

Frisbee also mentored charismatic Greg Laurie, who now has a global charismatic ministry. Frisbee was a primary influencer of both Chuck Smith, founder of the worldwide Calvary Chapel movement, and John Wimber, founder of the Vineyard Movement (now known as the "holy laughter" crowd, including Rodney Howard Browne and the "Toronto Blessing"). Frisbee was also embraced by Kathryn Kuhlman, who featured him on her CBS television specials. Kuhlman in turn, later profoundly influenced Benny Hinn and his ilk with her "falling out" methods.

The abominable leavening of sexual immorality.

Underneath the surface of these "Jesus People" ministries was pernicious sexual immorality, as well as many other ungodly lifestyles. Frisbee claimed to have quit his homosexual behavior after his lifestyle was exposed and his reputation was damaged, but it soon became apparent that he had only taken his behavior underground. He died at age 43, of AIDS. Norman was known by those around him as a "lothario,"(seducer). He got involved with a friend's wife, and was blamed for their divorce. He later married her.

Another product of the California Jesus movement was the Hawkins family singers. Their black Gospel music, as well as the Churches they pastored, were tainted by the widely-known fact that both Edwin and Walter Hawkins were gay, as were many in their congregations and professional circles. The enormously popular Gospel music legend James Cleveland was also gay. He died of AIDS at the age of 59. Many other homosexual scandals among Christian musicians have reproached and called into question the very spiritual integrity of the entire Christian music industry.

Overall, the last quarter of the 20th Century was a period of extreme apostasy for Christianity. The Baby Boom generation literally went wild, and took Christianity down with it. Denominational churches were going out of business by the hundreds as the new wave of non-denominationalism stripped Christianity of its structure, its hierarchy, its doctrines, its standards and its order. Christianity became a free-for-all. Anything of any size, any shape, any color, any sound could claim to be a Christian, and it was the worst taboo for anyone to dare stand in judgment of any of it.

The leavening of HYPOCRISY LEAVENED THE WHOLE LUMP!

A little leaven leavens the whole lump. Leavening causes fermentation, and fermentation causes intoxication. Just as fermented wine and all strong drink intoxicate the mind and body, **carnality, worldliness, sensuality and ALL SIN intoxicate the Church** in a very evil way.

A.A. Allen was one of the first to be exposed. In his early years, multitudes had been roused by his fiery Bible preaching, received the baptism of the Holy Ghost, and had countless miracles of healings. But Allen gave himself to liquor, and in the end, his entire ministry drowned in reproach. He died in a hotel room in San Francisco. The coroner's inquest blamed "acute alcoholism and fatty infiltration of liver."

Since those days, we cannot count all the ministries that have been tainted by drugs and illicit sex. In subsequent years, Jimmy Swaggart was ruined by multiple encounters with prostitutes, and Jim Bakker's ministry was taken down in part by both a homosexual scandal and an adulterous scandal.

God demands that His saints and His Church be **UNLEAVENED** – not intoxicated by things of the world or the old sinful nature. God does not want us to be stirred up or stimulated by the forbidden things of the flesh.

The WORLD gets drunk and gets high on the things of the world. But the Church must not. Old-time Pentecostals used to get drunk on the Holy Ghost.

The LIFE OF GOD, the Holy Ghost, is the only TRUE LEAVENING from Heaven. God wants us to be solely inspired by His Spirit, not by the world. The Holy Ghost is the life that God has given to enliven His people and His Church. ALL OTHER LEAVENING is sin.

On the Day of Pentecost, after the Holy Ghost fell on 120 believers, the crowds outside accused them of being drunk. Peter set the record straight.

> **"These are not drunken, as ye suppose**,
> seeing it is but the third hour of the day.
> But this is that which was spoken by the prophet Joel;
> And it shall come to pass in the last days, saith God,
> **I will pour out of my Spirit upon all flesh,"**
> Acts 2:15-17.

The Holy Ghost from Heaven is the TRUE LEAVENING, and the ONLY leavening that God allows.

PLEASE SEE THIS!

Jesus said, "**The Kingdom of Heaven is like leaven** which a woman took a put into three measures of meal until **the whole amount was leavened**," Matthew 13:33.

Put the HOLY GHOST in the lump. The Holy Ghost is the true leaven.

The real anointing that works in the Gospel of the Kingdom of Heaven will eventually leaven the whole world.

Jesus said it! This is the determined will of God – that His Spirit rule the entire world.

Make no mistake about it. The message of God's Spiritual Kingdom is not dead or dying. The Kingdom of God is still alive and well, and it will soon fill all the earth with the glory of God.

It DOES NOT MATTER how many IMPOSTERS come on the scene, they will NEVER negate or nullify the original Book of Acts Pentecostal experience.

But if you turn to a false leavening, you are going to be put out of business one of these days when the true Kingdom of God overthrows the kingdoms of this world.

BEWARE OF ALL OTHER LEAVENING, especially the leavening of the Pharisees, which is **hypocrisy**.

The Kingdom of Heaven is the most exciting thing in the universe.

But I am terrified of the **leavening of hypocrisy**. False leavenings cause us to find joy in perishing things. They cause us to glamorize and put value and importance on worthless things, while ignoring the great value of being a pure, sincere, Holy Ghost-filled believer in Jesus Christ.

We had better not get hooked on watered-down religion, cheap grace, easy believism, once-saved-always-saved, success-prosperity, human-potential, dream-your-own-dream, sports, entertainment, or anything else that does not belong in the house of God.

If we get drunk on the world's leavening, we are going to die of a rotten addiction. It **will** eventually destroy us. Heroine, crack cocaine, morphine, and hard liquor are harmless drugs compared to the leavening of **hypocrisy**.

If you pose as a Christian without actually being what a Christian is truly supposed to be and do, you are practicing hypocrisy.

When you come to Church with a mind full of the world's junk, TV, lust, etc. and play the role anyway - that is the leavening of hypocrisy!

If you take the world's show-business and entertainment to the platform, instead of pure, sanctified worship in Spirit and Truth, you are a hypocrite.

If you walk, talk and act like the world all week long, then step up on the platform on Sunday and pretend to be the spiritual leader and holy minister of God to that congregation, you are a hypocrite.

If you take the world's success-prosperity message (or sports, comedy, politics, fitness programs, or other cultural fads and fashions) to the pulpit, instead of the unadulterated Word of God, you are a hypocrite.

If you can fake it in Church once, you can fake it twice. You will have been leavened with the leaven of the Pharisees.

I don't want to be leavened by the flesh - by hypocrisy.

> "You serve me with your lips, but your hearts are far from me."

The Church I had pastored in Georgia had the #2 Softball team in the state. They were softball fanatics. They could call a ball game and have hundreds in attendance. It was literally the strength of that Church. But when I preached on the Baptism of the Holy Ghost, they got their feathers ruffled and wanted me to stop preaching on that subject. The day came when I resigned that Church because they literally did not want to hear the doctrine of the Baptism of the Holy Ghost. But they still wanted their softball team.

That is a perfect example of the leavening Jesus was talking about. They serve God with their lips, but their hearts are on baseball.

Much Gospel music and Christian music is also full of carnal leavening.

If there ever was an indictment about Christian music now, it is that **they love Him with their lips**, but their hearts are far from Him. It doesn't matter how pretty their song is, or how fine their band, or how big their orchestra, or if they have travelled every country in the world, or sung on every stage in America, or performed on every TV network, or raised millions of dollars for orphans or other humanitarian causes. If their hearts are far from **Him - from GOD and His Word -** I don't want to hear what their lips are saying.

Doctrinally, the Gospel music industry is "anything goes." Pentecostals and holiness people are regularly the butt of their stand-up comedy, and very few singers or musicians actually take the Baptism of the Holy Ghost seriously, let alone practice it or promote it in their concerts or "ministry."

Some of the best singers and musicians in the business are spiritually null and void. We should give them the boot. Stop buying their music. Stop watching their videos. Boycott them. No more putting up with junk in the Church. You cannot get the real thing until you kick OUT the wrong thing.

Beware the leavening of the Pharisees, which is hypocrisy! The body of Christ is being seduced by lips that have learned to sing a song while its heart is in love with someone other than God. We have seen some like Amy Grant and Kirk Franklin finally crossover from Christian to secular entertainment. Elvis, Whitney, and a thousand other secular stars have rendered their offering of enormously popular Gospel and Christian music. But it is the offering of Cain. It does not meet God's criteria, and God has no respect for it (Genesis 4:4-5). Neither should we. **Only a little leaven like that leavens the WHOLE LUMP!**

> "Therefore also now, saith the LORD,
> **turn ye even to me with all your heart**,
> and with fasting, and with weeping, and with mourning:
> And **rend your heart**, and not your garments,
> and turn unto the LORD your God: for he is gracious and merciful,
> slow to anger, and of great kindness, and repenteth him of the evil.
> Who knoweth if he will return and repent,
> and leave a blessing behind him,"
> Joel 2:12-14.

This is the CURE for HYPOCRISY. That is how to get rid of phony stuff.

REND YOUR HEART!

Tear your heart open. Be brutally honest with yourself about your thoughts. Weigh your actions. Judge your values. Own up to every wrong desire and every carnal, worldly habit.

God does not want, does not need, and will not use anything that is heartless, insincere, or made out of flesh.

> "They that worship him must worship him **in spirit and in truth**," John 4:24.

That would render "worship" from a double-minded person ineligible.

The further Dixie and I went with our daily prayer and Bible studies, the more we knew that we literally HAD to us great care and careful control over all our future associations. **We must not compromise** with unbiblical views OR with those who hold unbiblical views. We must not give place to the devil. We must not be careless with our souls.

I saw so very clearly that the Church of Jesus Christ has a somber responsibility to "PURGE OUT" the old leavening of carnality, sensuality, worldliness, and every sin.

Now the Devil's Advocate for purging the Church is the "once-saved, always-saved" crowd. They insist that God loves us more than we can imagine, and that His grace is taller than a mountain, and that He knows that we are just human, and forgives us anyway, and that there is nothing we can do to keep God from loving us. **But there are just too many scriptures that contradict that argument.**

> "God is angry with the wicked every day," Psalm 7:11.

Be not unequally yoked with anything unholy.

> "**Be ye not unequally yoked** together with unbelievers:
> for **what fellowship** hath righteousness with unrighteousness?
> and **what communion** hath light with darkness?
> And **what concord** hath Christ with Belial?
> or **what part** hath he that believeth with an infidel?
> And **what agreement** hath the temple of God with idols?

> **for ye are the temple of the living God;**
> as God hath said, I will dwell in them, and walk in them;
> and I will be their God, and they shall be my people.
> Wherefore **come out from among them, and be ye separate**,
> saith the Lord, and **touch not the unclean thing;**
> and I will receive you, And will be a Father unto you,
> and ye shall be my sons and daughters, saith the Lord Almighty,"
> 2 Corinthians 6:14-18

Unclean things must be cast out.

The **VERY FIRST THING** that Jesus gave His twelve disciples was **power to cast out unclean spirits.**

> **"He gave them power against unclean spirits, to cast them out,"**
> **Matthew 10:1.**

It is increasingly rare to find anyone anywhere casting out unclean spirits anymore. People argue that God does not care about things like this. Then why does the Bible say all these things??

"Jesus ...**cast out** all them that sold and bought in the temple," Matthew 21:12.

"If the salt have lost his savour, ...it is thenceforth good for nothing, but to be **cast out**," Matthew 5:13.

"That which beareth thorns and briers is **rejected**, and is nigh unto **cursing;** whose end is to be **burned**," Hebrews 6:8.

"**Put away** from among yourselves **that wicked person**," 1 Corinthians 5:6.

"He shall **separate them one from another**, as a shepherd divideth his sheep from the goats," Matthew 25:32.

"Every soul which will not hear that prophet [Christ], **shall be destroyed from among the people**," Acts 3:23.

Dozens of scriptures teach the doctrine of **CASTING OUT DEVILS**. If there are unclean spirits in the Church, it is the divinely-ordained purpose and duty of believers to **CAST THEM OUT!**

John the Revelator prophesied of a Great Whore – a Harlot Church – a phony, hypocritical Church - that would dominate the scene in the last days. A VOICE FROM HEAVEN said to the believers,

> "**Come out of her, my people**, that ye **be not partakers** of her sins,
> and that ye **receive not of her plagues**,"
> Revelation 18:4.

Jude obviously understood the perils of those who get mixed up with false religionists. He urged us not to sit idly by and watch them perish, but to actively work to **get them out of it**.

> "Others **save with fear, pulling them out of the fire**;
> hating even the garment spotted by the flesh,"
> Jude 1:23.

> "For we must all appear before the **judgment seat of Christ**;
> that every one may receive the things done in his body,
> according to that he hath done, **whether it be good or bad**.
> **Knowing therefore the TERROR of the Lord, we persuade men**,"
> 2 Corinthians 5:10-11.

> "Behold therefore the **goodness and severity** of God,
> on them which fell severity,
> but toward thee goodness **if thou continue** in His goodness,
> **otherwise, thou shalt also be cut off**,"
> Romans 11:22

Most Christian hypocrites do not want to see or hear any of this "SEPARATION" business. They think this kind of talk is itself of the devil.

Jesus cast out devils – *unclean spirits* – and they said, "**HE hath a devil**," Matthew 11:18; Luke 7:33; John 10:20. But Jesus called their bluff. "And if I by Beelzebub cast out devils, by whom do your sons cast them out?" Luke 11:19.

Look at that hypocritical crowd and see how often they cast out devils. Count the number of times they take a stand against real, unclean spirits. In the vast majority of cases, there are no devils being cast out.

So what does that mean? Evil spirits do not ordinarily cast out evil spirits, (unless it is to deceive).

But when the Holy Ghost is truly in a place, **demons tremble**. Sometimes, they will even BEG you NOT to cast them out! (Matthew 8:29).

When the **Holy Ghost** is free to operate in the Church, and in men of God, demons will be cast out. **Evil, unclean spirits will be exposed,** and they will be told to come out. And in the name of Jesus Christ, they HAVE to come out. **They do not get a choice.** Jesus said,

> "If I with the finger of God **cast out devils**, no doubt **the kingdom of God is come** upon you," Luke 11:20.

When the devils go, the Kingdom comes.

If I, in the very words of this book, am identifying an evil spirit that is working within the context of your life, then may the Truth of Jesus Christ EXPOSE and CAST OUT that spirit right now, in the name of Jesus.

And if you, a professing Christian, see an evil or unclean spirit that is working in your life, in your Church, or in your environment, it is your sacred duty to resist the devil.

> "**Resist the devil**, and he will **flee** from you," James 4:7.

Jesus said that when our adversary comes against us,

> "**Give diligence** that thou mayest **be delivered from him**," Luke 12:58.

A promise of a great reward goes with the effort.

> "To **him that overcometh** will I grant to sit with me in my throne," Revelation 3:21.

I do not think there is any other way to save and preserve the true Church. **We cannot continue to do the work of God if the Church is infested with unclean spirits.**

At what point will we finally admit that there is damnable hypocrisy in the Church, and it is KILLING whole congregations! When is enough finally ENOUGH?

Hypocrisy is nothing to laugh or joke about. It is not the figment of your imagination. Hypocrisy is an evil spirit. Hypocrisy is an unclean spirit. Hypocrisy is an enemy of the Holy Ghost. Hypocrisy is the LEAVENING that Almighty God HATES. That means that it absolutely MUST GO. **Any leavening beside the Holy Ghost** will ruin even the most seasoned Saint of God, and the most long-standing Church. Never doubt it.

"Purge out the old leaven... that there may be a new lump."

Chapter 19

Decision Time

I started preaching many of these things on Wednesday nights in the little church. Tapes of those sermons started flying all over Jefferson County. Some of my old friends started dropping in on Wednesday nights.

Scott and Vicki had been our friends for many years. They showed up several Wednesday nights in a row. One night, after I had invited everybody to the altar to pray, Vicki lingered long after everybody else had left. She was crying. After a while, I interrupted her.

"Vicki, what's going on?" I asked.

"Ken, all this stuff you've been preaching about holiness and godliness - it's real. I know it's real. I grew up around that kind of preaching, and I left it years ago, and I've been sorry ever since," she said, still crying.

I really didn't know what to say, so I let her talk. "The United Pentecostal people believe everything you've been preaching. If you are going to keep on preaching like that, you're going to have to go somewhere where they believe it. They believe it."

I was making a reputation for myself preaching so many hot and heavy convictions. In my heart, I knew that we were not going to be able to stay where we were.

Vicki's grandmother heard about my preaching, and sent word by Vicki to invite me to a special revival meeting at the Apostolic Church in Beaumont, where Rev. Marvin Cole was the Pastor.

I had encountered Bro. Cole briefly while Dixie and I were out of Church. He and his Associate came to our home to visit one day, to invite us to Church. I had only recently renounced my faith, and did not want to be bothered with any preachers. When he introduced himself to me at the door, I firmly told him that I was not interested, and rudely shut the door in his face. That had been a little more than two years earlier. Now I was being invited again to visit that Church. This time, I decided I would visit.

Long Winding Road

On a Tuesday night, I went alone to investigate. When I walked in the door, the service was already in progress. The place was packed. Probably 400 people were there on a Tuesday night. And they were definitely holiness people. I was impressed. The service was in high gear. The music and the worship were over the top, and the preacher was intense. After he had preached for about an hour, he gave an altar call.

I remained at my pew. I had only come to observe and no more. The evangelist came back to invite me to the altar, but I declined his invitation. But I stood there and continued watching all the goings on. What I saw utterly blew my mind. I watched hundreds of people engage in the most amazing prayer meeting I had ever seen. Before the altar service was over that night, fourteen people had received the Baptism of the Holy Ghost. I was absolutely stunned!

My extended family is inextricably linked to both the Assemblies of God and the United Pentecostal Churches. I have relatives on both sides. But up until that night, I had almost no experience with the United Pentecostal Churches. I had not attended one since I was a child.

When my aunt Norma's husband, Wallace, heard that I had visited the Apostolic Church, and that I had been preaching a lot about holiness at the Assembly of God Church, he knew what God was doing. He brought me a cassette tape with a sermon preached by his pastor, Johnny Harrell, at the United Pentecostal Church in Bridge City. He thought I would want to hear some of the things he was saying.

I sat down at the dining room table with a portable cassette player and put that tape on. Dixie stopped what she was doing to listen to it with me. It was entitled, "The Ashes of the Red Heifer," based on Numbers 19. He preached about purification and cleansing. It was an utterly amazing message on holiness. By the end of that sermon, we were both sitting there in tears. We could not believe that we had actually found someone that preached the kind of things that God was dealing with us about.

I asked my uncle, "Do you have any more tapes of Bro. Harrell that we can listen to?" That was like asking "Is there any snow on the North Pole?" Wallace had an enormous collection of Bro. Harrell's messages. He brought a cardboard box full of tapes.

Long Winding Road

The first tape I selected was entitled, "Four will let you down - One will lift you up." It was about the four men who let the crippled man down through the roof to Jesus. Four, Bro. Harrell said, is the number that represents the world. One, he said, is the number that represents God. All the world can do is let you down. But Jesus can lift you up. It was one of the most amazing sermons I had ever heard. I could hardly sit still as we sat at the table and listened.

Dixie and I went through that entire boxful of tapes. We listened to them day and night. We played them in the house and in the car. In one particular sermon, we listened as he spoke directly to the young people of the Church, passionately warning them against compromising with the world, and naming so many things that could cause them to lose out with God. Dixie and I looked at each other and shook our heads and wept. It was as if the windows of Heaven had opened up on our souls.

"One of these days, we're gonna drive over the bridge and visit that Church," I told Dixie.

The occasion presented itself to us during the week of Christmas. The little Church dismissed the Wednesday night service for the holiday. I found out that they would be having service in Bridge City, so we planned to go.

I called Scott and Vicki and asked them if they wanted to go with us to Bridge City Wednesday night. They said they did, so we all went.

Service was to start at 7:30, so we arrived at about ten minutes after seven. Scott and I walked in the door together. The lobby was fairly large, but it was empty. I could hear a noise echoing from down a hall somewhere. It sounded like a roar. For a moment, I couldn't figure out what it was. Then I figured out that there was a prayer meeting going on in a prayer room somewhere. I looked at Scott, and said, "You want to go to the prayer room?" He slowly responded an OK. He told me later that he almost turned around and left. It scared him at first. But we went. The girls took the kids and went into the auditorium.

I pushed open a door, and there were about forty or fifty men in the Church dining hall and they were all praying up a thunderstorm. It was mind-blowing. Scott and I squeezed into a place where we could pray, and joined in for several minutes. As service-time approached, the men just began leaving the room. We followed.

Service began right at 7:30. There was a good crowd for a holiday weeknight - probably about 300 people. C.R. Brown went to the pulpit to start the song service. They began singing a chorus and in moments, everyone in the building was on their feet, clapping and singing and worshiping God. I was utterly amazed. I could not remember ever being in a service in all my life where the people were so responsive. Dixie and I sang, and clapped and worshiped with them.

Then C.R. said to turn to page 369 in the song books. I grabbed a song book and turned to the song, "It's All In Him."

"Uh-Oh," I muttered to Dixie, "this is one of those Oneness songs." I didn't know what to expect. I was feeling so much mixed emotion, because I was absolutely loving the atmosphere of worship that I was feeling, but all of a sudden I was afraid we were going to get into their heresy, their false doctrine.

I had never heard this song before, so I followed the words carefully.

"The mighty God is Jesus, the Prince of Peace is He. The everlasting Father, the King Eternally" - so far, all of that was in the Bible.

"The wonderful in wisdom, by whom all things were made, the fullness of the Godhead in Jesus is displayed." Paul said that.

"It's all in Him, It's all in Him, the fullness of the Godhead, it's all in Him. It's all in Him, it's all in Him, the mighty God is Jesus and it's all in Him."

I couldn't find any fault with the song, so far. So, let's sing another verse.

"'Our God for whom we've waited,' will be the glad refrain of Israel recreated, when Jesus comes again. Oh, He will come and save us, our King and Priest to be, for in Him dwells all fullness, and Lord of all is He."

It's all in Him. I was loving this song. And a million wheels were spinning in my head. These people are not heretics! "Man, this is good stuff!"

Long Winding Road

Brother Harrell didn't even preach that night. He had a guest minister. It was good, but we had hoped to hear him preach.

Nevertheless, we had been wowed. Immediately, we had a decision to make. Are we going to take up with these people, or is this heresy?

Dixie and I and Scott and Vicki had a lot of things we needed to talk about. Later that week, Vicki made a fried shrimp dinner for all of us, and invited us over to their house. The whole night, we talked about God and Church.

"What about their doctrine? They teach that you have to be baptized in Jesus' name! They think you have to have the Holy Ghost and talk in tongues!"

Is it true? That was the million-dollar question.

We all wanted to know what to do. In all honesty, I did not have a problem with Jesus' name baptism, and here is why.

In 1976, while I was pastoring the Gospel Lighthouse, someone had given me a tape of a man named Marvin Hicks, a Pentecostal preacher from Corpus Christi. It was a recording of a public debate between Hicks and a Church of Christ preacher. Their subject was Jesus' name baptism.

I happened to have an evangelist visiting with me at the time, so he and I sat down late one night and listened to that tape. By the time the debate was over, the Pentecostal preacher had made mincemeat out of the Church of Christ argument. Jesus' name water baptism was clearly far more scriptural than baptism in the titles.

My preacher friend and I sat up late and discussed it all for nearly two hours. We took our Bibles down and started researching all the scriptures on the subject that we could find.

We figured out that Peter preached it, Peter practiced in, Paul practiced it, and every example we could find where the formula was mentioned, it was in the name of Jesus Christ. Acts 2:38 said, "Repent, and be baptized, every one of you in the name of Jesus Christ for the remission of sins, and ye shall receive the gift of the Holy Ghost."

It was almost two o'clock in the morning when this preacher and I decided to go out into the church and baptize each other in the name of Jesus. So we did.

I never told anyone. I never preached it. I rarely spoke of the subject. But in my heart, I knew I could not argue against it. BUT, I did not really understand all I needed to understand about it. Maybe I was a "closet" Apostolic, but I really did not know or understand the Oneness doctrine that they believed.

So as Scott and Vicki and Dixie and I talked about it, we all agreed that there was nothing wrong with Jesus' name baptism, and we all were willing to be re-baptized if we needed to be.

Then we had to talk about this business of the necessity of the Baptism of the Holy Ghost. Apostolics believe that the baptism of the Holy Ghost is essential to salvation. So we had to determine if that was scriptural.

"Does the Bible teach that a believer must receive the baptism of the Holy Ghost?" We argued and hollered at each other all night long over that one.

The parable of the ten virgins stumped me. The five virgins who had no oil could not go with the bridegroom. "So," I said, "if the oil is not the Holy Ghost, then what is it?"

Every preacher I could ever remember preaching on the subject compared the oil to the Holy Spirit. Anybody who has ever read the Bible knows that oil in the Bible is a type of the Holy Spirit. So, if the five virgins were left behind because they didn't have any oil - that was the same as saying that they got left behind because they didn't have the Holy Ghost! Didn't Jesus say that you have to be **born of both the water and the Spirit** or you cannot enter the kingdom of God? Water birth. Spirit birth. These are real events in a person's life. If you never have those events, you are never born again.

Scott stood up in the middle of the living room and raised his hands to get everybody's attention. "Alright, I'm admitting it. Everybody needs to be baptized in Jesus' name, and everybody needs to receive the Holy Ghost and talk in tongues."

We all looked at one another.

"I agree," I said.

"I agree," Dixie said.

"I agree," Vicki said.

It was a done deal. I didn't yet know if Scott and Vicki would end up moving to the Bridge City Church, but as far as I was concerned, I had just made my decision.

The Hair Issue

There was one more big hurdle before would could make the move.

The United Pentecostal people are known widely for their teachings about hair. So when it became apparent that we were going to make a move in that direction, we had to decide whether or not their teachings about hair were Biblical.

From the very beginning, Dixie and I had relied heavily on God's Word to guide us in our marriage. On my part, as early as the age of 13, I had memorized most of 1 and 2 Corinthians during my Bible Quizzing days.

I had memorized the eleventh chapter, in which Paul taught about the hierarchy of relationships between God, men, and women. Like an umbrella,

1. The Eternal Spirit of God is the covering for the Son of Man.
2. Jesus Christ is the covering for the Man.
3. The Man is the covering for the Woman.

God covers Christ. Christ covers the man. The man covers the woman.

Furthermore, Paul taught that a person's HAIR was a symbol of that hierarchy. Dixie and I had both been taught that a man's short hair corresponded to the fact that Jesus Christ was his covering. Paul also taught that the woman's long hair symbolized the fact that her husband was her covering. Dixie and I had discussed that subject many years earlier, and were in agreement.

Until the hippie rebellion of the 1960s, virtually all men wore their hair short. We had always considered long hair on a man to be a symptom of rebellion against God. For most of her life, Dixie had worn shoulder-length hair because of her beliefs that a woman should have long hair.

But we went back to 1 Corinthians 11 and studied it again.

This time, we saw clearly that Paul was not merely speaking about LONG hair on a woman. He was speaking about UNCUT hair on a woman. At that point, Dixie decided that she would stop cutting her hair.

(I have a complete Bible study of this subject on my website. You can Google it by typing "Ken Raggio Hair" or simply go to kenraggio.com.)

Dixie quickly decided that she would never cut her hair again. She had no reservations, and no argument. During the time we had been out of Church, she had cut her hair in a "Pixie," (extremely short), and had bleached it light blonde. But that was to be no more. She immediately committed to wearing long, uncut hair for the rest of her life. It was a really big deal.

It was not just a matter of cutting hair. It was a spiritual condition.

Dixie understood, like few women today understand, that God made the woman for the man. She had a mind of her own just like any other person. But she had learned from going to Church and reading her Bible all of her life that God requires the woman to be in submission to her husband. The husband is to be in charge of the marriage and the home, and he will give account to God for his wife and his family, based on his decisions and actions. Long, uncut hair on a woman corresponds to and bears witness to the fact that she is in willing submission to her husband, under God.

Of all the adjectives in the dictionary, I can think of none more appropriate or weighty to describe Dixie's relationship with me as her husband than "LOYAL." She had known from her youth what God's Word had said about a woman submitting to her husband, and she lived very dutifully, deliberately and conscientiously by that rule. It was something that she discussed and taught with great passion and conviction to young women that we pastored and ministered to.

She loved me and trusted me with deliberate intention and purpose, even when she was not sure if I was right. She stood beside me and supported me with her whole heart through many of the most difficult of times. And I sincerely believe that is the way that God meant it to be.

The woman is God-ordained to acknowledge that the man is her covering. The man is God-ordained to acknowledge that Jesus Christ is his covering.

If either the man or the woman fail in God's designated role, then all bets are off. A man who will not submit to Christ, and take the leadership role, is at 100% risk of calamity. And the woman who will not submit to her husband, and support his leadership under Christ is at 100% risk of calamity. (If the man will not submit to Christ, she must still obey Christ.)

Most women have no idea that when a woman insists on having her way, she is competing with God's authority and God's will for the man. It puts a man in a most difficult position of yielding to his wife and not unto God. Many men have compromised the will of God to please their wives. Only on Judgment Day will it become apparent how many strong-willed females have hindered their husband's Godly leadership roles, and in far too many cases, caused entire families, and many others in their circle of influence to be lost.

Dixie would have told you in a heartbeat that a woman should NOT "wear the pants in the family." She knew what the Bible taught about a woman's role, and she lived by it with an iron will, even when she did not agree with me.

And those values weighed heavily in her decision not to ever cut her hair again.

So the die was cast. The dice had been thrown, and it could not be recalled. We had made a series of profound, life-altering choices and decisions, and there was no going back to the Christianity we had come from. We had to stay the course as God was revealing it to us.

That night at Scott and Vicki's home in December of 1982, we decided to be baptized in Jesus' name and become Oneness Apostolic Pentecostals. I had just turned thirty-one years old in September.

That decision meant that we would be embarking on an entirely new life among people whose beliefs were much different from all our old friends and family members. I knew in my heart that we would fall out of favor with just about everyone we knew from that day forward. I just didn't know how quickly or how tumultuous it would be.

In the course of those four months of intense fasting, prayer and Bible study, God had shown me three visions.

In the first vision, God had warned me of specific adversities that I would soon be going through, and where they would be coming from.

In the second vision, God warned me of a demonic attack that Dixie would have to endure, how it would be resolved, and what the outcome of it would be.

In the third vision, God had showed me exactly how long our tenure would be in the house we were living in. He showed me the exact date we would be moving out of the house, and on that very day (months later) someone called and offered us a rent house, available immediately. We moved out that day.

I saw the first vision fulfilled in December. I saw the second vision fulfilled in January. It was absolutely mind-blowing how God had prepared us for those three events. Those visions were miraculous confirmations that God had known the end from the beginning, and as such, greatly encouraged us as the trials came to pass.

I told the pastor at the little church that Dixie and I were going to be making a change and we would be leaving. He wanted to know why, so I told him.

He knew exactly where I was coming from. His late wife was raised in a Oneness, Jesus' name church. He had had many dealings with Jesus' name Pentecostals in his lifetime. During a period of life-threatening illness, he had been laid up in the hospital for an extended period of time. During his hospitalization, two of the local Apostolic pastors had visited his bedside on numerous occasions, and prayed for him. They talked with him about the very same issues that Dixie and I had been facing. He had come face to face with some of the very same decisions that we were making right then.

He had been impressed with the holiness teachings, and understood the doctrine of Jesus' name baptism, but had decided not to make the change.

He wanted me to explain to the congregation why we were leaving. I told him that we were leaving because we wanted to obey the scriptures God was showing us.

> "Then Peter said unto them, Repent, and **be baptized every one of you in the name of Jesus Christ for the remission of sins**, and ye shall receive the gift of the Holy Ghost,"
> Acts 2:38.

I also explained that I wanted to go where holiness was being preached and practiced. Hebrews 12:14 was also on my mind;

> "Follow peace with all men, and **holiness, without which no man shall see the Lord**."

He asked me to take the pulpit on a Sunday morning and explain the things that made us leave. I couldn't believe he would want me to do such a thing. I told him that I didn't really think he should have me say those things in his pulpit. I sincerely did not want to cause him any trouble.

Nevertheless, he insisted. I warned him that if I preached on Sunday morning, I was going to preach on Acts 2:38. He said that was OK, just preach whatever I felt like I needed to preach.

So, that is what I did. On Sunday morning, I tried not to be offensive or even abrasive. I just told them what we were seeing, and how we felt like this is what God was showing us, and that is why we were making the move.

As soon as I finished preaching, service was dismissed. Someone met Dixie in the aisle and immediately launched a vicious verbal assault on her and against me.

I did not see it happen, but I noticed out of the corner of my eye that she left the building in a big hurry. I didn't know why.

As soon as I finished speaking with several people, I went next door to our house and found Dixie sitting on the floor in the corner of the bedroom.

She was weeping uncontrollably. I asked her what was going on, and she told me everything that had just been said to her.

That was the attack I had seen in the second vision about three months earlier. When I saw Dixie sitting in the corner of that bedroom floor, crying, I told her the vision God had given me, and it comforted her.

Sunday evening, we all got in the car and headed over the Rainbow Bridge to attend church in Bridge City. We planned to be baptized in Jesus' name that night.

We were already getting opposition from a lot of people. Several members of our family thought we were making a horrible mistake, and getting into heresy.

We were being lambasted about our convictions, and even accused of joining a cult. It was painful, agonizing and stressful. But we knew we had to do what we believed was pleasing to God.

I was so hungry for God. I was ready to find my place in God and spend the rest of my life there. And I knew that where we were was not it.

Everything seemed so abundantly clear to me at that point. We HAD to act.

I have always been exasperated by people who cannot plainly see the things that the Bible plainly teaches. But Jesus explained that many are blind and deaf by choice. I did not want to be one of those.

I did not want to be one of the multitudes who can see the will of God at a distance, but cannot leave the world behind. Many cannot leave the wrong Church. Many cannot disconnect from family or friends who would prevent them from doing the will of God. I refused to be one of them.

Chapter 20

Crossing The Bridge

As we drove up the old Rainbow Bridge which crosses the Neches River between Groves and Bridge City, the Holy Ghost impressed me to read Matthew 19. I didn't know what was in that chapter. I told Dixie to open up her Bible to Matthew 19 and read it out loud. She read it as we crossed the bridge.

At the end of the chapter, verse 29 says,

> "And every one that hath forsaken houses, or brethren, or sisters, or father, or mother, or wife, or children, or lands, **FOR MY NAME'S SAKE**, shall receive an hundredfold, and shall inherit everlasting life."

Dixie and I both were both amazed that God would give us that specific verse just as we were on our way to be baptized in Jesus' name – to officially become Jesus' Name Apostolic Pentecostals.

That was Sunday evening, January 24, 1983. That night, Brother Harrell baptized Dixie, our eight-year-old son, Brian, and me in Jesus' name at the United Pentecostal Church in Bridge City.

Everything forever changed that night.

It was a glorious night. God's presence was profound, and the praise and worship that went up from the few hundred people who were there was thunderous. People were shouting, dancing and running the aisles as we were baptized. It was a time of great victory and great rejoicing for us.

Scott and Vicki followed soon thereafter. Another couple we had befriended followed shortly after that. Then my brother, David and his family came along not long after that.

The transition was far from smooth, and far from easy. We had much opposition. I received a phone call at eight o'clock Monday morning.

"Did you get baptized in Jesus' name last night?"

"Yes, we did."

"Well, I want you to know that I don't ever want to hear your doctrine!"

"Hey, you called me. I didn't call you."

"Well, I just want you to know that I don't ever want to hear your doctrine."

"OK!"

Dixie and I had been in such intense prayer and fasting for so long, we could see God's hand in so many things. Our lives were so completely in the hands of God. We had no resources of our own. Every step we took was a step of faith.

Brother Harrell took us under his wings and gave us intensive care. Every Monday morning, at 7:00 o'clock, he called me to meet him for breakfast at a local restaurant. I filled his ear, week after week, with the goings on in our lives, and sought his counsel on so many things. Throughout the week, it seemed his phone calls were divinely timed. It seemed so amazing how that each time we faced another crisis, the phone rang, and it was Brother Harrell checking up on us.

He coached us through the enormous transition. During our first six weeks at the Bridge City church, a guest evangelist preached in every service. We didn't get to hear Brother Harrell preach until the seventh week after we moved there. Meanwhile, we built up a huge collection of his sermons on cassette tape. We listened to those sermons almost daily.

"Brother Ewing wants you to come preach for him," Brother Harrell announced to me in the third month at Bridge City. Murrell Ewing pastored the Eastwood United Pentecostal Church in Lake Charles.

It was early spring, and our first time to preach in a United Pentecostal Church. We arrived on Saturday evening, and they took us to our guest quarters. On Sunday morning, about 450-500 people were present, and I was loaded for bear. Dixie and I sang, "It's Worth It All," and then I preached from Genesis, the story of Cain and Abel. I talked about how Cain was **sincerely wrong** in his sacrifice, nevertheless **he had to change or forfeit God's blessing**. Cain did not make the change, and it cost him everything. I testified of how God had dealt with Dixie and me over the past several years, and how He finally led us to an Apostolic church - a church like the Apostles preached and believed in. I preached as hard and as fast as I could preach non-stop for two solid hours. The response was overwhelming. The people were with me the whole way. I couldn't believe I had preached for two hours, but they stayed with me full-force through it all. Eventually, I entitled that sermon "Sincerely Wrong," and I gave that testimony in every church we were called to for almost two years.

Calls came for other meetings. Immediately, my calendar began to fill with wonderful opportunities to preach around Texas and Louisiana, in some great churches. Shortly after that, Brother Harrell helped us purchase a Super-cab Ford truck and a nice travel trailer. We became full-time evangelists from the day we preached in Lake Charles. In the summer of 1985, I was invited to preach the Friday afternoon service at the Texas District Camp Meeting. The camp theme that year was "HE IS..." I was asked to take the topic, "HE IS HOLY."

I modified "SINCERELY WRONG" to fit the occasion. There were about 5,000 people present, and I preached for two hours. The crowd stayed with me. The response was amazing. I preached strong doctrine and holiness. Pastor James Kilgore of Houston came to me afterward to say how he appreciated my sincerity and attitude toward holiness in my presentation. The lady who managed the tape ministry for the Texas District informed me a few months later that she had never sold so many tapes of one service in all the many years she had worked at the camp.

People responded amazingly to that message where ever I preached it. Recordings of "Sincerely Wrong" went literally all over the world. More than twenty-five years later, I still have people contact me occasionally to discuss that message and tell me how helpful it was to them.

At the heart and soul of everything I preached in those days was a simple message, **"Don't be deceived by popular Christianity!"** I preached hard against easy-believism, name-it-and-claim-it, prosperity preaching, and all the popular, but unscriptural messages of our time.

In the early days of our transition, I had prayed earnestly that God would help me to understand the Oneness of God clearly so that I could articulate it to others.

My big revelation came one day while I was reading in the Book of Isaiah. I already understood that Moses had declared from the beginning to the Children of Israel, "Hear O Israel, the Lord our God is One Lord," Deuteronomy 6:4. I knew that God was a Spirit.

But it all became perfectly clear to me when I read Isaiah 42:13:

> **"The LORD shall go forth as a mighty man,**
> he shall stir up jealousy like a man of war:
> he shall cry, yea, roar; he shall prevail against his enemies,"
> Isaiah 42:13.

All of a sudden, it was a plain as daylight. God is A Spirit. He is ONE Spirit. He is the Father God. And He is the LORD.

Now THAT VERSE – Isaiah 42:13 – told me that the LORD shall go forth as a mighty man.

Suddenly, I realized that Jesus is NOT the second person of the Trinity. He is NOT the incarnation of one-third of the Godhead. Jesus Christ is the FATHER come in flesh.

THE LORD came forth as a mighty man. God the Father came down in the body of His earthly Son, Jesus Christ. Suddenly, I understood for the first time in my life what Jesus meant when he said to Philip,

> "Have I been so long time with you,
> and yet hast thou not known me, Philip?
> **he that hath seen me hath seen the Father;**
> and how sayest thou then, Shew us the Father?
> Believest thou not that **I am in the Father, and the Father in me**?
> the words that I speak unto you I speak not of myself:
> but **the Father that dwelleth in me**, he doeth the works.
> Believe me that **I am in the Father, and the Father in me**:
> or else believe me for the very works' sake,"
> John 14:9-11.

So God the Father is the ONE ETERNAL SPIRIT. Jesus Christ is the ONLY begotten **human Son of God IN WHOM the Father dwells**.

The Father is a Spirit. The Son is the Man who embodies, and is the IMAGE of the invisible Spirit.

Since those days, I have written quite extensively on the Oneness of God, and those writings have been read by literally millions of people around the world. See my website for all those articles (kenraggio.com).

I could never again, as long as I live, embrace or approve the Trinitarian doctrine. It is wrong, wrong, wrong, wrong, wrong. God is not three co-equal, co-eternal persons. God is a single, solitary, invisible Spirit. That is our Father.

There is no greater doctrine on earth than the Oneness of God.

The doctrine of the Oneness of God is the absolute BEDROCK of true Christianity.

It is impossible to build a true Church on Trinitarian doctrine. It cannot and will not stand.

That doctrine is the reason why I could no longer embrace the Trinitarian version of the New Birth. Once I realized that God is only ONE SPIRIT and not three, I could no longer believe that anyone can receive the Spirit of Christ without receiving the Baptism of the Holy Ghost. The Holy Ghost IS the Spirit of Christ. The Oneness doctrine is the basis for teaching that the Baptism of the Holy Ghost is absolutely essential to the New Birth.

I preached that the New Birth is represented in the **blood, water and spirit**; the **death, burial and resurrection** of Jesus Christ, or in our case, death by **repentance**, burial by **water baptism in Jesus' name**, and resurrection by the **infilling of the Holy Ghost, speaking in other tongues**.

"You must be born again - of the **water** and of the **Spirit**."

I had heard plenty of Assembly of God preachers as I was growing up preach that "the spirit that raised Christ from the dead will quicken your mortal bodies." Brother Clendennen used to preach that it was the Holy Ghost in you that was going to get you up in the rapture. But when it came down to taking a doctrinal stand, every one of them refused to say or preach that the baptism of the Holy Ghost was essential to the New Birth.

It was doublespeak. On one hand, they said you had to have the Holy Ghost to be in the rapture, but they made the exception that you had to get saved before you could get the Holy Ghost. There simply was no logic in that argument. They simply did not understand the Truth of the matter.

The Assemblies of God preaches that the Holy Ghost baptism is a second work, subsequent to being born again. But that is not how the Bible teaches it. Romans 8:9 says, "Ye are not in the flesh, but in the Spirit, if so be that the Spirit of God dwell in you. Now if any man have not the Spirit of Christ, he is none of his."

The Oneness doctrine is absolutely essential to the understanding of this matter. If the Spirit of Jesus Christ is a different Spirit from the Holy Spirit, then it is conceivable that you could be born of the Spirit of Christ and then receive the Holy Ghost later. But the Bible is abundantly clear to show that the Holy Ghost IS the Spirit of Christ. God is a singular Spirit. He is A Spirit, not three co-equal, co-eternal Spirits. Therefore, to be born again, of the Spirit of Christ, you MUST have the Holy Ghost. It is the ONLY Spirit of God. All the many other spirits that proceed from God are created spirits (angels). But there is only one DIVINE Spirit. God is A Spirit.

There are millions of Christians who think that it is possible to receive the Holy Spirit without speaking in other tongues, but the Bible does not support that view either. Jesus told the disciples in Luke 24:49 to tarry in the city of Jerusalem until they be endued with power from on high. Then He explained in Acts 1:8, "Ye shall receive power after that the Holy Ghost is come upon you."

The Holy Ghost did come upon them in the Upper Room on the day of Pentecost.

> "...there appeared unto them cloven tongues like as of fire,
> and it sat upon each of them.
> **And they were all filled with the Holy Ghost,**
> and began to **speak with other tongues**,
> as the Spirit gave them utterance,"
> Acts 2:3-4.

Some in the crowds nearby accused them of being drunk. Peter denied the charge saying,

> "**These are not drunken**, as ye suppose,
> seeing it is but [nine in the morning].
> But this is that which was spoken by the prophet Joel;
> And it shall come to pass in the last days, saith God,
> **I will pour out of my Spirit upon all flesh:**
> and your sons and your daughters shall prophesy,
> and your young men shall see visions,
> and your old men shall dream dreams:
> and on my servants and on my handmaidens
> I will pour out in those days of my Spirit,
> and they shall prophesy,"
> Acts 2:16-18.

When the first Gentiles received the Holy Ghost while Peter preached at Cornelius' house, the Jews who were present **knew they had received the Holy Ghost, "for they heard them speak with tongues and magnify God,"** Acts 10:46.

In Ephesus, when the apostle Paul laid hands on the believers, "the Holy Ghost came on them; **and they spake with tongues**," Acts 19:6.

Later, to the Corinthians, Paul made several bold statements about speaking in tongues.

> **"I would that ye all spake with tongues,"**
> 1 Corinthians 14:5.

> **"I thank my God that I speak in tongues more than ye all,"**
> 1 Corinthians 14:8.

And to the skeptics, a command: **"...forbid not to speak in tongues,"** 14:39.

This is a warning to all ministers and all denominations not to forbid speaking in tongues.

It is not good enough to argue that it is "jibber-jabber," or that it cannot be identified as any legitimate language. The scripture does NOT set a linguistic standard as a prerequisite. The facts are quite the opposite. Speaking in tongues is the equivalent of an encrypted language, **not intended to be understood by men**, including arrogant intellectuals.

> "For he that speaketh in an unknown tongue **speaketh not unto men, but unto God; for no man understandeth him**; howbeit in the Spirit he speaketh mysteries,"
> 1 Corinthians 14:2.

Furthermore, it is not good enough to argue that speaking in tongues is the babbling of fools. Paul said it is an asset to the believer,

> "He that speaketh in an unknown tongue **edifieth [builds up] himself**,"
> 1 Corinthians 14:13.

It is not good enough to argue that speaking in tongues is unprofitable, because Paul says otherwise:

> "Likewise the **Spirit also helpeth our infirmities**: for we know not what we should pay for as we ought: but **the Spirit itself maketh intercession** for us with groanings which cannot be uttered."

It is not good enough to argue that "tongues have ceased" - a false doctrine called cessationism. Peter declared that it was an open-ended, unending promise from God,

> "For the promise is unto you, and to your children, and **to all that are afar off**, even as many as the Lord our God shall call,"
> Acts 2:39.

The baptism of the Holy Ghost with the evidence of speaking in other tongues is the Spirit-birth that every believer must experience in the process of the New Birth.

A second gift, one of the nine gifts of the Spirit, enables a person to deliver a message from God in an unknown tongue, but this gift should only be used when another person present has the gift of interpretation of tongues.

Speaking in tongues is an individual gift for the individual believer; not intended for speaking to other people, but to God in prayer and worship.

Nevertheless, countless examples could be cited of modern instances similar to that in the Upper Room - where people of other languages heard a Spirit-filled believer speaking in his native tongue. One of my Bible college instructors, Charles Harris, wrote a book in the 1970s entitled, "Spoken by the Spirit," in which he documented hundreds of incidents where people heard a Spirit-filled believer speaking holy messages in their native tongue - over 60 distinct languages in all. It still occasionally happens as it did on the day of Pentecost.

It is not good enough to argue that an interpreter must be present every time when someone prays in the Spirit. That is NOT a scriptural requirement. That only applies to the gift of tongues when used in a public ministry.

The raw, hard, cold fact is that every single New Testament writer was a Spirit-filled tongue-talker. Matthew, Mark, Luke, John, Paul, Peter, Timothy, Jude, and James. They were all Pentecostals, and I don't suppose they would approve of all the naysayers and deniers who have such a major voice in so-called Christianity today.

If the Pope of the Roman Catholic Church is truly a successor to Peter, then why doesn't the Pope appear on world-wide television and preach, like Peter, "Repent, and be baptized every one of you in the name of Jesus Christ for the remission of sins, and ye shall receive the gift of the Holy Ghost?" Because he doesn't believe it. The Pope is a complete imposter. He is no more the successor of Peter than the Devil himself. The modern-day Acts 2:38 Apostolic church is Peter's successor.

Nicodemus came to Jesus in John 3:3-8,

> "Jesus answered and said unto him, Verily, verily, I say unto thee,
> **Except a man be born again, he cannot see the kingdom of God**.
> Nicodemus saith unto him, How can a man be born when he is old?
> can he enter the second time into his mother's womb, and be born?
> Jesus answered, Verily, verily, I say unto thee,
> **Except a man be born of water and of the Spirit,**
> **he cannot enter into the kingdom of God**.
> That which is born of the flesh is flesh;
> and that which is born of the Spirit is spirit.
> Marvel not that I said unto thee, **Ye must be born again**.
> The wind bloweth where it listeth, and thou hearest the sound thereof,
> but canst not tell whence it cometh, and whither it goeth:
> so is every one that is born of the Spirit."

Here are the emphatic points of Jesus' conversation with Nicodemus:

1. If you are never born again, you will never see the kingdom of God.

2. If you are never born of water and of the Spirit, you cannot enter the kingdom of God.

3. Flesh begets flesh. Only the Spirit of God begets a new spirit in us.

4. You must be born again (of the water and of the Spirit).

5. **You can HEAR the WIND, but can't see it.**
   You can HEAR the SPIRIT because it speaks through us in unknown tongues, but you can't see it.

The early saints knew that Cornelius' household had received the Holy Ghost because they HEARD them speak with tongues.

What is the conclusion of the matter?

Jesus was born again when He died, was buried, and came back to life. He was the FIRSTBORN from the dead. Death, burial, resurrection.

We become born again when we follow Him in the similar process. Death, burial, resurrection.

We do that through **repentance** (death to self), **baptism** ("Know ye not, that so many of us as were baptized into Jesus Christ were baptized into his death? Therefore we are buried with him by baptism into death," Romans 6:3-4) and being baptized in the **Holy Ghost**, speaking in other tongues.

There are similarities worth noting between natural birth and spiritual birth.

Water Birth

A natural baby is born of water: the amniotic sac in which the fetus develops bursts when it time for the baby to be delivered. Similarly, a spiritual baby is born of water: beginning in the days of John the Baptist, and ever since by Jesus Christ and His disciples and followers, repentance is to be accompanied with water baptism.

Spirit Birth

A natural baby must inhale the air of its new environment. It is no longer in the amniotic fluid of its mother's womb, but must receive the air of its new world.

A spiritual baby must "inhale" or be baptized in the Holy Spirit. Failing to be filled with the Holy Spirit is to be spiritually still-born. Failing to speak with other tongues is failure to give evidence of being filled with the Holy Ghost. That sign is the initial, scriptural and universal evidence that one has received the Holy Ghost.

Everywhere I preached, people swarmed me with affirmations and confirmations. They really believed what I was preaching. They knew that I was preaching the Bible. They knew that I was right about a lot of the phony junk in modern Christianity. They knew that God's real Church loves Truth above popularity. They knew that God's people are holy people, too.

Chapter 21

The Rest Of The Story

It has been almost thirty years since those days in Bridge City. Dixie, Brian and Chad accompanied me for about two years of travelling from Church to Church at first. Then we pastored two United Pentecostal Churches – in Comanche, Texas for six years, and in Birmingham, Alabama for 16 years. During those years, we saw about 1,500 people Baptized in Jesus' name, and about 3,000 people receive the Baptism of the Holy Ghost. We saw many wonderful healings and miracles in those days.

All those intervening years were jam-packed with more stories to tell – enough stories to write another book larger than this one. I have included many stories in my other books. Several of the most amazing stories are included in my book, **"Praying on Purpose – Praying for Results."** We witnessed many mighty works of God in our lifetime of ministry. Many other stories are scattered throughout the hundreds of articles available at my website online – kenraggio.com.

In 1997, Dixie was found to have Stage 3 colon cancer. The next six years were very trying times. I simply cannot retell all those experiences here. Those years were filled with many dramas and agonizing experiences. Dixie rebounded for a few years and enjoyed strength and good health for a while until the cancer returned with a vengeance.

On my fifty-first birthday, September 26, 2002, surgeons opened her up and found that she was completely consumed with malignant tumors. The lead surgeon told me that day that there was nothing else he could do.

She lived twelve more months. Despite the doctor's "terminal" prognosis, we adamantly prayed and believed that God would miraculously heal her. With much assistance from Dixie's sister and brother-in-law, we kept her on an extreme regimen of health and nutritional treatments, spending tens of thousands of dollars in an effort to keep her strong and reverse the cancer. But it was not to be.

Through the entire six-year ordeal with cancer, her faith never foundered.

Shortly before she died, as she lay sick in bed, I went searching through a dresser-drawer one day, looking for something. I came across her childhood Bible, one she had used in her schooldays.

I opened it and flipped through it. I saw many notes and underlines. But in the back pages, I found a hand-written note that she had made at least 35 years earlier.

"I love the Lord because of Psalms 116." I turned to Psalm 116, and saw that she had underlined this verse:

"Blessed in the eyes of the Lord is the death of his saints."

I asked her if she remembered writing that note in her little Bible. I read the note to her and then read that Verse in Psalm 116.

She said, "Yes, I remember it well. I was in a Sunday night service when I was a teenager, and the preacher was preaching, and for some reason, I thought I was going to die. Then I read that verse, and I underlined it. 'Precious in the sight of the Lord is the death of His saints.'"

From her childhood, Dixie had always taken comfort in God and in His Word. She believed every jot and every tittle of the Bible and lived by it. And to the very end, she trusted in Him.

Dixie believed in the Lord. She spent her life for Jesus. She lived the way that she believed He wanted her to live, and she expected to see Him at the end of the journey. I have no doubt that she did.

One of our most poignant moments happened as she lay in bed sick, shortly before she died. I had taken down John Bunyan's "Pilgrim's Progress" and was reading it aloud to her over a period of several nights. One night, we came to the episode where Christian encountered Apollyon. I want you to read it.

Christian's Encounter with Apollyon, from "Pilgrim's Progress"

> But now, in this valley of Humiliation, poor Christian was hard put to it; for he had gone but a little way before he espied a foul fiend coming over the field to meet him: his name is Apollyon.

Then did Christian begin to be afraid, and to cast in his mind whether to go back, or to stand his ground.

But he considered again, that he had no armor for his back, and therefore thought that to turn the back to him might give him greater advantage with ease to pierce him with his darts; therefore he resolved to venture and stand his ground: for, thought he, had I no more in mine eye than the saving of my life, it would be the best way to stand.

So he went on, and Apollyon met him. Now the monster was hideous to behold: he was clothed with scales like a fish, and they are his pride; he had wings like a dragon, and feet like a bear, and out of his belly came fire and smoke; and his mouth was as the mouth of a lion.

When he was come up to Christian, he beheld him with a disdainful countenance, and thus began to question him.

APOLLYON: Whence came you, and whither are you bound?

CHRISTIAN: I am come from the city of Destruction, which is the place of all evil, and I am going to the city of Zion.

APOLLYON: By this I perceive thou art one of my subjects; for all that country is mine, and I am the prince and god of it.

How is it, then, that thou hast run away from thy king? Were it not that I hope thou mayest do me more service, I would strike thee now at one blow to the ground.

CHRISTIAN: I was, indeed, born in your dominions, but your service was hard, and your wages such as a man could not live on; for the wages of sin is death, Rom. 6:23; therefore, when I was come to years, I did, as other considerate persons do, look out if perhaps I might mend myself.

APOLLYON: There is no prince that will thus lightly lose his subjects, neither will I as yet lose thee; but since thou complainest of thy service and wages, be content to go back, and what our country will afford I do here promise to give thee.

CHRISTIAN: But I have let myself to another, even to the King of princes; and how can I with fairness go back with thee?

APOLLYON: Thou hast done in this according to the proverb, "changed a bad for a worse;" but it is ordinary for those that have professed themselves his servants, after a while to give him the slip, and return again to me. Do thou so too, and all shall be well.

CHRISTIAN: I have given him my faith, and sworn my allegiance to him; how then can I go back from this, and not be hanged as a traitor?

APOLLYON: Thou didst the same by me, and yet I am willing to pass by all, if now thou wilt yet turn again and go back.

CHRISTIAN: What I promised thee was in my non-age: and besides, I count that the Prince, under whose banner I now stand, is able to absolve me, yea, and to pardon also what I did as to my compliance with thee.

And besides, O thou destroying Apollyon, to speak truth, I like his service, his wages, his servants, his government, his company, and country, better than thine; therefore leave off to persuade me farther: I am his servant, and I will follow him.

APOLLYON: Consider again, when thou art in cool blood, what thou art like to meet with in the way that thou goest. Thou knowest that for the most part his servants come to an ill end, because they are transgressors against me and my ways. How many of them have been put to shameful deaths!

And besides, thou countest his service better than mine; whereas he never yet came from the place where he is, to deliver any that served him out of their enemies' hands: but as for me, how many times, as all the world very well knows, have I delivered, either by power or fraud, those that have faithfully served me, from him and his, though taken by them! And so will I deliver thee.

CHRISTIAN: His forbearing at present to deliver them, is on purpose to try their love, whether they will cleave to him to the end: and as for the ill end thou sayest they come to, that is most glorious in their account.

For, for present deliverance, they do not much expect it; for they stay for their glory; and then they shall have it, when their Prince comes in his and the glory of the angels.

APOLLYON: Thou hast already been unfaithful in thy service to him; and how dost thou think to receive wages of him?

CHRISTIAN: Wherein, O Apollyon, have I been unfaithful to him?

APOLLYON: Thou didst faint at first setting out, when thou wast almost choked in the gulf of Despond.

Thou didst attempt wrong ways to be rid of thy burden, whereas thou shouldst have stayed till thy Prince had taken it off.

Thou didst sinfully sleep, and lose thy choice things.

Thou wast almost persuaded also to go back at the sight of the lions.

And when thou talkest of thy journey, and of what thou hast seen and heard, thou art inwardly desirous of vainglory in all that thou sayest or doest.

CHRISTIAN: All this is true, and much more which thou hast left out; but the Prince whom I serve and honor is merciful, and ready to forgive.

But besides, these infirmities possessed me in thy country, for there I sucked them in, and I have groaned under them, been sorry for them, and have obtained pardon of my Prince.

APOLLYON: Then Apollyon broke out into a grievous rage, saying, I am an enemy to this Prince; I hate his person, his laws, and people: I am come out on purpose to withstand thee.

CHRISTIAN: Apollyon, beware what you do, for I am in the King's highway, the way of holiness; therefore take heed to yourself.

APOLLYON: Then Apollyon straddled quite over the whole breadth of the way, and said, I am void of fear in this matter. Prepare thyself to die; for I swear by my infernal den, that thou shalt go no farther: here will I spill thy soul.

And with that he threw a flaming dart at his breast; but Christian had a shield in his hand, with which he caught it, and so prevented the danger of that.

Then did Christian draw, for he saw it was time to bestir him; and Apollyon as fast made at him, throwing darts as thick as hail; by the which, notwithstanding all that Christian could do to avoid it, Apollyon wounded him in his head, his hand, and foot.

This made Christian give a little back: Apollyon, therefore, followed his work again, and Christian again took courage, and resisted as manfully as he could.

This sore combat lasted for above half a day, even till Christian was almost quite spent: for you must know, that Christian, by reason of his wounds, must needs grow weaker and weaker.

Then Apollyon, espying his opportunity, began to gather up close to Christian, and wrestling with him, gave him a dreadful fall; and with that Christian's sword flew out of his hand.

Then said Apollyon, I am sure of thee now: and with that he had almost pressed him to death, so that Christian began to despair of life.

But, as God would have it, while Apollyon was fetching his last blow, thereby to make a full end of this good man, Christian nimbly reached out his hand for his sword, and caught it, saying,

> "Rejoice not against me, O mine enemy:
> when I fall, I shall arise,"
> Micah 7:8;

and with that gave him a deadly thrust, which made him give back, as one that had received his mortal wound.

Christian perceiving that, made at him again, saying,

> "Nay, in all these things we are more than conquerors,
> through Him that loved us,"
> Romans 8:37.

And with that Apollyon spread forth his dragon wings, and sped him away, that Christian saw him no more.

> "Resist the devil, and he will flee from you,"
> James 4:7.

In this combat no man can imagine, unless he had seen and heard, as I did, what yelling and hideous roaring Apollyon made all the time of the fight; he spake like a dragon: and on the other side, what sighs and groans burst from Christian's heart.

I never saw him all the while give so much as one pleasant look, till he perceived he had wounded Apollyon with his two-edged sword; then, indeed, he did smile, and look upward!

But it was the dreadfullest sight that ever I saw.

So when the battle was over, Christian said, "I will here give thanks to him that hath delivered me out of the mouth of the lion, to him that did help me against Apollyon."

And so he did, saying, "Great Beelzebub, the captain of this fiend, Designed my ruin; therefore to this end He sent him harness'd out; and he, with rage

That hellish was, did fiercely me engage: But blessed Michael helped me, and I, By dint of sword, did quickly make him fly: Therefore to Him let me give lasting praise, And thank and bless his holy name always."

Then there came to him a hand with some of the leaves of the tree of life, the which Christian took and applied to the wounds that he had received in the battle, and was healed immediately.

He also sat down in that place to eat bread, and to drink of the bottle that was given him a little before: so, being refreshed, he addressed himself to his journey with his sword drawn in his hand; for he said, "I know not but some other enemy may be at hand." But he met with no other affront from Apollyon quite through this valley.

Now at the end of this valley was another, called the Valley of the Shadow of Death; and Christian must needs go through it, because the way to the Celestial City lay through the midst of it.

The Valley of the Shadow of Death

Dixie and I wept hot tears as I read the whole of *Pilgrim's Progress* out loud as she lay in her sickbed. We had met Apollyon in the road, but were determined to overcome him. In her final year on earth, she suffered unspeakably, and I spent virtually all of my time at her side. In the same sequence that John Bunyan had chronicled Christian's progress, Dixie and I progressed from meeting Apollyon in the road, to passing through the Valley of the Shadow of Death.

Dixie passed away on September 29, 2003.

The angels of the Lord came to get her (Luke 16:22) in the wee hours of the morning. She immediately saw the face of Jesus (2 Corinthians 5:8), arriving there in a perfectly healthy, heavenly body (1 Corinthians 15:42-44), and receiving a white robe of righteousness (Revelation 6:11; 7:9-14).

On the great Judgment Day, she will have a great reward. In the twenty-two years that Dixie and I pastored Apostolic Churches, we baptized approximately 1,500 people in Jesus' name, and saw around 3,000 people receive the Baptism of the Holy Ghost. Many others received amazing healings and miracles by the hand of God.

I continued to pastor for about 20 months longer without Dixie, but it was very difficult. I finally resigned as Pastor of the Church, because I felt that God was leading me into writing and broadcasting.

That was an agonizing and painful choice that had many bitter consequences. Satan tried desperately to destroy me and a lifetime of ministry with enormous discouragement, and depressions like I had never known were possible. I gave myself to a forty-day fasting and prayer vigil at that time, seeking God's help and fresh direction.

During Dixie's last year, I had spent more time in prayer than in any one year of my life. I fasted 21 days for her on one occasion, and 30 days on another occasion. Many nights, while I attended to her at bedside, I spent the entire night on the floor in prayer, asking God to heal her.

You don't have to believe me, but I will tell you anyway that we never expected her to die. From the first day I learned she had cancer, I made up my mind to trust God for her healing. She did too. All the saints in the Church we pastored were there for us, too. Ministers and friends all over the country called and sent letters of prayerful support. Everybody believed that God would heal Dixie. Some preachers came hundreds of miles to pray for her and express their faith that she would be healed.

We never discussed her dying. Never bought a cemetery plot. Never discussed a funeral. We believed she was going to get well. Maybe you think I'm crazy, but I have seen too many miracles in my day to doubt that God can do a miracle like that.

So, just about two weeks before Dixie died, one night as she lay in bed, and I was tending to her, she said, "If I die, it's because God has something He wants to do with you, and He needs me out of the way."

She wasn't just saying that for naught. She really, really believed it. I am not saying that I agreed with her, because I really did not want to believe that was true. But I can never forget that statement.

I sit here adding this paragraph to an otherwise completed book, exactly nine years to the hour since she died in my arms, sitting on the edge of our bed at two in the morning. I will send this book to the publisher this week.

I will not know what the value of my life and ministry has been since Dixie died until the Judgment Day, but I now believe more than ever before that,

> "The steps of a good man are ordered by the LORD:
> and he delighteth in his way.
> Though he fall, he shall not be utterly cast down:
> for the LORD upholdeth him with his hand,"
> Psalms 37:23-25.

Since leaving Birmingham, I have written well over two million words, that will soon be published in at least nine books.

I ended up back at my home Church in Bridge City, where Pastor Harrell has been pastoring for more than 41 years. It is still a great Church, and his incomparable preaching, pastoral ministry and Godly example has been a great and immeasurable strength to me. I have been continuously involved in the music ministry there, while I continue the endless work on my writing and producing.

My Internet ministry has grown substantially, to become a real force in the world. On any given day, hundreds of thousands of people are exposed to my written, audio, and video material. That audience grows daily.

Readers in 215 nations have subscribed to my DAILY BIBLE STUDY by e-mail. Letters with prayer requests, Bible questions, and other requests come to me in an endless stream, twenty-four hours a day from my readers in every nation on earth. I try to answer as many as I can with personal responses, although it is impossible to respond to them all. In many ways, I feel like I am pastoring an International Church. Many of my readers are quite dependent on my teaching material because they do not have a good Church in their part of the world. Pastors and Teachers in Churches all over the world are using my lessons in their Churches and study groups.

My major life's work has taken the form of a 1488-page Bible Commentary and Study Guide entitled, "MY DAILY BIBLE COMPANION." It is a 2-Volume (Old Testament and New Testament) work that contains more than 4,800 mini Bible lessons from Genesis to Revelation. The response from those who have purchased those books has been extremely encouraging.

Another major project has been to build a large following on the social network TWITTER. I post Christian and Biblical quotes every 45 minutes which go to thousands of people around the world. Those quotes are regularly RETWEETED by my followers to their followers, which greatly extends my reach. At this writing, my TWITTER account is ranked as one of the most influential accounts in the world – regularly in the top 5,000 to 10,000 of more than 540 million users. Recently, I published a 188-page book containing more than 2,000 of those quotes, entitled, "TRUTH IN A NUTSHELL." There will probably be a second volume in coming months.

I have also produced several extensive and artful PowerPoint presentations with graphics that will be incorporated into a lengthy series of preaching and teaching videos, God willing. I am just beginning to produce those videos. Eventually, they will all be posted for free viewing on the Internet, and also available on DVDs and digital downloads as well.

And last, but not least, I have written dozens of songs that I hope to have recorded before time runs out. God willing, I hope to release an album of at least ten of my own songs, fully orchestrated, as soon as He enables me to get it done.

Invitations come frequently to preach and teach around the world, but so far I have declined almost all of them so that I can complete the books that are already near completion. As God directs, I hope to fulfill many of those missionary and evangelistic invitations in time to come.

Long Winding Road

Chapter 22

The Long Winding Road

The long winding road is not mine alone.

It is your road, too.

The long winding road stretches all the way back to Bethlehem.

The path that Jesus Himself trod was a long winding road. And the road for every seeker of Truth since that time has been a long winding road. Multitudes have traversed it.

The way has never been easy for anyone who set out to do the will of God. I know the Bible says that the way is straight and narrow (Matthew 7:14). If we could only see our lives from Heaven's point of view, we would see that it really is straight and narrow. But from our vantage point on earth, we can't see the forest for the trees.

From the bottom of the tapestry, the life of the true believer looks dark and chaotic, but from Heaven's point of view, it is beautiful and divinely impressive.

God in Heaven is guiding every true seeker of Truth, and He IS guiding us straight to Heaven. But from this lowly perspective, it does not look straight at all. It seems very long, and very winding.

I want to show you, before I finish, that this Apostolic Pentecostal Holiness Church is indeed descended from the original Mother Church found only in the Book of Acts (not in Rome). We did not get here accidentally. This Church is not a fluke.

Today's Oneness Pentecostals who continue to preach and practice holiness are not an aberration or a historical quirk. They are not a flash fire.

They are tried and true descendants of 120 disciples of Jesus Christ who met in the Upper Room on the Day of Pentecost nearly 2000 years ago.

The history of the modern Apostolic Pentecostal Holiness movement is largely unknown to most people, but it is profoundly important to know and understand **the long winding road that led us to modern Pentecostalism.**

The **Early Church** received the **Early Rain,** and the **20th Century Apostolic Church** received, and continues to receive, the **Latter Rain** prophesied in Joel 2:23, Zechariah 10:1, and James 5:7.

The outpouring of the Holy Ghost in the Upper Room on the Day of Pentecost was the beginning of the **Early Rain**, out of which the Early Church was born. The Early Rain lasted for most of the first two centuries AD. The outpouring that began at the end of the nineteenth century, and quickly spread around the world was the **Latter Rain**.

The original Early Church was Oneness, Jesus' name baptized, full of the Holy Ghost, and spoke in tongues. That was the universal modus operandi of the Church for most of the first two centuries.

I want to show you some of the firm evidence that modern Pentecostalism is a genuine outgrowth of generations of men and women who diligently searched for Truth until it was finally revealed.

I will be publishing a book in the near future entitled, "Greatest Doctrines of the Bible," in which I will not only explain the core doctrines of the Bible, but will also show where so many modern false doctrines came from and why we should reject them. I will not duplicate that material here.

The Council of Nicea (325 AD) - I do not have the time or space to elaborate on the details here (they will be in other books), but suffice it to say that Roman Catholicism displaced the Early Church. The Nicean Creed institutionalized the unbiblical doctrine of the Trinity, as well as many other heresies. By substituting heresies AND by murdering or otherwise silencing early Apostolic believers, Christianity became a complete hoax.

I know that is a hard pill to swallow, but it is the truth, and there are voluminous proofs that what I say is true.

Researchers have shown us that the Apostolic Oneness Pentecostal experience was apparently never totally extinct. In pockets of locales throughout history, we have found scattered evidence of them.

But due largely to the predominance of Roman Catholicism, the Bible was almost completely hidden from men, and the Gospel was abominably perverted for over a thousand years.

The Dark Ages is a term which generally refers to the 5th to the 15th Centuries, and accounts for the near extinction of anything resembling TRUE New Testament Christianity. This fact further supports the reality of the "Early Rain – Latter Rain" occurrence of the Holy Ghost outpouring, separated by the Dark Ages. During this period, the Roman Catholic Church effectively prevented the masses from having any access to the Bible. The few Bibles in existence were in Latin, Masses were in Latin, and most people were illiterate anyway. Nobody knew what the Bible said.

John Wycliffe (1320-1384) was one of the first great anti-Catholics of record. He was also a champion of the sacred scriptures. He translated the Latin Vulgate Bible into English by 1384. He was also one of the first to associate the Catholic Church with the Antichrist. After he died of a stroke, the Catholic Church decreed him to be a heretic, exhumed his body, burned it, and banned his writings. Wycliffe was called "The Morning Star of the Reformation," and was considered a precursor to the Reformation led by Martin Luther.

John Huss (1369-1415) was influenced by the martyrdom of Wycliffe, and the Catholic burning of Wycliffe's writings. A Catholic priest, Huss struggled to take the R.C.C. in a more Biblical direction, but was declared a heretic and condemned. He was burned at the stake July 6, 1415 by Catholic executioners. His writings inspired later reformers.

The Gutenberg Bible was the first printed Bible, following the invention of Gutenburg's printing press around 1455. Earlier Bibles were rare, hand-written manuscripts. The Gutenberg Bible was a copy of the Vulgate, published in Latin.

Martin Luther (1483- 1546) was a German monk given to much fasting and prayer who became repulsed by the selling of indulgences by the Roman Catholic Church. In 1517, he published his "Ninety-Five Theses," enumerating many unbiblical practices of the Roman Catholic Church. Copies of his theses quickly circulated all over Europe.

He furthermore denied that the papacy was any part of the Biblical Church, leading to his excommunication from the R.C.C. on January 3, 1521, and his condemnation by Holy Roman Emperor Charles V later on May 25, 1521. Luther's life was saved when Fredrick III of Saxony gave him safe harbor in Wartburg Castle. It was during Luther's exile (he called it "my Patmos"), that Luther translated the New Testament from Latin to German and published it in 1522; the Old Testament followed in 1534. Thanks to the newly invented printing press, it proliferated quickly. Luther's teaching about justification by faith is the core doctrine of Lutheranism to this day. Still, Lutheranism clings to many pre-Reformation practices carried over from Catholicism.

The Reformation: **Martin Luther**'s revolt against Roman Catholicism, beginning in 1517, triggered a tsunami of revolt among Church leaders across Europe.

Huldrych Zwingli (1484-1531) was a leader of the Reformation in Switzerland, who took great exception to many of the core practices within Catholicism, and wrote extensively to establish the primacy of the Bible over all Church authority.

John Calvin (1509-1564) was a Frenchman who broke from the Roman Catholic Church in 1530, and soon fled to Switzerland. His "Institutes of Christian Religion," (1536) was a seminal work that attempted to define the true Biblical doctrines of Christianity, as opposed to the historical heresies of the Roman Catholic Church. It was an introduction to Christian piety, and one of the first documents to assist in forming a Biblically-structured belief system (religion) for Protestant Churches, since the practices of Catholicism were all that had been known before that time. "Calvinism" stressed five points: 1. The total depravity of man. 2. Unconditional election. 3. Limited atonement. 4. Irresistible grace. 5. Perseverance of the saints. Many know it colloquially as "eternal security," or "once-saved, always-saved."

Unfortunately, Calvin took an adversarial position against **Michael Servitus**, a brilliant, multilingual, Spanish theologian, scientist and physician who was one of the first non-Trinitarian (Oneness) Christians to come to any influence in his day (with the publication of his treatise, "On the Errors of the Trinity" in 1531). Calvin finally had Servitus executed by a Catholic inquisitor – burned at the stake - on charges of heresy, for his Oneness and anti-predestination beliefs (predestination being one of Calvin's pet doctrines).

John Knox (1514-1572) was a revolutionary Scottish clergyman ordained to the priesthood in the Roman Catholic Church. His entire life was a horrific back-and-forth struggle with Catholicism in Scotland, the Church of England, Kings and Queens of Scotland and England, and the Reformation. Mentored in mid-life by John Calvin, Knox was finally afforded the opportunity in 1560, to draw up a Reformed confession of faith, called the Scots Confession, and Scotland abolished the authority of the Pope, forbade the Catholic mass, and condemned all theology contrary to the reformed faith. Knox is credited with being the founder of the (Calvinistic) Presbyterian Church.

William Tyndale (1492-1536) took up the torch left behind a century earlier by John Wycliffe. Tyndale translated the original Hebrew and Greek texts of the Bible into the English language. His writings influenced the King of England, Henry VIII, to sever ties between the Church of England and the Roman Catholic Church. Tyndale was convicted of heresy and executed by strangulation.

The Tyndale Bible was a prime factor in the Reformation. The subsequent **Geneva Bible** was drawn largely from the Tyndale Bible. That is the Bible that came to Jamestown, Virginia in 1607, and was on the Mayflower in 1620. In 1611, 54 scholars created the **King James Version** of the Bible, of which about 83% of the New Testament and 76% of the Old Testament is Tyndale's work.

Holiness - When, for the first time in history, the printed Bible became readily available to the general public, thanks to the invention of the Gutenberg printing press, holiness (piety) teachings were quickly rediscovered and put into practice. Holiness was at the very heart and soul of most Churches in the early Reformation – the **Anabaptists, Amish, Mennonites, Hutterites, Puritans, Quakers, Moravians, Presbyterians, Wesleyans, Methodists** and many, many others.

In the 1620s, **Puritans** in England became weary of being persecuted by the Church of England, as well as with its similarities to the Roman Catholic Church. As many as 20,000 Puritans migrated to New England.

By 1685, 8,000 **Quakers** came from England for similar reasons, many of them fleeing a reign of terror in England. They settled mostly in Pennsylvania, under the leadership of William Penn.

In the 1700s, **Lutherans, Reformed, Moravians,** and other German groups moved into the colonies.

Catholics gained dominance in Massachusetts, and the **Church of England (Anglicans)** became dominant in Virginia.

John Bunyan (1628-1688) influenced Christianity profoundly toward the end of the seventeenth century. A Calvinist (Baptist) and later, Puritan, Bunyan was a nonconformist who repeatedly offended the Church of England, which recurrently landed him in jail. From a severely underprivileged upbringing, and a quite profane lifestyle, Bunyan was converted by two books on Christian piety that were owned by his new wife. While imprisoned for preaching a nonconformist Gospel contrary to the Church of England, Bunyan wrote "The Pilgrim's Progress," which was published in two parts, 1678 and 1684. It is probably the second most widely read book ever published beside the Bible, and has been translated into more than 200 languages. It sold over 100,000 copies in his lifetime (and hundreds of millions since).

Bunyan's books, which also included "The Life and Death of Mr. Badman," "The Holy War," and "Grace Abounding to the Chief of Sinners," taught an entire generation the precepts of the straight and narrow life, with its many trials and tribulations, that leads from earth to Heaven. The depth of his spirituality clashed with the coldness of the Church of England, causing him great personal trials, but out of which came his powerful writings. "The Pilgrim's Progress," helped brand Protestantism into the entire Christian psyche of that day.

The First Great Awakening

By the late 1600s, the **Church of England** had mostly suppressed all other religions both in England, and in the American colonies. King Charles II of

England had become a great adversary of Protestantism, especially Puritanism. But a spiritual revolution was born in England under the voices of **John and Charles Wesley** and **George Whitefield.**

The colonists had not been inspired at all by Anglicanism, and spiritual complacency and ritual religion had taken a heavy toll on Christianity across the land. So the English Awakening quickly spread to the colonies.

In the 1730s and 1740s, men like **George Whitefield** and **Jonathan Edwards** began to call American colonialists to fervent prayer and consecration. In New England, Whitefield was heralded as a modern Apostle Paul.

Whitefield and Edwards preached that men's lives should be transformed by the Holy Spirit. Edwards denounced sin and warned of "sinners in the hands of an angry God." He called them to follow "the divine and supernatural light." Their followers came to be known as the "New Lights." The dead religions were called the "Old Lights."

Their revivalism urged people to be bold, even loud in prayer, and bold in faith. It also encouraged them to renounce religious oppression (from the Church of England), religious intellectualism, and demand freedom of religion. As the Awakening convinced people to abandon the Church of England, a great number of Protestant denominations began to pop up.

The colonialists no longer saw God's will being handed down through secular Kings and High Church prelates, but through His Word. Consequently, they began to believe that they should live their lives under God's sovereignty, not under the sovereignty of a secular King.

Therefore, the First Great Awakening is credited with spawning the American Revolution. It emboldened the people to renounce the evil controls of **King George III of England**, and declare their independence.

Many new Protestant denominations began to appear, and the influence of the older Churches, including the Church of England, the Puritans, and the Quakers was greatly diminished. In England, some said that the Great Awakening was a "**Presbyterian Rebellion.**"

Anti-Catholicism was at fever pitch throughout the colonies. The **Anglican Church was disestablished** in 1786 by Thomas Jefferson.

Christianity was becoming a much more communal, grass-roots religion. In place of institutional ceremonialism, they were learning to read their Bibles, pray, and seek God on a personal level. As a result, many were beginning to see, know and understand God on a level not seen since the days of the Early Church, sixteen centuries earlier.

The Second Great Awakening (1780-1840) was an Armenian revival, as opposed to Calvinistic "eternal security." A great consciousness and expectation began to arise about the prophesied Second Coming of Jesus.

Charles Finney, a great revivalist, preached an anti-Calvinist message that included the sinful depravity of man, free will, and the hazards of unrepented sins. He also preached against many vices, including Freemasonry.

Joseph Smith, founded the **Church of Jesus Christ of the Latter Day Saints** (the Mormons).

William Miller, the Millerites, Ellen G. White, and the Seventh Day Adventists rose during that period.

Barton Stone, Thomas and **Alexander Campbell, Campbellites,** the **Disciples of Christ**, and the **Church of Christ** began in this period.

Charles Haddon Spurgeon (1834-1892) of London, was called "The Prince of Preachers," of the Reformed Baptist tradition. A more-than-prolific author, both his writings and his oratory were known around the world.

Baptists and **Methodists** flourished in North America during the Second Great Awakening.

The Third Great Awakening (1850-1900) was marked by more preaching about the Second Coming of Jesus Christ. The Holiness movement and the Nazarenes arose in this period. **Dwight L. Moody** founded the **Moody Bible Institute**. The Gospel hymns of **Ira Sanky** proliferated. Social issues were tackled, including liquor (prohibition), pornography, prostitution, even child labor and women's suffrage. Churches of all kinds began to develop missionary programs to take the Gospel around the world.

The Wesleyans and Methodists brought a fresh **Holiness** context into which the Pentecostal experience would eventually be restored. Had there been no **Holiness movement,** it is not likely that **Pentecostalism** would have been manifest as widely as it did. That is a moot point, however, considering that Almighty God promised to pour out His Spirit in the last days. It was the prophesied **Latter Rain.**

Since God always intended to pour out His Spirit in the last days, it was inevitable that a holiness movement would precede it. God would not have poured out the **Latter Rain** if there had been no one willing to separate themselves from their worldly fascinations and addictions.

Naturally, the Trinitarian doctrine had been embraced almost universally in those days, because from the days of Martin Luther, the entire Reformation had remained Trinitarian. Although Luther accomplished a watershed revolution when he posted his "Ninety-Five Theses" in 1517, renouncing the Roman Catholic Church, the reformers did not yet realize the error of the Trinity Doctrine they had always known. Consequently, the Lutherans and all subsequent "Protestants" continued in the doctrine of the Harlot Mother Church (Revelation 17:5), failing to protest that.

Pentecostalism is counted as a part of the Third Great Awakening. Some of the earliest Holy Ghost outpourings were in Scotland, Wales and Great Britain in the 1800s. **Smith Wigglesworth** (1859-1947) was one of the earliest proponents of the Pentecostal outpouring, having received the Holy Ghost in 1907. From his home in Britain, he traveled to more than a dozen countries around the world, preaching the Holy Ghost baptism, healing the sick, and raising the dead (as many as 23 were reported).

In the late 1800s, men like **John Alexander Dowie**, of Zion City, Illinois; **Frank Sandford**, of Shiloh, Maine; and **A.B. Simpson,** founder of the Christian and Missionary Alliance, were forerunners of the modern Pentecostal movement. They all advocated holiness lifestyles, preached and practiced divine healing, and preached that there would be a full restoration of Apostolic Pentecostal manifestations in the last days.

As the twentieth century approached, ministers and laymen of many religions seemed to have a sense that something of enormous spiritual significance was about to take place.

On New Year's Eve, 1900, Howard Goss' mother-in-law recalled how her neighbor came out into the yard at eleven o'clock and said, "I feel as if the Magi and their camels might suddenly come down the street," to which his mother-in-law replied, "I shouldn't be surprised if the heavens opened at midnight, and the angels sang."

1901 would indeed prove to be a great milestone in the annals of Christianity. According to **Shirley Nelson**, in "Fair Clear and Terrible," members of Frank Sandford's ministry in Maine experienced speaking in other tongues in 1900. The "Lewiston [Maine] Evening Journal," reported on January 6, 1900 that **"the gift of tongues has descended**," on a New Years Eve prayer and praise service at **Sandford's Shiloh** Bible School.

According to Harold D. Hunter, in "Beniah at the Apostolic Crossroads," **Charles Parham** visited **Shiloh** in the summer of 1900. Parham told **C.W. Shumway** that he first heard tongues being spoken by two male students as they emerged from one of the prayer towers at Shiloh.

Then on **January 1, 1901, in Topeka, Kansas, at Bethel Bible College** (a small start-up school meeting in an unfinished house called "Stone's Folly"), led by Charles Parham, the Holy Ghost fell on a prayer band of Bible students. For three weeks, forty students had prayed and fasted, asking God to show them exactly what the true evidence of the Baptism of the Holy Ghost really was. Their answer came shortly after midnight, on January 1, 1901.

The first to speak in tongues was a lady named **Agnes Ozman**. Ozman had studied under **A.B. Simpson**, and briefly attended **Dwight L. Moody's** school, (Charles W. Nienkirchen, "A.B. Simpson and the Pentecostal Movement," p.31-32). Within a week, a dozen students had spoken in other tongues in Topeka.

Parham was apparently the first in modern times to publicly affirm that **speaking in tongues was "Bible evidence"** of the Baptism of the Holy Spirit. Parham encouraged the phenomenon as being the modern version of the original **"Apostolic Faith."**

In 1902, Parham wrote a book entitled, "A Voice Crying in the Wilderness," in which he said, "Then how quickly we recognized the fact that we could not be buried by baptism in the name of the Father, and in the name of the Holy Ghost, because it stood for nothing, as they never died, and were never resurrected. So if you desire to witness a public confession of a clean conscience toward God and man, and faith in the divinity of Jesus Christ, **you will be baptized by single immersion, signifying the death, burial, and resurrection**; being baptized in the name of Jesus, into the name of the Father, Son, and Holy Ghost; **they are one when in Christ you become one with all**," (from "United We Stand," by Arthur L. Clanton).

Parham thus became a trailblazer for water baptism in Jesus' name.

Parham was invited to bring his "Apostolic Faith" message to Galena, Kansas. Thousands were drawn to his meetings, and hundreds were converted. In the winter of late 1903, Parham baptized over 100 converts in the Spring River, in Jesus' name.

Robin Johnston, in his book, "Howard Goss: The Pentecostal Life," reported that **Howard Goss was converted in that meeting in Galena, and Goss recalled Parham baptizing him in the name of Jesus.** Goss would eventually become one of the most influential Pentecostals of his time.

In "The Winds of God," Ethel Goss (Howard's wife) reported that Charles Parham, who was formerly a Methodist minister, strongly emphasized divine healing, and many were healed of cancers, blindness, and many other diseases.

Howard Goss, who had almost no previous exposure to Christianity, and whose brother had impressed upon him the atheistic infidelity of Voltaire and Ingersoll, said, "it became evident to me that some superhuman power was at work here. ...I became fully convinced that infidelity was wrong."

Goss watched as "several hundred were baptized in the Holy Ghost, as evidenced by their **speaking in strange tongues according to Acts 2:4**." He added, "I feel that I owe my conversion to Christianity to hearing people speak in other tongues. The 14th Chapter of 1 Corinthians tells us that tongues are a sign to the 'unbelievers.' Today, I still thank God that I saw and heard this sign from heaven."

Howard Goss elaborated on Parham's preaching. "He preached a **clean, holy life** of victory for all believers [similar to what he had heard preached by A.B. Simpson]. He emphasized the words and commands of Jesus and taught a **clean separation from the old life."**

Goss added, "Although I had been enthusiastically interested in all types of sports, I now felt that God had a different work for me to do. ...I belonged to two secret lodge orders, but felt they were not God's best for me, so I resigned from them, as well as from the football team. These and many other decisions I made for myself before hearing them mentioned from the pulpit. God somehow made it plain to me what he wanted me to do, and I did it. All my plans for the future were changed.

I was disconsolate over the time I had wasted reading newspapers. So, for two years after my conversion, I read nothing but my Bible. What a love I had for the Word of God! Many nights I could not bear to lay it down even to sleep. I would lie all night with the Bible folded in my arms upon my chest while I slept, so intense was my love for that Blessed Book.

This exclusive reading of the Scriptures soon became a fixed habit. I would read it in every spare moment, even while at work if it was possible."

So, here we have the record of the **FIRST MAJOR OUTPOURING OF THE HOLY GHOST** in modern times, in Galena, Kansas. Several major elements of that outpouring are noteworthy.

1. It occurred under the ministry of people who were given intensely to **prayer, fasting, and the study of God's Word**.

2. **Holiness and separation from the world** was believed, preached, and practiced.

3. Whereas earlier preachers (i.e., Simpson, Dowie, Sandford) had preached that sanctification was the baptism of the Holy Ghost, Parham believed that **the baptism of the Holy Ghost was always accompanied by the physical evidence of speaking in tongues**.

4. **Divine healing, miracles, signs and wonders** were present.

5. Parham **baptized his converts in the name of Jesus**.

This was an epic breakthrough!

No other ministry since the Early Rain of ancient times had been so clearly pronounced, and so explicitly defined. This was indeed the Latter Rain beginning to fall.

In early 1905, Parham moved to Orchard, Texas (on the west side of Houston) where his "Apostolic Faith" message began to proliferate by his workers, one of whom was **Howard Goss**. They preached the Pentecostal message all around the region of Houston, Galveston, and Alvin, Texas. Goss finally received the baptism of the Holy Ghost on a train ride with a group of other believers.

A black preacher by the name of **William Seymour** enrolled in Parham's local Bible school, and that is where Seymour embraced speaking in tongues as the initial evidence of the Baptism of the Holy Ghost (although he had not yet experienced it). Both Seymour and Goss continued to be trained by Parham in those days.

In February, 1906, Seymour received an invitation to become the pastor of a small Holiness mission in Los Angeles, California. He went there, only to have his Pentecostal message rejected by that congregation.

Seymour, not having the money to return to Texas, was received into the home of **Edward and Mattie Lee**, where prayer meetings were held until the attendance outgrew their home, and they moved to another home. Edward Lee was the first to receive the Baptism of the Holy Ghost, and in April, 1906, **Seymour received the Holy Ghost**.

Then they moved to the dilapidated African Methodist Episcopal Church building (which had been turned into a horse livery) on Azusa Street, where, in the next three years, almost non-stop prayer meetings were held, and many hundreds would receive the Baptism of the Holy Ghost. The Azusa Street mission is legendary in its role in the history of modern Pentecostalism.

Seymour became the Pastor, and named it the **Pacific Apostolic Faith Mission**. By 1907, the Azusa Street ministry had ignited Pentecostal fires that spread like wildfire across the United States and around the world. **Frank Bartleman's** periodical, **"The Apostolic Faith,"** was written and published from the Azusa Street mission and circulated to tens of thousands all over the world.

Some estimates say that by 1909, around 50,000 people had received the Baptism of the Holy Ghost, speaking in other tongues, in connection with the Azusa Street mission.

The Wesleyans had taught holiness, using the mantra, "Saved, sanctified, and baptized in the Holy Ghost." William Seymour's teachings in "The Apostolic Faith" publication reflected a Wesleyan influence on his holiness beliefs. Seymour wrote, "God is calling His people to **true holiness**...He means for us to be **purged from uncleanness and all kinds of sin**."

Glen Cook left the Azusa Street mission to go preach the Apostolic Faith message in Churches all over the country. His ministry was instrumental in the Apostolic Faith message being well-established in St. Louis, Indianapolis, and Memphis.

Author Robin Johnston records that **Charles H. Mason** was subsequently converted to the Apostolic Faith message, and "**transformed the Church of God in Christ to a Pentecostal organization**." (from "Howard A Goss: A Pentecostal Life").

Johnston also reported that Seymour laid hands on **G.B. Cash**, of Dunn, North Carolina, and he received the Holy Ghost. Cash played a key role in transforming the **Church of God of Cleveland, Tennessee into a Pentecostal organization.**

In 1908, **Frank Ewart** attended a Pentecostal Camp Meeting in Portland, Oregon and received the Baptism of the Holy Ghost. His periodical, "Meat in Due Season," and his book, "The Phenomenon of Pentecost," put forward the Apostolic doctrines, and had immeasurable influence on multitudes of people.

In 1911, **William Durham** preached for **Howard Goss and E.N. Bell** in Malvern, Arkansas, abandoning sanctification as a second work, calling it the "Finished Work of Calvary." It was the abandonment of the Wesleyan idea of sanctification as a second work of grace.

Durham founded the Seventh Street mission in Los Angeles, and Frank Ewart became the associate minister for Durham. In 1912, Durham died at the age of 39 of tuberculosis, but his "Finished Work" message persisted into the Jesus' name movement that soon erupted. When Durham died, Ewart became the pastor.

William Durham's "Finished Work" message has similarities to teachings of that day by **E.W. Kenyon**. Kenyon is thought to have influenced Durham to believe that **Jesus is the New Covenant name of God**. It was one of the first hints of a revelation of the **Oneness of God**.

In 1913, Ewart attended the **World Wide Apostolic Faith Camp Meeting in Arroyo Seco** (Los Angeles) California, where **Maria Woodworth-Etter** was preaching and practicing a healing ministry. It was attended by hundreds of Pentecostal ministers from around the U.S., and large numbers of people were receiving healings, miracles, and the Baptism of the Holy Ghost.

In that camp, Ewart also heard **R. E. McAlister preach about Jesus' name baptism**. McAlister said, "The apostles invariably baptized their converts once in the name of Jesus Christ; …that the words Father, Son, and Holy Ghost were never used in Christian baptism." (From "United We Stand," A.L. Clanton).

Ewart met with **McAlister and Glenn Cook** in private to better understand the Jesus' name doctrine. In that Camp Meeting, **Ewart, McAllister, and John G. Scheppe,** all declared that God had shown them that they should be baptizing in Jesus' name, that it was indeed the proper New Testament baptism. Others who heard those things included **G.T. Haywood** and **Frank Morse**, both of whom were soon baptized in Jesus' name.

On April 15, 1914, Frank Ewart and Glenn Cook re-baptized each other in the name of Jesus and preached Jesus' name baptism in a tent meeting in Belvedere, a suburb of Los Angeles, California.

That triggered the "New Issue," Jesus' name baptism.

Unknown to Pentecostals in North America, **Andrew Urshan** had been baptizing his converts in Russia in Jesus' name since 1910. In fact, a group of **Latinos in the Azusa Street mission** had also been baptizing their converts in Jesus' name since 1909.

But the New Issue was not merely about baptism. It demanded a rethinking of the doctrines of the Godhead and of the New Birth.

Those were the first clear signs that the ancient Oneness doctrine was about to be restored and reinstated in the Pentecostal Church worldwide.

In 1914, about 300 preachers from 20 states met in **Hot Springs, Arkansas**, and founded **The General Council of the Assemblies of God in the United States of America**.

The next year, 1915, the New Issue of Jesus' name baptism and the Oneness of God was denounced. Several key proponents of the New Issue were openly ridiculed. The New Issue stirred up considerable disagreement at that time. According to "The Historical Development of the Statement of Fundamental Truths," by Glenn W. Gohr (in the Assemblies of God archives), "many of the doctrinal matters discussed in the 1915 Council arose from the Oneness controversy."

E.N. Bell, the first General Superintendent of the Assemblies of God ,was one of the highest-profile individuals in the New Issue debate. According to Matthew Shaw, in "The Old Landmark," Bell published, in May and June of 1915, a four-part series for the "Weekly Evangel" (the official publication of the new Assemblies of God) ardently defending Trinitarian baptism, and discounting the need for Jesus' name baptism. However, in July, Bell was re-baptized in the name of Jesus at the Third Interstate Encampment of the Assemblies of God in Jackson, Tennessee, making front-page news in the "Word and Witness" publication in August. Frank Ewart also reported it in his publication, "Meat for Men." Then, in September, Bell wrote an article attempting to say that he yet retained his Trinitarian views. Nevertheless, the explanation of God in Christ that he put forth in that article was entirely consistent with the Oneness position of the Mighty God in Christ. According to Richard A. Lewis, in his article, "A Voice of Restraint in an Era of Controversy," E. N. Bell "briefly identified with the unorthodox position of 'Oneness.'"

By the time the 1916 Council rolled around, the Oneness issue was the centerpiece of the discussions. **D.W. Kerr**, a former Christian and Missionary Alliance minister, had done extensive research on "The Eternal Sonship," and prepared to defend the Trinitarian position.

The Oneness ministers in the early Assemblies of God were effectively pushed out on their own at the 1916 General Council. 156 ministers and many assemblies departed the Assemblies of God at that time.

Nevertheless, shortly after the Oneness ministers were ostracized in 1916, a group of Oneness ministers met in Eureka Springs, Arkansas, and formed the **General Assembly of the Apostolic Assemblies,** on January 2, 1917. **Howard Goss, H.G. Rogers, and D.C.O. Opperman** were leaders in that new group.

World War 1 began in April. Around January 1918, that group merged with a slightly older group called **The Pentecostal Assemblies of the World, Inc.** (P.A.W.). **G.T. Haywood,** who had re-baptized 456 of his Church members in Jesus' name at Christ Temple in Indianapolis soon became the General Secretary of the **P.A.W.**

A number of other Oneness groups organized over the following twenty years or so.

Andrew Urshan had preached in the 1913 Arroyo Seco Camp Meeting, and had fellowshipped with the Assemblies of God early on, before leaving for missions work overseas. But when he returned to America in 1919, he promptly abandoned the Assemblies of God to join with the Oneness brethren. He preached the Oneness, Jesus' name message throughout the United States and many nations, including Russia and Persia (modern Iran). He was a major figure, and a pioneer trailblazer for the Apostolic message.

On August 20, 1920, **E.N. Bell** wrote to a friend, Pastor J.C. Brickey, of Jackson, Tennessee, clearly **articulating his rejection of the Oneness, Jesus' name position**.

> "I could not conscientiously baptize in this way alone. For to do so I would be misunderstood as to truths of far more vital importance than the matter of the baptismal formula. I was more concerned not to teach that Jesus Christ is the only person in the Godhead, not to teach that the name of Jesus is the Name of the Father, and of the Son, and of the Holy Ghost; not to teach that Jesus is the Father; not to teach that water baptism is necessary to salvation; not to teach that baptism with the Spirit is the birth of the Spirit."

Bell died suddenly of a heart attack on June 15, 1923 at the age of 57.

In Biblical fact, and in contradiction to Bell's objections, Jesus is the only body of God. God the Father is an infinite, invisible Holy Spirit, embodied in the man Jesus. Therefore the name of Jesus (Yehoshua - Jehovah Savior) is the name of the Father, Son and Holy Ghost. Water baptism AND Spirit baptism are in fact necessary to salvation (see John 3:3-5; Acts 2:38; 1 Peter 3:21).

The Oneness message continued to fuel impressive growth.

In November of 1931, the Pentecostal Assemblies of the World (P.A.W.) merged with the Apostolic Church of Jesus Christ to form the **Pentecostal Assemblies of Jesus Christ (P.A.J.C.)**, which was incorporated in Indianapolis, Indiana.

In 1945, the two largest Oneness organizations at that time were **The Pentecostal Assemblies of Jesus Christ (P.A.J.C.)** and the **Pentecostal Church Incorporated (P.C.I.)**. They met together in General Conference in the Kiel Auditorium in St. Louis, Missouri on September 20-26, 1945, and elected to merge together to become the **United Pentecostal Church**. There were 1,838 ministers and about 900 church congregations involved in that merger. Howard Goss became the first General Superintendent of the United Pentecostal Church.

I did not realize what an Apostolic heritage that I had been born into, until after I was baptized in Jesus' name in 1983. I knew that my grandparents, John and Margaret Raggio had attended the First Pentecostal Church in Port Arthur, Texas as far back as the 1920s. Rev. J.T. Pugh was their pastor for many years.

But I soon learned that my Great-Grandfather, **William E. Workman**, of McAllen, Texas was originally ordained by Elder **G.T. Haywood** of the **P.A.W.** in the early days of his ministry. I now have a copy of his official ordination papers which came later, from the **Pentecostal Assemblies of Jesus Christ**, dated December 19, 1936.

I also found that my Great Uncle, **V.A. Guidroz** (married to my Grandfather's sister, Dora Raggio) was licensed by the **P.A.W.** on October 15, 1926. He joined the **P.A.J.C.** in 1931. He was present when the **P.C.I.**

and the **P.A.J.C** merged to become the **United Pentecostal Church** in 1945. He was the Superintendent of the **Texas District U.P.C.** for 19 years, and one of the founders of **Texas Bible College**. Many of his sons and grandsons are now Apostolic ministers.

I was licensed with the **United Pentecostal Church** in 1983, and ordained on July 15, 1986.

I also began to discover several interesting facts about the Trinitarians whose writings and ministries had formerly impacted my own ministry.

After the Trinitarians and Oneness ministers parted ways in 1916, the Assemblies of God began to emphasize their Trinitarian beliefs more than they had before, in large part, in reaction against the New Issue. They eventually compiled what would become known as "The Sixteen Fundamental Truths" to which they would adhere. Naturally, the Trinitarian doctrine and Trinitarian baptism were at the top of the list. Those sixteen beliefs were codified in a seminal book entitled, "Knowing the Doctrines of the Bible"(1937), written by a Jewish Pentecostal named **Myer Pearlman**.

Pearlman's writings were essentially position papers. That book became, by far, the most influential doctrinal handbook for all Assemblies of God ministers and Bible college students for half a century.

Pearlman also taught for more than twenty years as an instructor at Central Bible Institute (later Central Bible College) in Springfield, Missouri. Pearlman's book was one of my textbooks while I attended college there. According to the Assemblies of God, "Heritage" magazine, Winter 1994 edition, Myer Pearlman "experienced a 'breakdown' and died in a Veteran's Hospital on July 13, 1943 at the age of 45."

Stanley Frodsham

During the time that Dixie and I were going through our four month transition into the Apostolic Faith, we spent about a week in fellowship with an elderly minister who had been the Pastor of one of the largest Full Gospel Churches in the wealthy Heights neighborhood of Houston, Texas during the 1950s and 60s.

Modest Pemberton had been one of the very first to join with Oral Roberts in establishing the Full Gospel Business Men's Fellowship in the city of Houston. In those days, they conducted parades down Main Street in downtown Houston promoting their inter-denominational ministries.

But in his old age, Pemberton denounced the ecumenical, charismatic movement, and returned to the holiness convictions he had held in his earlier years. He said to me, "They can tell you that SPAM is as good as HAM, but don't you believe it!" He was speaking negatively of the compromised, charismatic movement.

For many years, Pemberton had been a close personal friend of Smith Wigglesworth, the world-renowned miracle and healing evangelist. Wigglesworth had left his personal Bible with Pemberton when he died, and this old preacher decided to pass Wigglesworth's Bible on to me! I was ecstatic! For weeks, I pored over Wigglesworth's Bible, which was heavily notated by hand on virtually every page from Genesis to Revelation. After a couple of months passed, the old preacher had second thoughts, and asked me if he could have that Bible back. I reluctantly returned it to him.

But another of his old, personal friends had been **Stanley Frodsham** (1882-1969), who in 1920, became the Editor of the "Pentecostal Evangel" magazine, which was the official house organ of the Assemblies of God. Frodsham and Wigglesworth had also been closely associated for many years. In 1948, Frodsham wrote "Smith Wigglesworth: Apostle of Faith."

Frodsham had been a pivotal figure in the Assemblies of God for many years, but later left the Assemblies and took up with free Pentecostals and the Elim Bible Institute. Frodsham wrote a book entitled, "With Signs Following - The Latter Day Pentecostal Revival," which was the Trinitarian version of modern Pentecost. Frodsham had circulated with virtually every major player in 20th Century Pentecost.

According to Keith Malcomson, in "Pentecostal Pioneers Remembered," Frodsham traveled for the last thirteen years of his life without a permanent home or base, living out of a suitcase. In 1965, Frodsham issued a long, extensive prophecy, warning about a coming great falling away, and the rise of many seducing spirits and doctrines of devils that would plunge Pentecostalism into great darkness. That prophecy is well known.

He died four years after publishing that prophecy. In his final days, Frodsham lived for a while with Modest Pemberton and his wife in their home. Pemberton told me personally that Frodsham renounced his faith in God in Pemberton's presence sometime before he died. Apparently, that fact was never made public, as I have searched widely without finding any corroboration of it.

For whatever reasons, it seemed to me at the time, that God had sent Pemberton across my path for a simple reason. I needed to be reminded that ALL MEN are fallible. All preachers are fallible. All Christians are fallible.

More than a dozen times in the four Gospels, Jesus had said to various men, "**Follow me.**" Peter said, "**Ye should follow His steps**," 1 Peter 2:21. Paul had said in 1 Corinthians 11:1, "Be ye followers of me, even **as I also am of Christ**."

We should only follow a man as far as he follows Christ. Any time a man ceases to follow Truth, Righteousness and Holiness, we must redirect.

When any man's doctrine becomes significantly in error, we must turn away from that, and meticulously maintain our allegiance to Truth.

Here is a hard saying - hard because few people are willing to stop and contemplate it:

> "Every spirit that confesseth not that
> **Jesus Christ [Jehovah Savior, the anointed One]**
> is come in the flesh is **not of God:**
> and **this is that spirit of antichrist,**
> whereof ye have heard that it should come;
> and even now already is it in the world," 1 John 4:3.

That verse does NOT merely qualify EVERYBODY who believes that Jesus Christ was a real human. Billions of people believe that Jesus was a real human, come in the flesh, but they are not of God.

The POINT of John's radical statement is that a man MUST BELIEVE that Jesus Christ is Jehovah Savior come in the flesh. That is a Oneness doctrine, embedded in your Bible in 1 John 4:3.

You must believe that Jesus Christ is the One True Invisible Spirit incarnate in a man.

In John 8:19, the Pharisees said to Jesus,

> **"Where is thy Father?**
> Jesus answered, **Ye neither know me, nor my Father:**
> **if ye had known me, ye should have known my Father also."**

But Jesus must have shocked them with what He said in verse 24:

> **"If ye believe not that I am he, ye shall die in your sins."**

If you do not believe Jesus is the Father… "ye shall die in your sins."

It is right there in your Bible. What will you do with it? It is not good enough to believe that Jesus is the incarnation of the Second Person of the Trinity. That is NOT who Jesus is. **He is the incarnation of "the fullness of the Godhead** bodily," Colossians 2:9. **ALL** of God is in Christ.

Nearly all of the early Pentecostal pioneers came face-to-face with the New Issue of Jesus' name baptism and the Oneness of God, and many of them were quite adversarial, working feverishly to defeat the New Issue.

I have seen, in the forty-seven years since I began preaching the Gospel, every kind of phenomenon that a man can imagine. I have seen great and impressive "moves of God," and immediately afterward, I've seen devastating scandals and contradictions. I have watched many of the greatest Christian leaders of modern times ultimately self-destruct, huge world-wide ministries implode, and some of the most highly-regarded figures in Christianity turn out to be impostors.

I have learned that RELIGION is not about you or me. Religion is about knowing God. It is not good enough that we make celebrities out of religious leaders. Our task is to show GOD to men. If we fail to show the TRUTH of GOD to men, we have failed the task we were called to.

Therefore, my confidence is not in men. My confidence is in the Word of God.

I have NEVER seen a preacher or a Christian who was perfect. I have rarely seen a ministry of any kind, any denomination, or any size that did not have a taint on it somewhere.

And I am not referring merely to those who fell under great scandals of sexual immorality or financial improprieties. I also include men and women who, without ever committing the major sins, were nevertheless tainted by a love for money, or narcissism, or power-mongering, or abuse of authority, or any other of a thousand vices.

You know EXACTLY what I am talking about.

Let me leave you with one last thought.

God did not send angels to preach the saving Gospel. He chose sinners, saved by grace, to bring hope to the world. It is important to remember that ministers come from common stock. Otherwise, you are certain to become disillusioned with ministers.

God chose His ministers from all strata of men. That is His divine way. God has intentionally filled the ministry with ALL KINDS of men – the good, the bad, the ugly!

From ancient days, the Priesthood was taken from among ordinary men.

Paul explained to the Hebrews and to us that God, instead of revealing Himself to mankind by an audible voice, or a visible figure, or a tangible body, chose to reveal himself through MEN - men who were "taken from among men." God's ministers/priests are from the very same stuff as those they are required to minister to.

> "For **every high priest taken from among men is ordained for men in things pertaining to God**,
> that he may offer both gifts and sacrifices for sins:
> Who can have compassion on the ignorant,
> and on them that are out of the way;
> for that **he himself also is compassed with infirmity**.
> And by reason hereof he ought, as for the people,
> so also for himself, to offer for sins,"
> Hebrews 5:1-3.

Men "who can have compassion on the ignorant," Paul interjected. Who can be more compassionate to the ignorant than one who has suffered the painful effects of his own ignorance?

Quite intentionally, God, incarnate in Christ, revealed Himself to a few ordinary men – twelve "ignorant and unlearned" disciples, and left the entire Gospel solely in their hands to communicate what they knew to all the rest of the world.

"Himself ALSO is compassed with infirmity."

Every man of God is compassed with infirmity. He is a long way from a polished, flawless specimen. God's man is pockmarked by mistakes, accidents and injuries. Certainly, those who are in leadership are expected to hold themselves to a higher standard of performance than the general populace, but notwithstanding, these men are still made of the SAME flawed material that all the rest of the populace is made of!

Why do I say these things in the end of this book? Because there is something infinitely more important about the Christian's calling than finding a preacher or a Church that is perfect.

And that thing is believing and living by absolute, Biblical Truth.

> "Ye therefore, beloved, seeing ye know these things before,
> **beware lest ye also, being led away with the error of the wicked,
> fall from your own stedfastness.** But **grow in grace,
> and in the knowledge of our Lord and Saviour Jesus Christ**,"
> 2 Peter 3:17-18.

It is too easy to become comfortable with a preacher or a Church congregation that we like, or enjoy being around. But that has never been a trustworthy criteria for being saved. Our lives must be founded on Bible Truth, not on men. We must KNOW THE WORD OF GOD, and live by it.

If we find a man of God who preaches everything in the Bible just exactly right, he will be a rare find, and we will be extraordinarily blessed.

But whether we do or not, we will eventually stand before Almighty God on Judgment Day, where we will NOT be judged by the question, "who was your Pastor?" or "what Church did you go to?"

We will be judged on our personal compliance with the Word of God.

These are the things that we know by the Word of God, and these are the things that we will be judged by.

1. The Lord our God is One Lord. We must have no other gods.

2. We must cease from sins, by repentance and a changed life.

3. We must be born again, of water in the name of Jesus, and of the Spirit, speaking in other tongues.

4. We must follow peace with all men, and holiness, without which no man shall see the Lord.

If we think that we have a better revelation of God than earlier generations, even as we spend our evenings absorbed in godless television shows, weekends full of sports and pleasure, prayerless days and nights, ignorance of God's Word, and generally unspiritual lives, we have fallen under a deadly, damnable delusion.

We have no reason to believe that we can win Heaven wholesale when all the saints and patriarchs of times gone by paid for it with their blood, sweat and tears.

There are no discounts to a walk with God.

If you want what the greatest men and women of God ever had, then you must be prepared to give what they gave, live like they lived, sacrifice like they sacrificed, and pay the kind of price that they paid.

Yes, I know that salvation is free. But a supernatural relationship with God is not. You must deny yourself, take up your cross, and follow Him.

Chapter 23

No Going Back

I have never been one to want to stay in a place where I knew I didn't belong. At least, not for very long. When it's time to go, it's time to go. Some people have a mortal fear of burning bridges to the past, but the Bible said of Abraham and the other heroes of faith,

> "If they had been mindful of that country from whence they came out, they might have had opportunity to have returned,"
> Hebrews 11:15.

In other words, if Abraham had continually thought about Ur of the Chaldees, he may have eventually returned. But he burned that bridge.

That precept is true with you and me. If a Christian continually looks back at the world, he will eventually be enticed back to it.

When I came into the Oneness Apostolic Pentecostal movement in 1983, I was overwhelmed at its holiness, its integrity, and its spiritual forcefulness.

But I have watched in horror in recent years as the Apostolic movement has begun to go backward. While I have struggled incessantly to keep to a Northbound course, I have been shocked to see many of my brethren in the Southbound lane.

I cannot shake the 2,000-year perspective from my head. Pentecost began in prayer, fasting, holiness, miracles, signs, wonders, baptism in Jesus' name, speaking in tongues, prophesying, casting out devils, healing the sick, raising the dead, and preaching the pure, unadulterated Word of God, even as all Hell assailed them.

Now what I see is an Apostolic movement that is in many places almost totally abandoning those fundamental components of Christianity, and following after large non-Apostolic movements that have never experienced the power of God, and never been filled with the Holy Ghost.

Many of our Apostolic ministers would rather attend conferences held by non-Pentecostal "gurus" and see smoke and mirror and light shows, and rub shoulders with celebrities than to see the kind of Church that was born on the Day of Pentecost, and restored to us in the 20th Century through much blood, sweat and tears.

The Pentecostal movement, rather than being characterized by sanctification and holiness, is now characterized by its wide acceptance of secular means and methods of drawing crowds. The same Pentecostal Church that once taught men to turn their backs on worldly activities and amusements now uses those very same worldly activities and amusements as enticements to draw their crowds.

This is not the same Pentecost. It is not the same Apostolic Church.

The Apostolic movement is falling away. It is embracing things that no Church since the Reformation began would have consented to. Five hundred years of preaching about holiness, sanctification and consecration have been burned on the altar of sports, recreation, rock and roll music, television, movies, and whatever other fleshly amusement happens to be the latest social and cultural trend.

Jesus said, "**No man, having put his hand to the plough, and looking back, is fit for the kingdom of God**," Luke 9:62. If you cannot keep your eyes off the world, you are never going to make it.

The sandy shoals of treacherous temptations are littered with the shipwrecks of countless "super-saints" and once-powerful men of God.

If you cannot burn the bridge that takes you back to the world, back to sin, carnality and worldliness, you will not be Pentecostal very much longer. You will wake up one morning in the hog pen, and find yourself filling your belly with corn husks and hog swill.

Go ahead, Noah. Tell your family that you are not going to ride in the Ark.

Go ahead, Abraham. Tell Isaac you are going back to Ur of the Chaldees.

Go ahead, Ruth. Tell Naomi that you are going back to the land of Moab.

Go ahead, Joshua. Tell Moses that you are going back to Egypt.

That is why God closed the Red Sea behind Israel.

Paul said that they "were all **baptized unto Moses** in the cloud and in the sea," 1 Corinthians 10:2. That meant that God permanently cut them off from Egypt. They were baptized unto Moses. They HAD to stay with Moses. They could not go back to Egypt. GOD burned that bridge.

I have been baptized into Christ. I cannot go back. There is no way back.

To go back would be suicide. God does not intend for us to ever go back. God builds no bridges to the past.

Have you been baptized into Christ? Or do you still belong to the world? Do you still belong to your unsaved family? Do you still belong to your football team? Do you still belong to your worldly social circle?

Now here is a great truth. You cannot have both your past and your future. If you will do the will of God, you will have to sell all you have, and purchase the field that has the treasure in it. Like the merchant, you will have to sell all you have if you really want the pearl of great price.

If God wants you to go forward, then going backward is a sin. If God wants you in Canaan, it is a sin to be in Egypt. When God makes you a square peg, you will never again fit in a round hole.

If you are going to be a Pentecostal, you have to get out of a non-Pentecostal environment and get into a Pentecostal environment.

If you are going to preach and practice holiness, you have to get out of a non-holiness environment and get into a holiness environment.

If you are going to believe in the Oneness of God, as did the entire Early Church, you have to get it fixed in your head and in your heart that Trinitarianism is false doctrine concocted by Roman Catholicism centuries later, and you will have nothing to do with it or its preachers and Churches.

Compromise is treason against a holy God.

And if you want to genuinely see the glory of God - the signs, the wonders, the miracles, the multitudes receiving the Holy Ghost, the anointing, the dreams, the visions, the revelations that the Early Church experienced, you will NEVER have them without the kind of consecration that THEY had.

You have no choice. You will HAVE to pray extensively. You will HAVE to fast longer than you ever fasted. You will HAVE to consecrate. You CANNOT continue holding on to the world, the flesh and the devil and STILL see the glory of God.

It has NEVER happened that way, and it will NEVER happen like that for you or me.

> "When they speak great swelling words of vanity,
> they allure through the lusts of the flesh,
> through much **wantonness**,
> those that were clean escaped from them who live in error.
> While **they promise them liberty**,
> **they themselves are the servants of corruption**:
> for of whom a man is overcome, of the same is he brought in bondage.
> For if after they have escaped the pollutions of the world
> through the knowledge of the Lord and Saviour Jesus Christ,
> they are **again entangled** therein, and **overcome**,
> **the latter end is worse with them than the beginning.**
> For it had been **better for them not to have known**
> the way of righteousness, than, after they have known it,
> to **turn from the holy commandment** delivered unto them.
> But it is happened unto them according to the true proverb,
> **The dog is turned to his own vomit again;**
> and **the sow that was washed to her wallowing in the mire**,"
> 2 Peter 2:18-22.

We must consecrate ourselves to doing everything strictly by the Book - by God's Holy Word. Otherwise, you are reverting back to error, and you are putting leaven of false doctrine in your heart and in the Church.

Don't do it.

Buy the Truth.

Sell it not.

**I want you to pray with me before you close this book.
Will you? Pray aloud with me.**

Holy God,

I want to do your will. I do not want to play games any more. I want to embody Your Spirit.

I want to put away every false way, and be filled with everything that is holy, true, and that only comes from You.

Deliver me from all evil. Purge my heart, my soul, and my mind of everything sinful, carnal, worldly, proud and vain. Fill me instead with all that is eternal, worthy and divine.

Stir my Spirit to hunger and thirst after righteousness. Crush my selfish will underneath a Heavenly burden. Give me a heart that is filled with love for You and Your glorious Kingdom.

Help me to mortify all my worldly desires, and give myself wholly and completely to You. O, to be Your hand extended; to be a voice for You; to go where You want me to go; to be what you want me to be.

I love your laws and your commandments. Your Word is a lamp to my feet and a light to my path. I will hide Your Word in my heart that I might not sin against Thee.

Show me the path of righteousness. Lead me, guide me, help me to be and do everything You desire me to be and do.

In Jesus' name.

_____
      (Your name)

Long and Winding Road

Song by Johnny Cook

Verse 2

"There are some times when the rocks hurt my feet;
My body burns from the sweat and the heat;
My strength completely drained
till my face marks the pain;
My back is bent from the strain.

I could turn around, for the road is still there,
but every mountain that I've climbed I again would have to bear,
so I really can't turn back, some may be using my tracks.
I see one more bend, and that just might be this road's end.

Chorus

Long and winding road keep on leading me.
Up ahead I see a sign, and it points me straight ahead to victory.
I know I must be traveling right, for I remember passing Calvary.
And although it's dusty and old, for years it's borne this traveler's load,
Some day this road will turn to gold.

For some this road's already turned to gold.

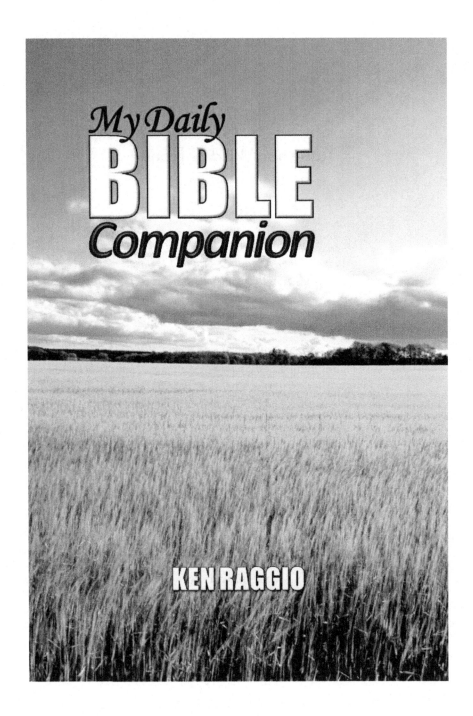

Over 4,800 Point-by-Point Mini-Lessons through the entire Bible!

KEEP THIS AWESOME 1200+ PAGE BOOK BY YOUR FAVORITE
EASY CHAIR, OR ON YOUR NIGHTSTAND.

It is a unique Daily Reader that is packed with
amazing Genesis-to-Revelation Bible lessons.

Read as many as you want each day: 2, 3, 4 or more.
Presented in easily understandable 100-Word topics
in four general categories:

- **PRAYER** Illustrations, Examples, Lessons about Prayer
- **PRINCIPALS** People, Places and Things in the Bible
- **PRINCIPLES** Virtues, Vices, Values in the Bible, Great Precepts
- **PROPHECIES** 1200+ Prophecies (Fulfilled and Unfulfilled) Explained

Order Vol. 1 Old Testament – 650 pgs: https://www.createspace.com/3839857

Order Vol. 2 New Testament – 788 pgs: https://www.createspace.com/3856644

Order KINDLE e-Book (Entire Bible): http://amzn.com/ Search "Ken Raggio"

Coming soon in PRINT & Amazon KINDLE

HOW THE WORLD WILL END – What The Bible Says

Here is God's Revealed Plan for our future!

Bible Prophecy foretells key major, even epic events all the way to Armageddon, the Millennial Kingdom of Jesus Christ, and beyond - to the eternal Kingdom of God. This book covers so much exciting material that most people have never seen, heard or studied. It is a must-read - showing absolutely amazing revelations of many rarely discussed events to come. You will never again think of the future in the same terms.

This is one of the most comprehensive books on Last Days Prophecies you will find anywhere. In-depth studies of Daniel, Revelation, and scores of other major prophecies.

TO ORDER, VISIT http://kenraggio.com

Now Available in PRINT & Amazon KINDLE

PRAYING ON PURPOSE – PRAYING FOR RESULTS

This is a powerful book that will effectively help you improve your practice of prayer with more effective, thorough, and dynamic prayer. Learn better prayer habits, ways to pray, and even what to pray for.

Chapters include: I Give Myself Unto Prayer | Daily Intercession | No Time To Pray | Making A Prayer List | Praying By Notes | Why People Don't Pray | Priorities In Prayer | All About Intercession | How To Intercede | How To Pray | You Can Call On That Name | Angels And Answers | Praying In The Spirit | Unimaginable Miracles | Life-or-Death Prayers | A Place To Pray | Let Us Pray | and more…

TO ORDER PRINT: VISIT https://www.createspace.com/3861983

TO ORDER KINDLE e-Book: Visit http://amzn.com/ Search "Ken Raggio"

Coming soon in PRINT & Amazon KINDLE

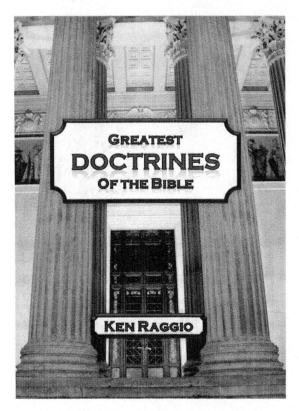

GREATEST DOCTRINES OF THE BIBLE

This is not a theological textbook, but an electrifying look at some of the most primordial of all divine precepts – an extraordinary, provocative look at the most fundamental, foundational and universal truths of the Bible. For some, it will be a revelation of never-before-seen glories of God, as well as an awesome faith builder!

Christianity is suffering the blight of multitudes of false teachers, false preachers, charlatans, pseudo-Christians and worse. Ken Raggio will take you back to the original New Testament doctrines that the Apostles fervently believed and preached. You will sense the authenticity of these great and core doctrines of the Early Church – the faith that was once delivered to the saints. You need this book. Every believer needs it.

TO ORDER, VISIT http://kenraggio.com

Coming soon in PRINT & Amazon KINDLE

TREASURES OF DARKNESS

How to see the glory of God in the darkest trials of your life.

This book was born in the furnace of a great personal trial, and is nothing short of a revelation of how God works behind the scenes during your greatest difficulties. God wants you to be able to see clearly in the dark. This book is a fascinating journey into the world of the Spirit, and will definitely enhance your night vision, and show you how to see the Treasures of Darkness!

Chapters include:

Blinded By The Light | God Plays Hide-And-Seek | Let There Be Light | Dark Matter | String Theories and Spin | and much, much more.

TO ORDER, VISIT http://kenraggio.com

Coming soon in PRINT & Amazon Kindle

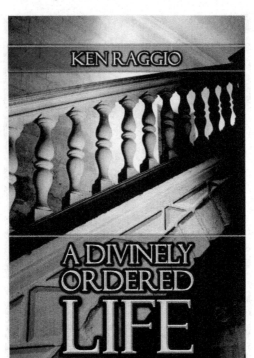

A DIVINELY ORDERED LIFE

What appears to be chaos in the eyes of a true Christian is quite the opposite in the eyes of God. It is possible to analyze your own situation intellectually without ever understanding how things will ever work out.

But this book explores a broad spectrum of Biblical analogies and metaphors that demonstrate the exact processes by which God orders your life, even when it seems like everything is falling apart.

The steps of a man are ordered by the Lord. This book will help you identify, understand and appreciate many of the principles that God uses to meticulously order your Divine Destiny.

TO ORDER, VISIT http://kenraggio.com

Coming soon in PRINT & Amazon KINDLE

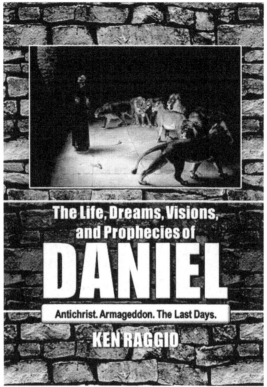

THE LIFE, DREAMS, VISIONS AND PROPHECIES OF DANIEL

A rich, in-depth look at the life and prophetic essence of the prophet Daniel. It includes a close-up character study of Daniel's life, followed by a point-by-point examination of each dream, vision and prophecy.

Includes MAJOR Last-Days Prophecies you need to understand.

Nebuchadnezzar's Image | The Four Beasts Of Daniel | The Iron and Clay Feet and the Four-Headed Leopard | Daniel's Dreadful Beast | Daniel's Seventy Weeks Prophecy | Daniel Chapter 11 (Revelation of the coming Man of Sin), and much more. This is a very powerful book.

TO ORDER, VISIT http://kenraggio.com

NOW AVAILABLE! $4.95 PRINT | $2.95 KINDLE

THE TRIALS OF JOB

Lessons about facing God-ordained adversities.

Before going to press with MY DAILY BIBLE COMPANION, I felt that it would be good to introduce this work in a sample version.

Since the Book of Job is probably the oldest book in the Bible, and since it contains many priceless and poignant life lessons, I decided to extract the 58 mini-lessons from the Book of Job and publish them ahead of the major work. This is only a tiny sampling of over 4,800 lessons in the MDBC. This MINI-BOOK is an excellent way to introduce your friends to the larger work, MY DAILY BIBLE COMPANION.

Order PAPERBACK Version here: https://www.createspace.com/3827423

Order the KINDLE E-Book here: http://amzn.com/B007M8A1H0

Now Available in PRINT $14.99 - also in KINDLE e-Book

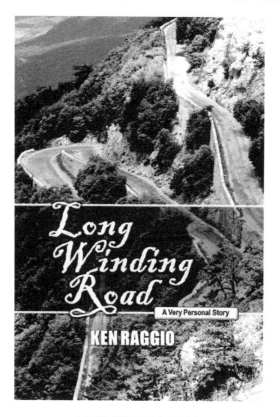

LONG WINDING ROAD

...a very personal story about forty years in the ministry.

Chapters Include:

The Groves | The Call | Facing the Music | Apprenticeship | The Work of an Evangelist | A Word, A Dream, A Miracle | Planting A Church | A Major Paradigm Shift | Which Way From Here? | Catch the Spirit of Love | Holy Ghost or Nothing | Crash and Burn | Separation Time | and more...

TO ORDER IN PRINT, VISIT: https://www.createspace.com/3862073

TO ORDER KINDLE e-Book: Visit http://amzn.com/ Search "Ken Raggio"

Now Available in PRINT $12.95 - also in KINDLE e-Book

TRUTH In A Nutshell

2,000+ Christian Quotes

Affirming the Biblical Way of Life

TO ORDER IN PRINT, VISIT: https://www.createspace.com/3913302

TO ORDER KINDLE e-Book: Visit http://amzn.com/ Search "Ken Raggio"

Long Winding Road

VISIT MY BLOG!
Personal Musings On God, Religion, and Daily Christian Living

kenraggio.blogspot.com

SUBSCRIBE to "Today's Bible Study"
FREE! - BY E-MAIL

Four 100-Word Mini-Bible Lessons Each Day in your Email Box
Subscribe here: **kenraggio.com**

Long Winding Road

"FRIEND" ME on FACEBOOK!

Read my Daily Inspirational Posts!

ALSO…

JOIN the KEN RAGGIO FACEBOOK "FANPAGE"

Ken Raggio – Bible Resources – Lessons – Sermons - Prophecy

Read the daily PROPHECY MINI-LESSONS on my FB Fanpage!

Click "LIKE" at this site.

Long Winding Road

"FOLLOW ME" on TWITTER!

Daily Power Quotes, Mini-Lessons, and Prophecy Updates

Twitter ID:

http://twitter.com/**kenraggiocom**

Long Winding Road

VISIT KENRAGGIO.COM

Thousands of pages of
Bible Studies – Sermons – Lessons – Prophecy Articles

Long Winding Road

Dear Friend,

For almost six years, I have worked feverishly, researching and writing in excess of 50 hours every week to produce, first of all, my major life-work, a 1438-page Bible Commentary entitled **MY DAILY BIBLE COMPANION**.

It is the compilation of over 4,800 100-word mini-Bible lessons, written for **"TODAY'S BIBLE STUDY,"** most of which have already been read in every nation on earth. My subscribers are in 215 nations at this writing. Having written step-by-step, point-by-point Bible lessons from Genesis to Revelation, virtually every topic in the Bible has been dealt with. I have already received literally thousands of testimonial letters from around the world expressing thanks and appreciation for these daily lessons. Letters continue to arrive daily. I hope and pray that you will enjoy them, too.

Because it is quite comprehensive in going point-by-point through the entire Bible, it became necessary to publish the work in two volumes.

Volume 1 contains lessons from the **Old Testament**.
Volume 2 contains lessons from the **New Testament**.
The **Kindle e-Book edition** contains the **entire book in ONE volume**.

I urge you to get **MY DAILY BIBLE COMPANION**. You won't be sorry.

In addition, I will soon release several other books that I have been writing: a powerful book on **PRAYER**, a book on the **GREATEST BIBLE DOCTRINES**, a MAJOR work on **BIBLE PROPHECY**, and at least three other **inspirational books** in the coming year or so.

Thank you for purchasing this book. I pray that God will bless the teaching of His Word to you.

Please visit my website (**kenraggio.com**) and enjoy the

vast FREE Bible resources that you will find there.

God bless you.

Sincerely,

Ken Raggio

Ken Raggio

ABOUT THE AUTHOR

A Pentecostal minister since 1966, Ken Raggio has been a Pastor, Evangelist, Singer, Songwriter, Musician, Broadcaster, Journalist, Editor and Author. Ken has maintained a major Internet presence since 1996 at kenraggio.com and has many thousands of subscribers in 215 nations to "Today's Bible Study," a daily email containing four 100-word mini-Bible-lessons. He is now focused on writing and producing video teaching series.

Made in the USA
Monee, IL
31 October 2020